THE
GOLDEN
ATLAS

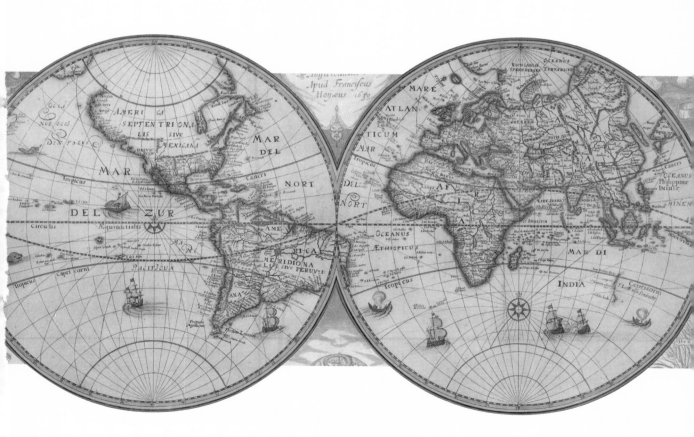

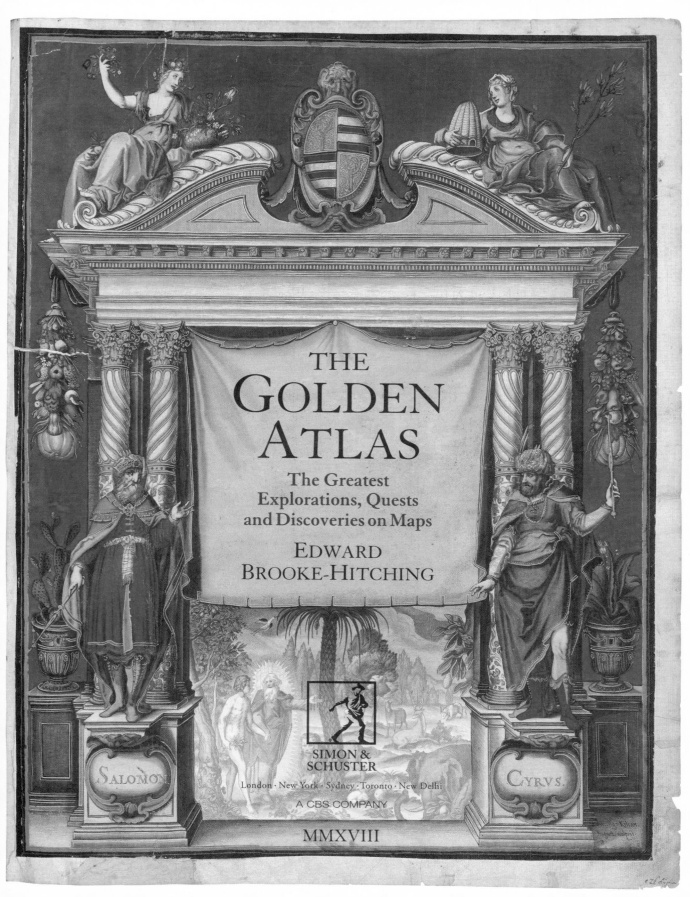

THE GOLDEN ATLAS

The Greatest
Explorations, Quests
and Discoveries on Maps

EDWARD
BROOKE-HITCHING

SALOMON

CYRVS.

SIMON &
SCHUSTER

London · New York · Sydney · Toronto · New Delhi

A CBS COMPANY

MMXVIII

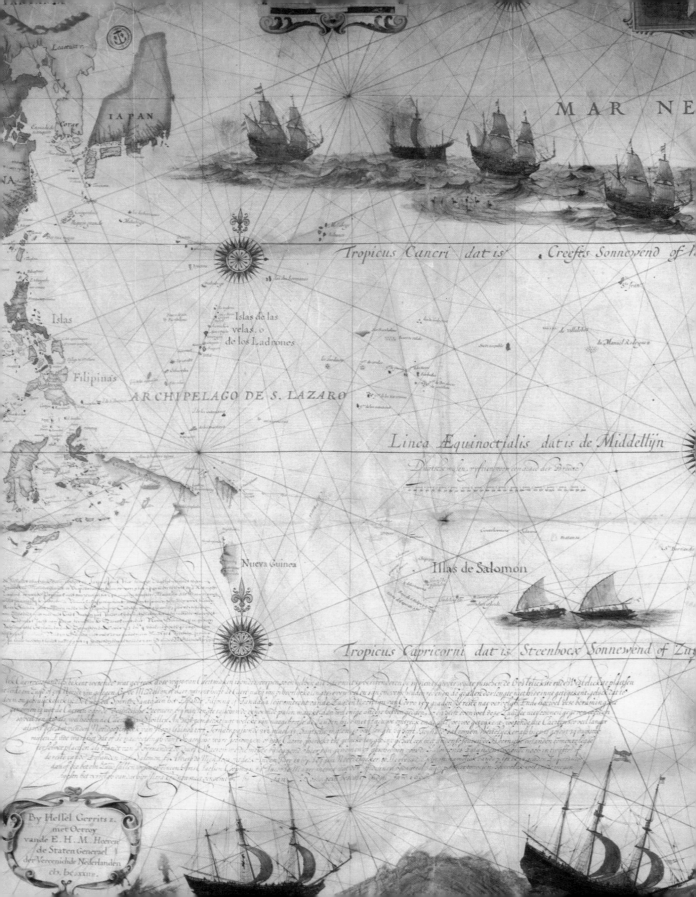

IAPAN

MAR NE

Tropicus Cancri dat is ... Creeftis Sonnewend of

Islas

Islas de las
velas, o
de los Ladrones

Filipinas

ARCHIPELAGO DE S. LAZARO

Linea Æquinoctialis dat is de Middellijn

Nueva Guinea

Illas de Salomon

Tropicus Capricorni dat is Steenbock Sonnewend of Zu

By Heſſel Gerrits z.
met Octroy
vande E. H. M. Heeren
de Staten Generael
der Vereenichde Nederlanden
cɔ. ɔc. xxxiv.

To Emma and Franklin
Treasure, treasured

CONTENTS

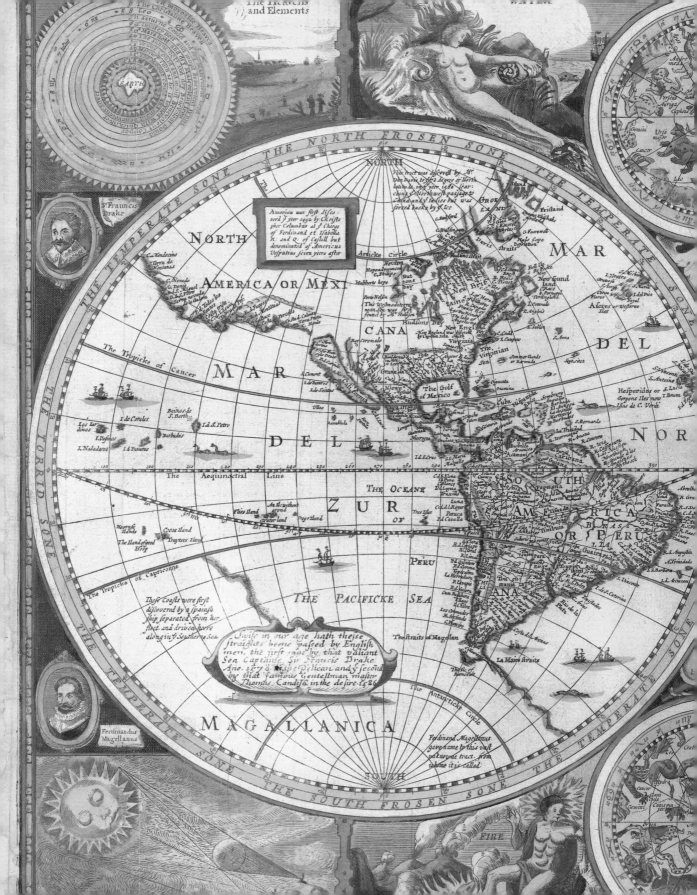

INTRODUCTION

'Following the light of the sun, we left the Old World.' CHRISTOPHER COLUMBUS

Maps, it should be said, are not quite what they appear to be. Throughout history cultures have carved, painted and printed their spatial understanding of the world using every material to hand. The Permian sandstone of Italy's Camonica Valley carries the Bedolina Petroglyph, chiselled *c.*1500 BC by an Iron Age people trying to make sense of their surrounding landscape. The vellum of the 'portolan' navigators' charts that first appeared in the thirteenth century formed the vanguard

John Speed's world map from Prospect of the Most Famous Parts of the World *(1627), the first English atlas of the world.*

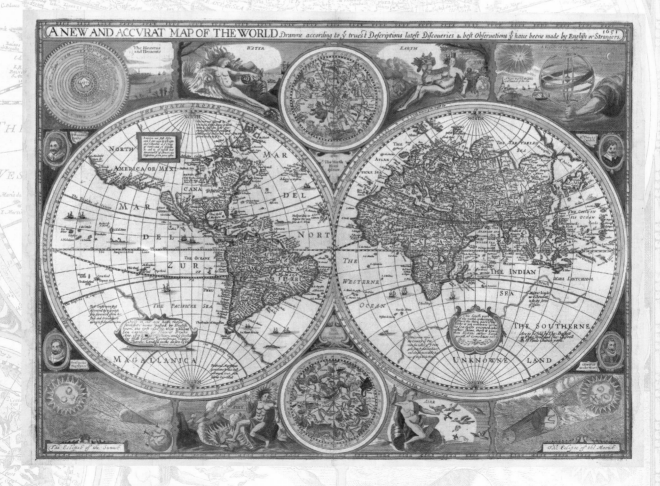

of a new practical cartographic accuracy, the animal hide able
to withstand the sea spray that would otherwise dissolve paper
in seconds. And then there are much rarer curiosities, like the
giant canvas sheet maps of nineteenth-century missionaries,
declaring the number of heathens awaiting conversion (see
David Livingstone, Henry Morton Stanley and the 'Dark
Continent' entry on page 216-19) or the collapsible cotton
umbrella globes and finely engraved silver coins of the Victorian
map-lover wishing to carry the world with them around town.

And yet with all this diversity there is one material common
to every map ever made, an essential ingredient imbuing
every cartographic particle: story. Maps are *alive* with stories,
crowded and raucous with the centuries of endeavour that

*Large portolan chart of the
Mediterranean across three
vellum sheets, by Giovanni
Battista Cavallini, 1641.*

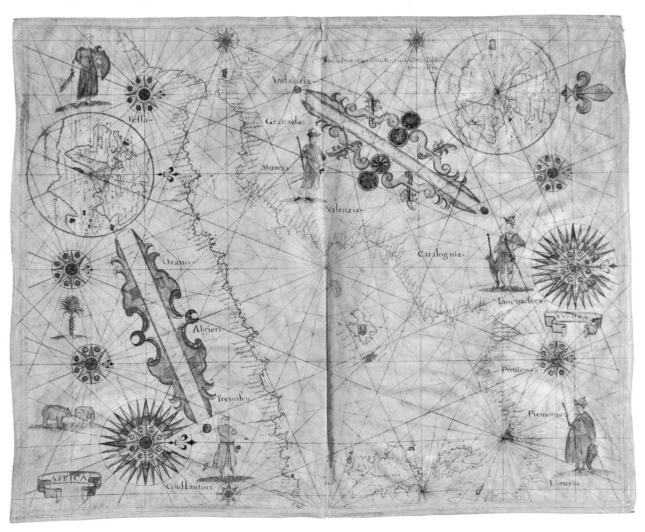

combined to piece together the knowledge they display. Consider each minute curve of coastline and brushstroke of river for what they were to their discoverers: jewels of data snatched from an unmeasured darkness beyond the known horizon, trophies potentially more valuable than a full hold of treasure because of the infinite continental riches to which they could lead. Maps function as intricate tapestries of these adventures, interlacing explorational enterprises of kings, conquerors, corporations, scientists and lone treasure hunters, ultimately all united by a common motive: to bring definition to the blizzard of the blank space.

The idea behind *The Golden Atlas* is to provide this narrative context with the stories of the greatest of these discoverers, revealing how their trailblazing exploits are woven into the historical fabric of the map, as the modern world took shape on the cartographer's canvas. In equal measure, too, is the intent to illustrate these histories with the most beautiful collection of cartography ever published. Some of these maps, in their role as the 'birth certificates' of new nations might be recognizable in their infamy. Other rare examples are published here for the first time, thanks to the wide variety of sources: not only museums and libraries but also private collections and the archives of antiquarian dealers around the world. As such, there are objects of phenomenal worth. The Maggiolo Portolan for example, illustrating 'Verrazzano Traces the East Coast of North America', is currently valued at $10 million (the most precious to ever go on the public market). And each map, from the local to the global, has stories to tell.

John Bett's 1860 invention of a collapsible globe with an umbrella mechanism.

Though we start with the earliest documented explorers of the Ancient World, the story of how we found our way begins much earlier with the first great explorers, the Polynesian wayfinders. Between 3000 BC and 1000 BC these extraordinary seafarers set out on voyages throughout the Pacific ocean using only outrigger canoes and knowledge of currents, wave forms and star patterns passed down through oral tradition – in a sense, maps in verbal form. No written or cartographic evidence exists of these earliest ventures, but archaeological traces record the diaspora from Melanesia to Tonga and Samoa, and then east to the Society Islands, the Hawaiian Islands and Easter Island, and south to New Zealand. Surviving records of explorations begin to appear with the navigators of the Ancient World like those of the Egyptian kingdom investigating the

Nile, the Red Sea and beyond, with slim paragraphic mentions in the writings of Greek and Roman authors like Herodotus, Strabo and Pliny, who scoured documents long since lost to us.

While the early establishment of trade networks made for piecemeal progress, the most monumental advancement in geographic discovery came with the conquerors. With the fourth-century BC campaigns of Alexander the Great in his pursuit of the 'ends of the world', and the spread of the Roman Empire, the great geographer Claudius Ptolemy was able to illustrate the world AD *c.*140 with unprecedented detail using a revolutionary mathematical system of coordinates. As Romanized Europe fell into the Dark Ages of the first millennium with the Empire's collapse, the most notable explorations were conducted by those far beyond its borders: the wildfire spread of Islam unified a vast medley of lands from Spain to the East, allowing scholars free passage throughout; while at the same

Sebastian Münster's map of the monsters thought to terrorize the Scandinavian waters, 1550.

time Scandinavian expeditions took to the tumultuous North
Atlantic to reach Iceland, Greenland and then, by sheer
accident, 'Vinland' (North America) in the late tenth century.

With the rest of Europe largely oblivious to these Viking
discoveries, it was the unstoppable expansionism of the Mongol
forces that delivered the next great impact, with the order
brought by the Great Khan allowing European merchants
(most famously, Marco Polo) to travel with relative safety
throughout Asia in the thirteenth century. The wealth of
the East was now evident to European eyes but the overland
journey was impractically long and arduous – a sea route was
needed, so that entire ships could be filled with bartered silks
and spices. Thus the fifteenth century saw the opening of the
great Age of Exploration. Portuguese expeditions crept down
Africa's west coast, the Crown hoping to establish itself in the
Saharan gold and slave trade while searching for a way to
India, until Bartolomeu Dias rounded the Cape of Good Hope
in 1488 and Vasco da Gama reached India ten years later. At
around the same time a British expedition made a remarkable
transatlantic crossing to discover Newfoundland (see John
Cabot Journeys to North America entry on pages 58-63), while
the Spanish also looked to the West, agreeing in 1494 to leave
eastern routes to the Portuguese. Christopher Columbus struck
out across the Atlantic to win the race to reach China, arriving
instead at the New World (and never accepting that he had
failed to find the Orient).

The riches of the Americas would transform Europe to the
devastation of the continent's indigenous cultures, but they
were not immediately apparent. The way to the East remained
the priority, and Ferdinand Magellan set out to uncover a way
around the continental obstacle – this he found in the storm
corridor of the Strait of Magellan, emerging into the Pacific
for the first time in 1520. With the discovery of the golden
civilizations of the Aztec and Inca, however, a new breed of
ruthless explorer began to arrive in South America for the
treasure-hunting opportunities. The hunger for gold led Juan
Ponce de León to his discovery of Florida in 1513, as it did
Hernán Cortés to his sacking of Mexico between 1517 and
1521, which would seal the destruction of the Aztec Empire.

On the tail of the Spanish came the English. Francis
Drake left England in 1577, appearing in the Pacific via the
Strait of Magellan to the shock of the Spaniards, who were

FOLLOWING PAGES: *Pieter van der
Aa's* Planisphere Terrestre ...
*(1713), displaying the extent of
French exploration.*

completely unprepared for the ensuing pillaging campaign
that would turn into the first English global circumnavigation.
Sir Walter Ralegh arrived in search of his own prize, chasing
the myth of El Dorado with disastrous consequences, just as
a new obsession gripped his peers: the search for a Northwest
Passage. This would theoretically allow easier sailing from the
Atlantic to the Pacific across the top of, if not through, North
America, and in anticipation of easier commerce with the East
the seventeenth century saw the appearance of the trading
company phenomenon. These monopolistic organizations
grew to possess the wealth and power of nations. The English
Muscovy Company sent trading missions into Russia and
Central Asia, scanning for a Northeast Passage to China;
while the British East India Company sought the treasures
of the Orient via more southern routes in competition with
the Dutch East India Company (VOC). The latter became so
astonishingly rich from its secret trade routes (locked away in
a hidden atlas called *The Sea Torch*) that to this day it remains
the wealthiest company in history, valued at a modern 7 trillion
US dollars. (For context, today's most valuable company,
Apple, is at the time of writing worth a mere $750 billion.) The
VOC's westward explorations from their base in Java led to the
discovery of a new land to obsess over: Australia and, shortly
after, the first European sighting of New Zealand.

With the eighteenth century came a gradual shift to
a scientific approach to discovery, embodied by more
mathematical and less decorative mapping, and our cast
of characters morph from gold-greedy privateers to more
regimented pragmatists. Vitus Bering led his extraordinary
fact-finding expedition across Russia's frozen entirety to
grant the last wish of Peter the Great; while between 1766
and 1769 Louis Antoine de Bougainville carried out the first
French circumnavigation, which also featured the remarkable
forgotten story of the first woman to sail around the world.
But the gold standard of this Scientific Age of Exploration was
set by Captain James Cook, who before meeting his grisly end
in Hawaii made three epic voyages around the Pacific on a
meticulous research mission of unparalleled success. Countless
explorers were inspired to follow Cook's example, and maps of
continental coastlines grew ever more detailed with the likes
of La Pérouse (before his mysterious vanishing) and George
Vancouver. In the nineteenth century this developed further

with explorers like the Scotsman Mungo Park setting out into the giant empty space on the map that was Africa's interior; while Alexander von Humboldt and Aimé Bonpland wrote, mapped and measured their way through South America's exotic nature; and Meriwether Lewis and William Clark made the first crossing of America's western vastness at the behest of Thomas Jefferson.

Though Arctic exploration had remained a preoccupation, the mid-nineteenth century saw a renewed British drive to find the Northwest Passage, with William Parry, John Ross and most famously Sir John Franklin's lost expedition among those combing the frozen labyrinth for a navigable route. The obsession persisted into the twentieth century, in what is known as the Heroic Age of exploration, when Roald Amundsen finally managed the feat between 1903 and 1906, and the last great challenge of discovery became the race to the poles, open to any with sufficient amounts of funding, courage and foolhardiness. While the contest to be the first to the North Pole remains unresolved due to the extraordinary unreliability of its two competitors, with the First World War engulfing the world this last great explorational age drew to a close with the gripping tales of Antarctic rivalry between British and Norwegian teams battling to raise the first flag at the South Pole, their inspirational bravery punctuating a story of catastrophic misfortune.

All of these stories inhabit the maps that carry their traces, the triumphs brightening the gilt, the tragedies tingeing the colours. As the art of exploration, maps string like lanterns along the story of how the world came to be known,

page 37

THE ORAN = OOTAN

The first European depiction of an orangutan, from Daniel Beekman's To and From the Island of Borneo *(1718).*

embodying each stage of our developing knowledge with both scientific and artistic beauty, quite unlike any other kind of document. Today, of course, with the technological achievement of satellite mapping this artistic and narrative quality of cartography is arguably now lost, the mystery replaced by convenience. But what were the voyages, battles and sacrifices that brought us to this point? How, and at what cost, was our knowledge of the world gathered, for the cultivation of its bloom on the page? It's a story with a global cast of characters that goes back over four thousand years, and it begins – as all stories really should – with the delivery of a dancing pygmy.

The only known example of W. Marsham Adams's Coelometer, invented c.1874 as a complete instructional tool for navigating by the stars.

EXPLORATION AND MAPPING OF THE ANCIENT WORLD 2250BC–AD150

'There is nothing impossible to him who will try.'

ALEXANDER THE GREAT

Ortelius's 1584 two-sheet map of Ancient Egypt, drawing on data from the historians Diodorus Siculus, Herodotus, Strabo and Pliny.

To find the stories of the very earliest named explorers we need look to Ancient Egypt, a kingdom more traditionally thought of for its fierce attitude of superiority and isolationist policies. There is no better figure of this time to single out than Harkhuf, a noble expeditionist of the Sixth Dynasty (c.2345-2181 BC) whose tomb in the hills of Aswan, surveying the Nile, includes an autobiography carved into the stone. Harkhuf's story is the earliest attributed chronicle of exploration, referencing his four epic voyages made to the faraway land of 'Yam', the exact location of which remains a mystery but is thought to be somewhere in modern Sudan along the Upper Nile. 'I did it in only seven months', boasts Harkhuf of his first journey to Yam, 'and I brought all [kinds of] gifts from it … I was very greatly praised for it.' He returned from each of the next three voyages with equally exotic gifts as tribute, on his final trip thrilling the 8-year-old boy-pharaoh Pepi II with the news he was bringing home the gift of a 'dancing dwarf of the god from the land of spirits'. 'Come northward to the court immediately', writes back Pepi, in a letter that Harkhuf proudly had engraved on his tomb. 'Thou shalt bring this dwarf with thee … take care lest he fall into the water.'

Even more mysterious, again to the southeast and with its exact location unknown, was the land of 'Punt', which was first visited by a party dispatched by the pharaoh Sahure c.2450 BC. For its luxurious goods this became a regular destination, despite it necessitating the lugging of boat-building materials some 150 miles (250km) from the Nile to the Red Sea. After 2000 BC Punt was forgotten for 500 years, until the reign of Queen Hatshepsut, the first female pharaoh of Egypt, who ruled from 1479 BC. In the hope of achieving immortal remembrance for herself she sent a force of 210 men to re-establish contact with Punt and return with exotic trees to populate the grandest garden Egypt had ever seen. This they did with myrrh, frankincense and more, even gifting her with whole Puntian families. The success meant that Hatshepsut's wish to never be forgotten was achieved: her grand mortuary temple was adorned with triumphal reliefs celebrating the Punt expedition, and is today filled daily with tourists.

Some 860 years later, Necho II took the Egyptian throne and tackled the problem of the overland crossing between the Nile and the Red Sea by ordering the digging of a canal, a forerunner to the Suez. The project was abandoned after

Harkhuf in a relief from his tomb.

Egyptian soldiers from Hatshepsut's expedition to the Land of Punt as depicted from her temple at Deir el-Bahari.

12,000 lives were claimed by collapsing sands (there was also the worry that the hated Babylonians could use it as an invasion approach), and so Necho turned his attention to exploration farther south than previous Red Sea navigations. At some point between 610 BC and 594 BC he commissioned a force of expert Phoenician pilots to lead this unprecedented journey. The only source for the expedition is a single paragraph from Herodotus's *Histories*. The men sailed south along Africa's east coast until finally turning westward, around South Africa, with the sun on their right. (Herodotus, without a concept of the Earth's curvature, found this baffling.) Eventually they returned to Egypt via the Mediterranean, having sailed around the African continent. How much of this actually occurred has been debated for more than two thousand years. Pliny believed the story while Ptolemy rubbished the idea, holding the notion, as one finds exhibited on his maps, that Africa could not be circumnavigated due to it being a promontory of a vast southern continent.

Another figure mentioned by Herodotus is Scylax of Caryanda, a Greek in the service of the Persians who explored the coasts of the Indian Ocean and rounded the Arabian Peninsula in 515 BC. While Scylax trailblazed for honour and glory, the reason for the 470 BC voyage of Sataspes, nephew of Persian King Darius, was quite different. After being caught defiling a nobleman's daughter, Sataspes avoided the standard sentence of impalement by choosing a punishment 'even more severe': a journey around Africa. He sailed from Egypt via the Strait of Gibraltar, following the African coast south for

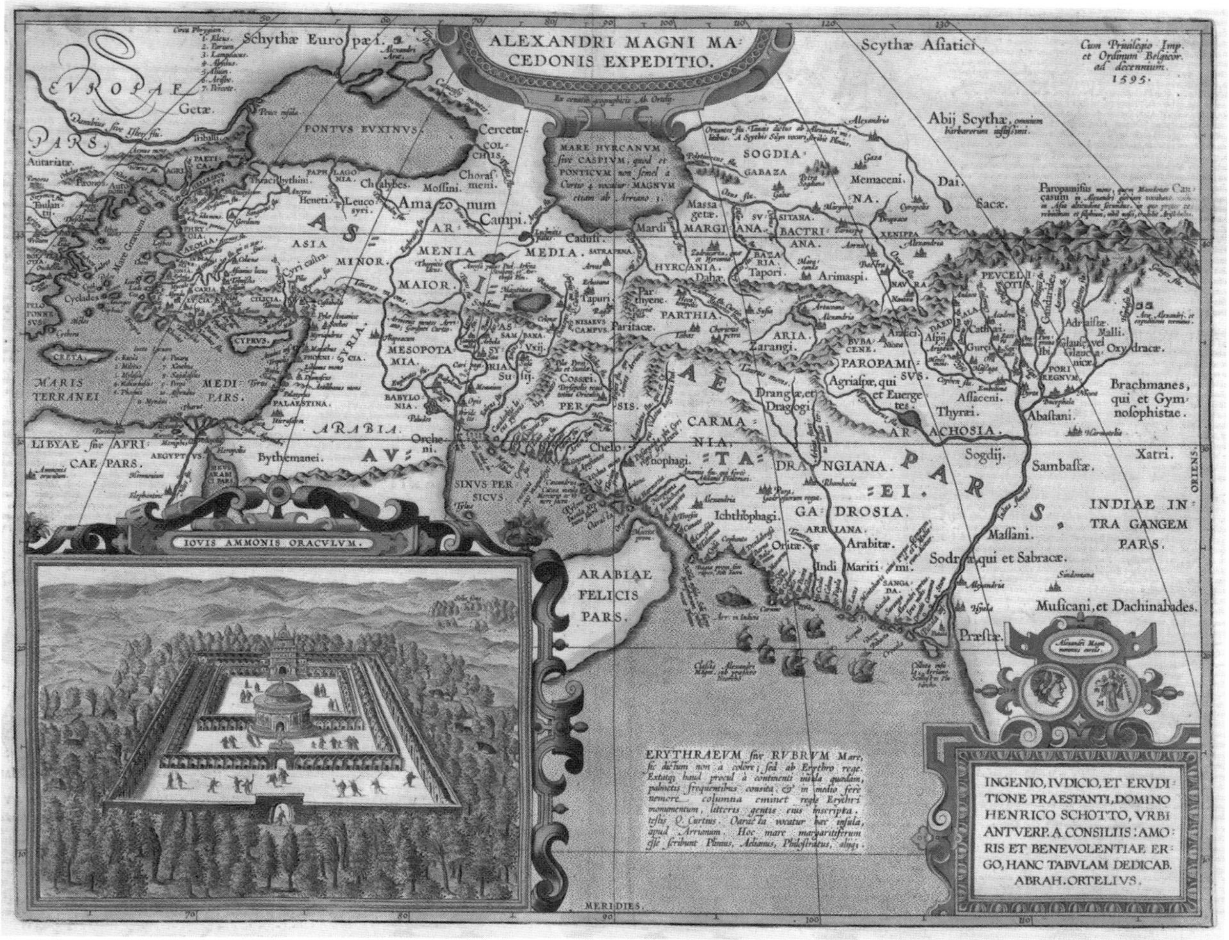

Ortelius's 1608 map of Alexander the Great's conquests in the Middle East and Persia.

months until he discovered a land of pygmies wearing palm leaves. Unable to progress past adverse currents, he returned to Persia in the hope his discoveries merited a pardon. They didn't. Xerxes deemed the voyage a poor effort, and Sataspes was impaled regardless.

The fourth century BC belonged to Alexander the Great, who inherited the Ancient Greek kingdom of Macedon at the age of twenty when his father Philip was assassinated. Awarded the generalship of Greece with a formidable army at his command, he crossed the Dardanelles (a waterway that effectively forms the border between Europe and Asia) in 334 BC and embarked on an unprecedented military campaign that tore through Asia and northwestern Africa, creating, by the age of thirty, one of the greatest empires ever constructed with an unbeaten battle record. Alexander had been tutored by

Aristotle until the age of sixteen, but his concept of the world that lay beyond was bound by the limits of Greek knowledge: that which lay to the east of the Caspian, and south to the Arabian Sea, was merely hypothesized. There was no understanding of Asia's true extent, just the Aristotelian idea of the world as a giant island surrounded by a single continuous ocean.

The desire to push on through to find the coast of this 'Great Outer Sea' drove Alexander across many thousands of miles, from Egypt to Mesopotamia to Persia, discovering the endless plains of Central Asia, and finally reaching the Indus Valley in 326 BC (where, among other demands, he requested to be brought the famed yeti for examination, but was told this was impossible as the creatures couldn't survive the low altitude). When he gave the order to cross the mighty Ganges, his exhausted men refused to march any farther.

In 325 BC a geographer named Pytheas of the Greek colony and trade centre Massalia (Marseilles) made his own extraordinary voyage of discovery, documenting for the first time the coastline of Great Britain, northern Europe and lands beyond. Though his record of the journey, *About the Ocean*, did not survive, it was celebrated in Antiquity and fragments

Martin Waldseemüller's map of the British Isles, with a lopsided Scotland likely a result of Ptolemy relying on Pytheas's imprecise coordinates.

UNIVERSALIS TABULA IUXTA PTOLEMÆUM

Mercator's 1578 map of the world based on Ptolemy's writings.

survive as echoes in other geographies. He was the first to describe the Midnight Sun of the north that shone for months at a time, the first scientific examiner of polar ice and the Germanic tribes, and the first to introduce the mythical island of Thule, which would pervade geographic imagination for more than a thousand years as a name for every unfounded rumour and fantasy of northern territory. It appears Pytheas's route took him from the Bay of Biscay, round modern Brittany to cross the English Channel and reach Cornwall. He then circumnavigated 'the islands of the Pretanni' [Great Britain], investigating the Orkney and Shetland Islands, and headed north to Thule, which is thought to be either Iceland or the Norwegian coast.

Though he had his doubters – Strabo sums up Pytheas as an 'arch falsifier' – *About the Ocean* was cited by historians and geographers for centuries with a visible influence on early cartography, like the map by Ptolemy (on page 22) which shows Scotland bent off at a right angle, most likely because of a reliance on Pytheas's erroneous coordinates.

Into the new millennium and the shadows cloaking the heartlands of France, Germany, Spain and Britain were blazed away by the explorations of Imperial Rome led by Julius Caesar and his successors, producing for the first time detailed documentation of the geography and native cultures encountered. By AD 84 the Gallo-Roman general Agricola was in Scotland. Oblivious to Pytheas's journey, he dispatched a party to circumnavigate, which claimed the Orkney Islands and sighted their own 'Thule' – in this instance, the Shetlands. Meanwhile, in Africa Suetonius Paulinus crossed the Atlas Mountains in the north in AD 42, and in AD 60 a tiny group of Praetorian Guard was dispatched by Nero to navigate the Nile in search of its source, eventually losing the river in the giant Sudd swampland of south Sudan, a mire that would swallow up future search attempts.

Little is known of the Greek cartographer Marinus of Tyre of the second century AD, who painstakingly assembled an atlas attaching coordinates for the first time to every known feature of geography so far collected. The work has since been

A section from the c.1200 copy of the 300 BC original Tabula Peutingeriana, *a 22ft- (7m-) long road map of the Roman Empire marking c.4000 settlements. The British coast is in the top-left corner.*

Opposite: Gallic War, *1753. The burning of a human-filled 'wicker man' by druids of ancient Britain, as described by Julius Caesar in his* Commentary on the Gallic War. *In fact there is no evidence that this form of sacrifice was ever used – the story was likely an invention to exaggerate the barbarity of the natives.*

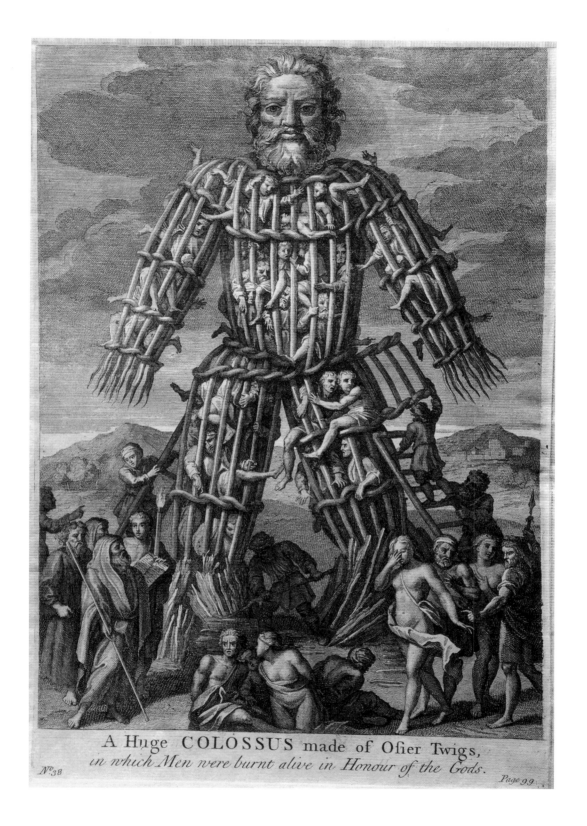

A Huge COLOSSUS made of Ofier Twigs,
in which Men were burnt alive in Honour of the Gods.

N.º 38

Page 99.

TRANSEAS VEL CIRCIVS
SEPTENTRIO VEL APERC
A SEPTENTRIONE
LIBYA
INTERIOR
TROPICVS
CAN CRI
Equinoctialis Circulus
AETHIOPIA INTERIOR
AETHIOPIA
SVB
AEGYPTO
ARABIA
FELIX
SARMATIA
DACIA
SINVS BARBARICVS
SINVS HESPERIVS
TROPICVS
LIBANOTVS
AVSTER

lost but underpinned the only book on cartography to have survived Antiquity, *Claudius Ptolemy's Geography*, written AD *c.*140-150. Ptolemy's work was also lost for centuries, and seems to have been virtually unknown to geographers until the ninth century when it was discovered by Muslim cartographers. Its equally influential European rediscovery was made in the early fourteenth century by the Byzantine-Greek monk Maximus Planudes, who translated it into Latin and made the first of many reconstructions of Ptolemy's maps based on the information in the text.

Being the only survivor of its age, *Geography* neatly summarized the history of ancient exploration. With his maps reproduced in medieval manuscripts, supplanting the religious *mappae mundi* (maps of the world), Ptolemy continued to hold sway over popular geographical perception for the next 200 years.

The world as it was mapped by the second-century Greek mathematician Ptolemy, this copy printed in Rome, 1478.

ISLAMIC GEOGRAPHERS AND THE SEARCH FOR KNOWLEDGE 833

'Seek knowledge, even if you have to go to China.'

THE PROPHET MUHAMMAD

With their inheritance of the work of the Alexandria-based Claudius Ptolemy, Arab and Persian scholars in the ninth century were incorporating Hellenistic geography for their foundation to build the world on maps. The Islamic geographers revised Ptolemy's centuries-old *Geography* with their own genius and the knowledge accumulated from Arab traders and expeditions to China, Africa, India and the East Indies, together with Eastern data accrued over centuries and unobtainable to the Greeks and Romans.

Rectangular world map from the Book of Curiosities, *c.1020-50, an illustrated anonymous cosmography, compiled in Egypt during the first half of the eleventh century.*

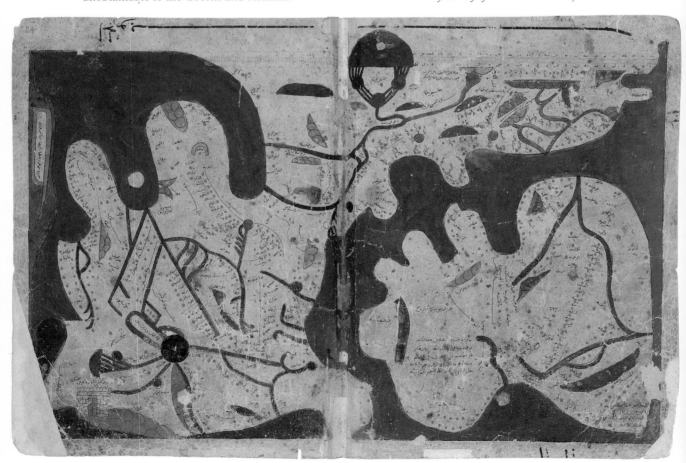

By 833 Muhammad ibn Musa al-Khwarizmi, a Persian
scholar of Baghdad's House of Wisdom, made the first major
reworking of *Geography* with his *Book of the Description of the
Earth*. Hampered by a lack of the original maps, al-Khwarizmi
set about refining the work with more modern information,
correcting, for example, Ptolemy's wild overestimation of the
length of the Mediterranean Sea from 63 degrees of longitude
to a more accurate 50 degrees, and showed the Atlantic and
Indian Oceans as open bodies of water, rather than landlocked
seas as Ptolemy had asserted.

Following this, Ibn Khordadbeh wrote the earliest surviving
Arabic book of administrative geography, detailing the trade
routes all the way to the Indies with maps and recording the
land, people and culture of the southern Asian coast as far
as Brahmaputra, the Andaman Islands, Peninsular Malaysia
and Java. As well as making early references to the lands of
Tang China, Unified Silla (Korea) and Japan, Ibn Khordadbeh

*Circular world map by Al-Sharif
Al-Idrisi from manuscript in
Bodleian, 1154.*

also mentions the mythical land of Wak-Wak, which is most
famous for its tree of screaming human heads, which roared
in salutation of the sun at dawn and dusk: 'East of China are
the lands of Wak-Wak, which are so rich in gold that the
inhabitants make the chains for their dogs and the collars
for their monkeys of this metal. They manufacture tunics
woven with gold.'

In the early tenth century, a remarkable journey was made
by the Arabic traveller Ahmad ibn Fadhlan, who crossed the
Caspian Sea in 922 as part of an embassy to the Volga Bulgaria,

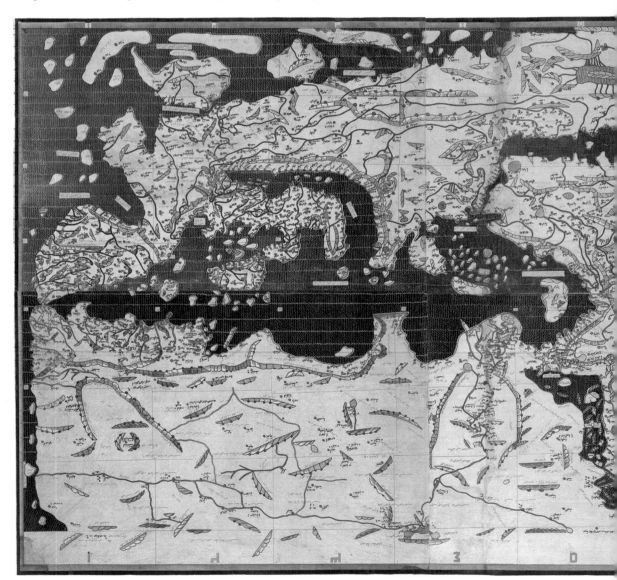

in what is now European Russia. A large part of his journal – a complete version of which was discovered only in 1923 – is devoted to his study of the 'Rusiyyah' people – better known as Vikings. To his Arab eyes the blond-haired men were extraordinary, as tall as palm trees and tattooed with dark 'tree patterns' from 'fingernails to neck'. Ibn Fadhlan proclaims the Rusiyyah to be perfect physical specimens, though utterly vulgar and completely lacking in personal hygiene, and he reports with horror the gruesome sight of human sacrifice as part of a ship funeral of one of their chieftains.

The world map from the Tabula Rogeriana, *created by the Arab geographer Muhammad al-Idrisi, in 1154. The map is shown here upside-down for familiarity, as it is drawn with south at the top, common to Islamic maps of this period as those in the many territories north of Mecca turned south to pray.*

An even more revered traveller is the Iraq-born Abu'l-Hasan al-Mas'udi, sometimes called the 'Herodotus of the Arabs', whose ravenous curiosity led him out to see the world for himself. His travels took him to Syria, Iran, Armenia, the shores of the Caspian Sea, the Indus valley, Sri Lanka, Oman and the east coast of Africa as far south as Zanzibar, possibly even to Madagascar. Though much of his writing has not survived, more than twenty works are attributed to al-Mas'udi, on subjects ranging from sects to poisons. The most impressive is the encyclopedic *Akhbār al-zamān* (The History of Time), which forms thirty volumes, a towering study of the kingdoms within the Islamic world – and beyond. Al-Mas'udi compares himself to a man 'who having found pearls of all kinds and colours gathers them together into a necklace and makes them into an ornament that its possessor guards with great care'.

The tree of screaming human heads, said to be found on the mythical island of Wak-Wak, common to early Islamic maps.

The nearest intellectual successor to al-Mas'udi appears some forty years after his death in the form of the polymath Abu Rayhan al-Biruni, who in 990 at the age of only seventeen accurately calculated the global latitude of his town. A shining figurehead of the Islamic Golden Age, often described as the father of geodesy and anthropology, al-Biruni travelled extensively throughout India, providing meticulous geographical detail and writing on the various customs and creeds he encountered, for which he was given the title 'al-Ustadh' (The Master). Most remarkably, he also devised a new technique to measure the Earth's circumference, calculating it to within 10.44 miles (16.8km) of the accurate measurement. Plotting the

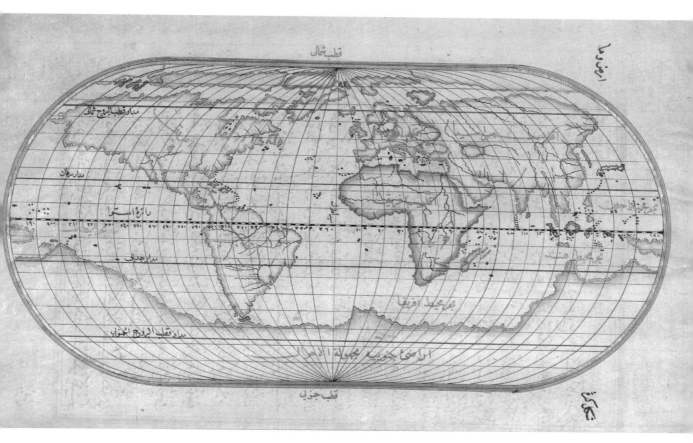

World map of Piri Reis (1465/70-1553), Turkish admiral and cartographer.

coordinates of known cities and geographical features on his globe, he realized the entirety of Eurasia took up only two-fifths of the planet. Traditional thought dictated that the rest took the form of a 'World Ocean', but from his studies of specific gravity there logically had to be a continent in the ocean between Europe and Asia. Through pure deduction, he had proposed the existence of the Americas in 1037.

Coincidentally, this unseen continent had been found by Europeans just a few years before al-Biruni published his theory in *al-Qanun al-Mas'ud* (Codex Masudicus). What's more, the discovery had been made by the same 'unsophisticated' race that had so horrified ibn Fadhlan: the Vikings.

THE VIKINGS DISCOVER
AMERICA 986-1010

'He who has travelled can tell what spirit governs the men he meets.' FROM THE OLD NORSE POEM *THE HÁVAMÁL*

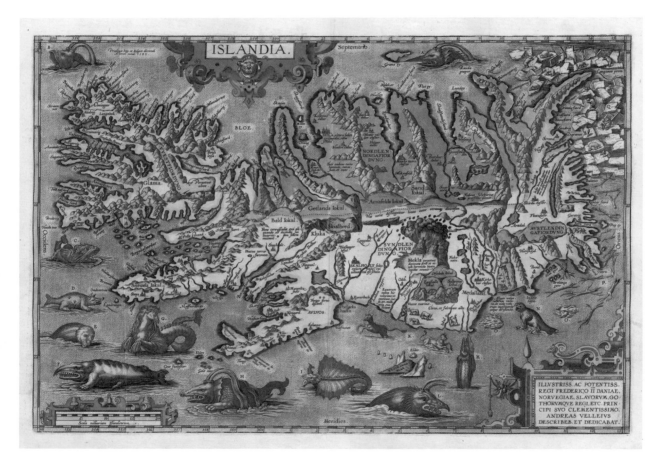

Ortelius's famous 1587 map of Iceland, with exploding volcanoes and mythological sea creatures.

Centuries before Columbus, the Vikings trod the sands of American shores. In Greenland, Eirik Raudi, also known as Erik the Red, had successfully colonized a new home for himself, his family and followers, after being banished from Norway for the crime of manslaughter. Stories of his vast, fertile new country were propelled by Eirik's cunning invention of 'Greenland' as an alluring name for the new settlement, three-quarters of which is actually covered by

A painting by the nineteenth-century artist Jens Erik Carl Rasmussen of a Viking vessel off the Greenland coast.

a permanent ice sheet. Rumour of abundant walrus tusk ivory – one of Medieval Europe's most valuable trade materials – reached Norwegian and Icelandic ears, and the northern waters soon teemed with vessels carrying families determined to stake their claim in the new land rush. And so perhaps it was inevitable that among this throng of traffic a ship would slip from its course by accident, and its passengers stumble onto an even greater discovery.

In 986 the Norseman Bjarni Herjólfsson made landfall in Iceland, intending to meet up with his family. To his dismay he was told that his father had left the country, having sold his home to join Erik the Red on his quest to colonize Greenland. Herjólfsson set out again, this time for the new settlement, but things didn't quite go to plan. On the third day of his journey his ship was swept up by a northern wind, carrying him a great distance until finally he met with strange terrain – he had discovered Labrador (northeast Canada). Herjólfsson explored the forests and hills, and then made another attempt for Greenland, this time successfully. Little was made of his sightings until fifteen years later when Leif Erikson, son of the Red, bought Herjólfsson's own boat and headed for the land he had described. (Incidentally, it is Erikson, not Herjólfsson, who is given credit for the discovery in the saga of Erik the Red.)

Around the year 1000, Erikson and his fifteen-man crew retraced Herjólfsson's voyage and arrived at 'a land of flat stones' they called Helluland, according to the sagas that record the story. It is generally agreed that this is Baffin Island, the fifth-largest island in the world, in what is today the Canadian territory of Nunavut. The barren ground and mountains were not the most suitable for settlement though and Erikson moved on, south to 'Markland'. Here again he found inhospitable shores thick with woodland and so continued his journey, making for another shore in the distance which he found to have a more agreeable terrain and climate. He remained there for a winter, and sung the country's praises on his return: temperate, rich with vegetation, its freshwater teeming with fish. Most wonderfully he told of lush grapes on the vine, and so it was named 'Vinland', the land of wine. (Whether this last feature was true, or whether Erikson had as great a gift for false advertising as his father, is debatable.)

Regardless, Vinland was now on the Norse radar and another expedition was dispatched, led by Leif's brother Thorvald, as Erikson had to remain behind to maintain the Greenland colony. This time, however, the Vikings encountered resistance from the native population and Thorvald was felled by an arrow. For a while the Norse were put off from making further efforts at exploring the new country until 1010, when Erikson's brother-in-law, Thorfinn Karlsefini, landed with a contingent of sixty-one men with their wives and farming animals in tow, determined to form a settlement. From this point the story is told with variation among the sagas, but it can be gathered that the Norse base was situated on the northern tip of Newfoundland. There is currently little evidence as to how much of their surroundings they explored, but it seems they maintained a presence on the American continent until the mid-fourteenth century. In 1960 an archaeological site at L'Anse aux Meadows at this general spot produced evidence of such a settlement, confirming this extraordinary pre-Columbian transoceanic contact.

Another related discovery of recent times is decidedly more controversial. 'The Vinland Map' is purported to be a fifteenth-century world map showing these Norse discoveries in the New World, including 'Vinlanda Insula', as well as Africa, Asia and Europe. The map was found in 1957 (three years before the unearthing of the Viking site at L'Anse aux Meadows) among the pages of a medieval text *Hystoria Tartarorum*, after a London book dealer named Irving Davis offered the slim volume for sale to the British Museum. It was treated with deep suspicion right away. The position of wormholes in the document did not match those in the book, although this appeared to be resolved a year later when the same dealer happened to come across a third volume with the

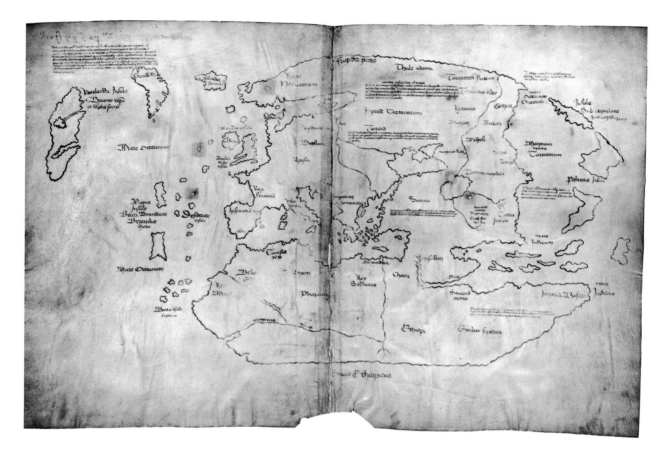

corresponding markings. Since this time, the Vinland map has been subjected to increasingly intense and technologically complex scrutiny, with chemical analysis of the ink, photomicrography, spectroscopy and radiocarbon dating all carried out over the years. No official consensus has so far been reached as to its authenticity.

Yale University, to which the map was donated in 1965, have refused to officially come down on either side. 'We regard ourselves as the custodians of an extremely interesting and controversial document', said university librarian Alice Prochaska in 2002, 'and we watch the scholarly work on it with great interest.' However, in 2011 Yale's Professor of History, Paul Freedman, stated that the map is 'unfortunately a fake', and this is the position generally held today.

The Vinland map of Norse discoveries, likely a forgery.

THE TRAVELS OF MARCO POLO
1271-95

'I did not tell half of what I saw.' Marco Polo

By the late eleventh century the end of the Viking age
was in sight as Scandinavia underwent enormous cultural
change. The Catholic Church was growing in power, and the
kingdoms of Norway, Denmark and Sweden were taking
shape. The last reference to a voyage to Vinland is recorded
as having taken place in 1121, when the Icelandic bishop Eric
Gnupsson 'went to seek Vinland'. Nothing more was heard
from him, and soon, for reasons that remain mysterious,
the colonial experiment of Vinland was abandoned (as
Greenland would be in the mid-fifteenth century). Central
Asia, meanwhile, was also experiencing enormous change,
engineered by one man – Genghis Khan. In the early
thirteenth century the Mongol warlord had brought together

The Catalan Atlas *of 1375, one
of the earliest portolan charts
(used by marine navigators)
to incorporate geographic data
drawn directly from Marco Polo's
record of his travels.*

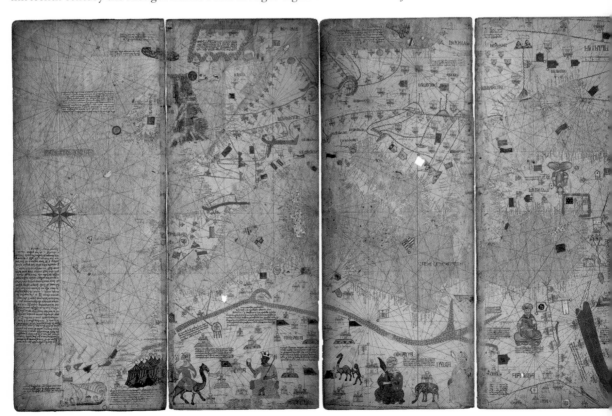

the warring tribes of Central Asia into one unstoppable force, a unity that also created an unprecedented stability to Eurasia, the Pax Mongolica (Mongol Peace), which allowed, for the first time, travellers to have a relatively safe passage from Europe to China.

In 1298 the Italian writer Rustichello da Pisa languished in a dank Genoese prison when a recently arrived prisoner, a merchant traveller in his mid-forties, began to tell the story of his life. For months the man shared with his fellow inmates his wild tales of travel over impossible distances to the East, past the rivers of jade lined with wild flowers in Khotan, through the merciless deserts of Persia and the lush countryside of Badakhshan. Most impressive of all were the stories of life at the court of the Mongol emperor, the Great Khan, of the savage forces known to them as Tartars, who, as the merchant put it, 'had made up their minds to conquer the whole world', and who held all of Eastern Christendom in abject terror. The writer and the raconteur decided to collaborate. The merchant sent for his notes from Venice and the romance author penned

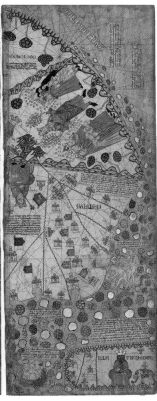

the tale, the love interest in this case being adventure itself. The result was a book that is still in print after 700 years, and has been variously titled *Book of the Marvels of the World, or Description of the World*, or in Italy *Il Milione* (The Million). English readers know it best as *The Travels of Marco Polo*.

In 1269 a 15-year-old Marco met his father Niccolò Polo and his uncle Maffeo for the first time, when the men returned to Venice from a mammoth journey to the East. According to *The Travels*, Niccolò and Maffeo had travelled from Constantinople in 1260 to the Crimean port of Sudak in search of trading opportunity. (Their timing was fortuitous – soon after they left, the Byzantine emperor Michael VIII Palaiologos seized the city, and any Venetians were captured and blinded.) They travelled to the Volga to sell goods, but their return was disrupted by local warfare. They took refuge in Bukhara (in modern Uzbekistan), and accepted an invitation

Lorenz Fries's 1522 map of China, the first to depict Marco Polo's writings (e.g. the port of Quinzay [Hangzhou] on the eastern coast and Zinpangri [Japan]) on a map devoted purely to the Far East.

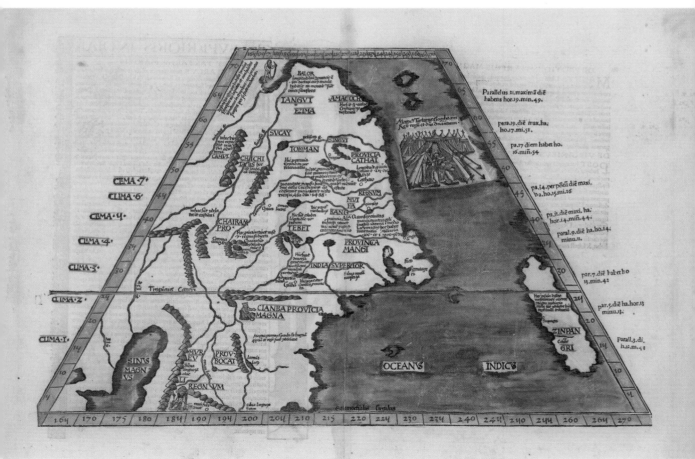

from the Tartar khan of the Levant to visit his overlord,
Kublai, the Great Khan of all the Tartars, in his distant palace
at Khanbalik (Peking) in Cathay (China). Kublai had a cast
of mind more inquisitive than that of his predecessors, and
received the two visitors from the Far West courteously.
After learning of their Christian faith, he bid them return
to Venice, to fetch 100 learned men to teach him of the
Christian religion.

It was this mission that Niccolò and Maffeo Polo had
arrived home at Venice to complete. The new pope,
Gregory X, gave his blessing to the endeavour but not to
the 100 men, and so in 1271 Niccolò and Maffeo began their
journey back to distant Cathay with just one escort – 17-year-
old Marco. The trio sailed to Acre, Israel, and rode camels
to the Iranian port of Hormuz. The plan was to sail to
Cathay but the ships were defective, and so they began their
infamous overland journey along the Silk Road, the ancient
web of trade routes that led through the Asian continent. The
extraordinary expansion and power of the Mongol Empire
had unified the region to the point that such a journey could
be made successfully, but not without risk. For safety the Polo
men travelled much of the way in the company of a caravan
of merchants, but even so had to fend off assaults by bandits,
sandstorms and other scourges. After an estimated three-
and-a-half years of travel, the Venetians arrived at the palace
of Kublai Khan. The Polo men were received with great
enthusiasm, and the emperor was presented with papal letters
and blessed oil of Jerusalem.

From this point, Marco Polo's story is of his, Niccolò's and
Maffeo's time in China at the pleasure of the khan, serving the
Mongolian court in an honorary official capacity. Although
his book was initially dismissed as mostly fantastic (which,
of course, did nothing to diminish its popularity throughout
Europe), over hundreds of pages he relays wonderful details of
the geography and cultural history of the empire. Highlights
include local histories such as that of Princess Khutulun, a
cousin of Kublai Khan, who Polo describes as a superb warrior.
To the despair of her parents, Khutulun would only consent
to marriage if the suitor agreed to wrestle her. If he won they
would marry, if he lost he would forfeit his horse. By the
time she died, she was unmarried and possessed a collection
of 10,000 horses.

Polo also debunks popular fables and misconceptions of the landscape and inhabitants of eastern Asia provided by other earlier writers. For example, Odoric of Pordenone (1286-1331) declared the Yangtze river to flow through a country of pygmies only three spans high (a span being the width of the hand from tip of thumb to little finger); while Giovanni da Pian del Carpine (1185-1252) reported 'wild men, who do not speak at all and have no joints in their legs', as well as monsters who looked like women with dogs for husbands, and other equally fantastic details that one can trace back to the mythology of Antiquity. Polo also makes the first European mention of kite-flying, albeit in a rather unusual context. This can be found only in the rarest form of the manuscript, a Latin translation in two documents dating to the fifteenth century. Here Polo relates to Rustichello that, when a Chinese merchant ship is to depart, the crew divine the auspices by sending up a giant man-carrying kite:

The men of the ship will have a wicker framework ... Next they will find some fool or drunkard and lash him to the frame, since no one in his right mind or with his wits about him would expose himself

Giacomo Gastaldi took much of his information (over 140 toponyms) for his 1574 mapping of Asia from Marco Polo's stories, even leaving out the existing Lake Aral (east of the Caspian) because Polo does not write of it.

to that peril. This is done when the wind is high; then they raise the framework into the teeth of the wind and the wind lifts up the framework and carries it aloft, and the men hold it by the long rope.

Even before weighing the reliability of Polo himself, there is the age of his manuscript to consider and the inherent issues this brings. Because it was written before the time of the printing press, copies were reproduced by hand, and so surviving manuscripts vary considerably in nuance of translation. Critics also point to the suspicious omissions made by Polo of key aspects of contemporary life – Chinese characters, tea, chopsticks, the practice of foot-binding. Rather damning, too, is the fact that not once does Polo mention the Great Wall of China; but then neither do the earlier travellers Giovanni de' Marignolli (1290-1360) and Odoric of Pordenone (1286-1381). It has also been pointed out that what we know today as the giant wall is a larger structure built two centuries after Polo, and that during his time its antecedent was of less significance.

Perhaps, then, the best way to enjoy *The Travels* is to recognize the impossibility of conclusively winnowing the myth from the matter and enjoy, with a pinch of salt, the combination of Rustichello's languid, poetic prose with Polo's rich accumulation of anecdotes; and forgive him for maybe not personally experiencing all of his 'recollections'.

One of the greatest maps of the Age of Exploration, the Fra Mauro map of 1459. It features information provided by Marco Polo, such as the note of northeast Asian tribes in the land of Tenduch named 'Ung and Mongul'. The map also carries the Polo reference to northern China as 'Cathay', and the southern region controlled by the Song Dynasty as 'Mangi'.

THE EXTRAORDINARY VOYAGES OF CHINESE ADMIRAL ZHENG HE 1405-33

'Our sails, loftily unfurled like clouds day and night, continued their course as swift as a star.' ADMIRAL ZHENG HE

By 1368 the Great Mongolian state that had offered such welcome to European missionaries and traders like the Polo family finally fell, disintegrating into competing khanate factions. The Han Chinese Ming Dynasty took control, and set about reinforcing the homeland, with an army over a million strong and the largest naval docks in the world. When the third Ming emperor Yongle rose to power in 1402, the Chinese gaze extended farther, beyond its borders, with the dispatching of an enormous expeditionary force into the South Pacific and Indian oceans as an unprecedented show of strength. To lead this venture, the Yongle emperor appointed a favourite palace eunuch and commander named Zheng He (pronounced jung-huh).

Never has there been a spectacle of such might as the colossal Chinese fleet of Admiral Zheng He (1371-1435), considered China's greatest explorer. In seven voyages over twenty years, Zheng He opened up much of south and western Asia, and even east Africa, to his traditionally insular nation. He did this with ships of massive size: giant junks known as 'treasure ships', accompanied by an armada of support vessels. Reputedly the largest of these ships had four decks and measured 450ft (137m) long and 180ft (55m) at the beam, the widest part of a ship. The

Section of the Mao Kun woodblock map, from the Wubei Zhi, *the most comprehensive Chinese military book ever produced, running to 10,405 pages. Shown here is Zheng He's passage through Malacca (Malaysia) on the* Mao Kun *map, commonly referred to as* Zheng He's Navigation Map.

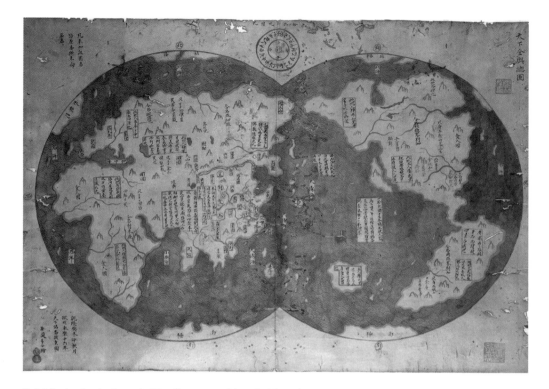

British sinologist Joseph Needham considered this to be a conservative figure, estimating the length could have been as much as 600ft (183m).*

To put these measurements in context, this is twice the width and just over half the length of the *Titanic* (at 92½ft/28m wide and 882¾ft/269m long). The vessels would also have completely dwarfed Columbus's largest ship, *Santa María* – in fact, if you took every ship involved in the explorations of Columbus and Vasco da Gama, you'd be able to fit them all on the top deck of just one of Zheng He's treasure ships. Individually the Chinese vessels were impressive; together, as they moved in formation, one would have had the impression of an entire wooden city sliding across the water.

When construction was finally completed in 1405 the Treasure Fleet was dispatched on a mission of exploration. Sixty-two of the behemoths, together with 225 smaller vessels (a total of 27,780 men) all under Zheng He's command, headed

A recently discovered copy of a world map claimed by some to have been based on information provided by Admiral Zheng He's voyages. Distinctive errors, however, betray it as a copy of an early seventeenth-century European map.

* These sizes have been contested on the grounds of sheer impracticability. Although there is to be expected a degree of hyperbole to such legend, it is interesting to note that two of the dry docks at Longjiang, where the ships were probably built, were 210ft (64m) wide, sufficient for the construction of vessels of such monstrous dimensions.

for the Indian ocean to Calicut (Kozhikode) with orders to examine territories on their way along India's east coast, establish trade networks and collect tributes to the emperor. After stops at Champa (southern Vietnam), Siam (Thailand), Malacca and Java, they reached Calicut, where they purchased huge quantities of spices. On their return to China the fleet was intercepted by the Indonesian pirate Chen·Zuyi, who rather ill-advisedly attempted to seize the fleet. The Chinese killed more than 5000 of the pirates, sank ten of their ships and continued on their way unfazed.

For the next seven years the fleet ranged the Indian ocean. By the fourth voyage (1413-15) the crew totalled 28,560 men, and the massive force had progressed along Arabian coasts, reaching as far as Jeddah in Saudi Arabia. Their holds were filled with exotic goods and live cargo with which to honour and delight their emperor, such as the nineteen foreign envoys collected, with the task of paying homage. From the next voyage to India came an even more precious haul of ostriches, zebra and camels. But the jewel of the floating menagerie was a giant giraffe from Kenya via Bengal, which caused a sensation on its arrival in China. Having never seen such a creature the giraffe was deemed to be a qilin, a mythical creature said to herald good fortune, and readily accepted by the imperial court from the Bengali envoy.

As impressive as Zheng He's travels are, there are unsubstantiated theories that his Treasure Fleet may have reached even farther than previously thought. The one piece of documentary evidence to support this idea is Fra Mauro's world map of 1459 (see The Travels of Marco Polo entry on page 43 for full image), which features a junk rounding the southern tip of Africa, accompanied by the intriguing inscription:

About the year of Our Lord 1420 a ship, what is called a Zoncho de India [junk from India], on a crossing of the Sea of India towards the Isle of Men and Women, was driven by a storm beyond the Cape of Diab, through the Green Isles, out into the Sea of Darkness on their way west and southwest. Nothing but air and water was seen for forty days and by their reckoning they ran 2000 miles and fortune deserted them.

Though Mauro records this as the journey of a single ship, and includes no mention of Zheng He, it has been taken by

Shen Du's painting on silk of the giraffe given by Bengali envoys as tribute to the Yongle emperor on 20 September 1414.

A section from Fra Mauro's world map drawn in 1459, which shows a junk rounding the southern tip of Africa.

some to indicate the possibility that the Chinese admiral made it at least as far as the Atlantic. (There is, however, little other evidence to support this.) The source of this quote is thought to be the Portuguese merchant explorer Niccolò de' Conti, who roamed the Indian Ocean in the same era as Zheng He. After leaving his home in Damascus to cross the desert to Baghdad, De' Conti spent more than twenty years exploring the trade routes that brought goods to the emporia of the Levant and on to India, Sumatra, Java and modern Vietnam in his quest to trace the source of the exotic spices. (The information gathered by de' Conti was added to that of Marco Polo by Fra Mauro to embellish his mapping of the East.)

After a sixth and seventh voyage, during which he explored the east African coastline possibly as far south as the Mozambique Channel opposite Madagascar, Zheng He returned home to a changed China. Now ruled by the Xuande emperor, the principal state concern was the swelling threat of Mongol resurgence. An end was put to seaborne exploration, with funds instead devoted to internal development.* 'We have traversed more than 100,000 li [about 500 miles/800km] of immense water spaces', wrote Zheng in summation of his voyages, 'and have beheld in the ocean huge waves like mountains rising in the sky, and we have set eyes on barbarian regions far away hidden in a blue transparency of light vapours, while our sails, loftily unfurled like clouds day and night, continued their course as swift as a star, traversing those savage waves as if we were treading a public thoroughfare.'

The anonymous Selden map of early seventeenth-century China is extraordinary in that it charts not just China but also the whole of east and southeast Asia, and with its illustration of shipping routes with compass bearings is the earliest known example of Chinese merchant cartography.

---

* Europe would exist beyond China's knowledge for decades to come. When the Portuguese entered Canton harbour in 1517, Ku Yin-hsiang, minister of maritime affairs, would be forced to break the news to his countrymen that 'Fulang chi [Portugal] is the name of a country, not that of a cannon as generally assumed'.

THE PORTUGUESE EXPLORE
THE AFRICAN TROPICS 1435-88

'The Lusitanian prince, who, Heaven-inspired,
To love of useful glory raised mankind.'

JAMES THOMSON ON HENRY THE NAVIGATOR, FROM *THE SEASONS*, 1730

As China was breaking apart its formidable treasure ship armada and turning her back on the rest of the world, the greatest era of European maritime adventure was just beginning to unfold. The Age of Discovery, loosely defined

Stefano Bonsignori map of western Africa including Senegal, Guinea, Mali, Sierra Leone, 1580.

as the period between the late fifteenth to the eighteenth centuries, was a period of prodigious transoceanic expansion, of ruthless empire-building driven by an insatiable rapacity. The history of this period is traditionally dominated by the voyages of Christopher Columbus (see Christopher Columbus entry on pages 52-7), who, though a citizen of the Genoese Republic, carried out the enterprise under the auspices of the Catholic monarchs of Spain. But, in fact, an earlier engineer of this European shift in fortune was Portugal, a nation whose contributions are often overlooked, and whose catalysis was most unexpected at the time. No one could have imagined that, within 100 years, Portugal would possess the most extensive naval empire ever built, ranging the waters from the North Atlantic to the China Sea.

In the fifteenth century the lust for African gold and the aspiration of a sea route around the southern tip of the continent to cash in on the spice trade of the East fired plans for exploration down Africa's west coast. This was an endeavour previously viewed with pessimism, because of the inherent danger of the wild currents, barren coastlines, scorching heat and hostile natives. But for the Portuguese the significant step was made by one of their own, the navigator Gil Eannes, when he rounded the fearsome Cape Bojador in 1435, a prominent headland on the northern coast of the western Sahara (in Arabic its name is Abu Khatar – 'the father of danger'). Beyond this point lay the deathly zone of unexplored Atlantic ocean labelled by Arab geographers as the great 'Green Sea of Darkness', a region riddled with ship-breaking sea monsters, where the sun shone so close to the Earth at its equator that the heat was said to incinerate ships and the men they carried.

Directing Portugal's southern exploration was Prince Henry, whose determined expansionism earned him the nickname 'The Navigator' (despite the fact that he never took part in any of the voyages himself). Though he has in the past been lionized as an agent of scientific motive, the reality – as is usually the way – was far more mercenary. Henry envisioned for himself a North African empire built on the Saharan gold and slavery trade, but when these ambitions came to naught he refocused exploration to the Senegal and Gambia rivers, hoping these would yield access to a golden hinterland. Under Henry's sponsorship a new kind of ship, the caravel, was developed in 1451, replacing the clumsier and more fragile, fixed single-mast balinger. With its triangular sails, the caravel allowed for beating, or tacking, meaning the ships could travel on a zigzag pattern upwind, and with these new nimble vessels navigators flying Henry's colours pushed as far south as Sierra Leone and Cape Verde by his death in 1460.

In 1469 the merchant Fernão Gomes was granted a monopoly on trade by King Afonso V in the Gulf of Guinea, with the condition that Gomes investigate a further 100 leagues (3 nautical miles/5.5km) of the African coast each year for five years. This, with his captains, he enthusiastically exceeded. He established a trading post at Elmina ('The Mine') in present-day Ghana in 1471, the first European settlement in west Africa. He then crossed the equator in 1474 to find the islands of the Gulf of Guinea. Gomes's monopoly was withdrawn the following year, however, when the task of further exploration fell to Prince João. In 1481 the 26-year-old prince became King João II, and immediately set about re-establishing the power of the Portuguese throne, curtailing the influence of the aristocracy and renewing efforts to find a route to the Orient. The outpost at Elmina was fortified, and João engaged a navigator named Diogo Cão to exploit this position and to continue the discovery of the African coastline on the way to a sea route to India.

Cão was to mark his progress with padrões, large stone crosses bearing the coat of arms of Portugal. He investigated every river mouth, pursuing each inland to acquire data on the terrain and native populations. Most importantly of all he was to detect clues as to the whereabouts of the mythical kingdom of Prester John (see Sir Walter Ralegh Searches for El Dorado entry on pages 120-3). It was by following these instructions that Cão became the first European to sight and explore the Congo river, before proceeding to southern Angola and finally turning for home armed with his discoveries. On his second voyage, launched in 1485, he travelled even farther, reaching as far as Cape Cross on the barren Namibian coast, but his efforts were frustrated by the contrary Benguela current and he was unable to round the southern tip of the continent.

The voyages of Cão had shown that an expedition of multiple vessels would have the best chance of success, and so in 1487, with three caravels and a support ship, Bartolomeu Dias set out to finish Cão's work. After passing Cape Cross, the expedition approached the mouth of the Orange river, the longest in South Africa. A violent storm swept the sailors westwards, away from the coast into open ocean, but they continued on their southern course until, having turned northeast to ride the strong Antarctic winds of the South Atlantic, they realized they had finally (at distance) rounded the cape. After thirty days without a glimpse of land, they entered what is known today as Mossel Bay on the Southern Cape, watched by natives herding their cattle. They then travelled as far as Algoa Bay, about 425 miles (684km) east of the Cape of Good Hope, where they erected a padrão. Shaken by the encounters with such wild sea weather, Dias originally named the Cape of Good Hope the Cabo das Tormentas ('Cape of Storms'), but on their return to Portugal in 1488 a delighted King João II devised its modern toponym, for to Portugal it represented the gateway to a new era of empire expansion and extraordinary profit. All that now remained was to complete the final leg of the sea route to India.

A Portuguese nautical chart of the North Atlantic by Pedro Reinel, 1504.

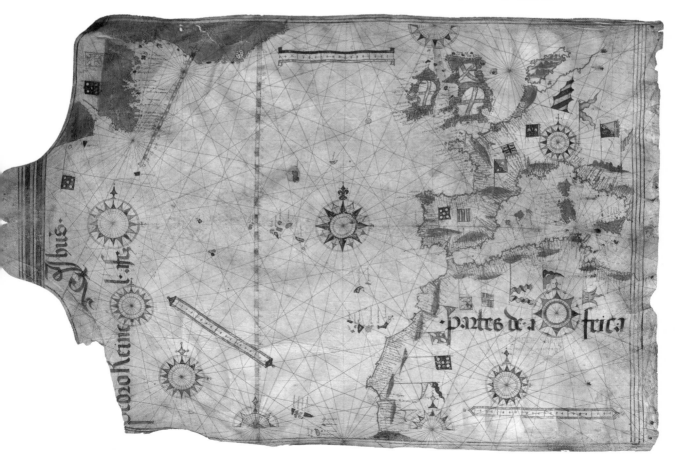

CHRISTOPHER COLUMBUS CROSSES THE ATLANTIC OCEAN 1492-1504

'The sea will grant each man new hope, and sleep will bring dreams of home.' Cʜʀɪsᴛᴏᴘʜᴇʀ Cᴏʟᴜᴍʙᴜs

With the Portuguese progress, the seaway from Europe to the Eastern world via Africa was materializing amid a frenzy of competition. The focus on forging a maritime highway had come through necessity. With the fall of Constantinople to the Ottoman Turks in 1453, the stability of the Silk Road – the land route to Asia traversed by Marco Polo – had deteriorated and the risk to caravans of traders was too great. The Portuguese had succeeded in edging down Africa's west coast and around its southern tip, and although it wouldn't be until 1497 that Vasco da Gama would build so spectacularly on this headway, by 1492 it seemed clear that it was, by following this African route, that the treasures of Asia would be found.

In the mind of Christopher Columbus, a Genoan of Portuguese nobility by marriage, there formed a different idea. It was a plan variously inspired by his years trading around the ports of Europe, along the west coast of Africa and perhaps also Iceland; by the chatter and rumour of the mariners that filled the streets of Lisbon, his home from 1477 to 1485; and from communications with the astronomer Paolo dal Pozzo Toscanelli, who provided Columbus with a copy of a letter and map he had originally sent King Afonso V of Portugal in 1474 outlining the idea of reaching the Indies

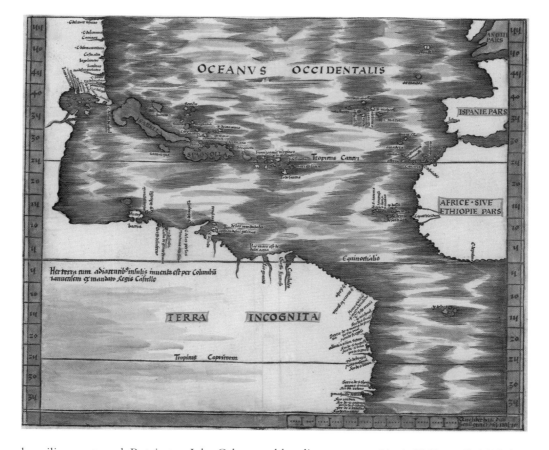

by sailing westward. But, just as John Cabot would realize (and indeed it is thought that the two men might well have originally collaborated on the plan before falling out), a venture of such scale would require greater funding and security than private financiers could bring. His expedition needed the aegis of a monarch, not least to guarantee part-ownership of any discoveries and yields of wealth. Attempts to convince royal councils of the feasibility of a westward heading, however, were roundly rejected. The Crown of Portugal twice turned down the proposal in 1485 and 1488, and applications to the courts of Castile, England and France were also in vain. The same objections were made by each: the Portuguese route was proven, it made no sense to diverge. There was also the issue of Columbus's calculations. He had planned his journey using Pierre d'Ailly's cosmographical work *Imago Mundi* (1410), but misinterpreted the span of a degree of latitude being '56⅔ miles' (91km) – Columbus assumed these to be Roman miles, not the longer Arabic mile used by d'Ailly. This simple

Martin Waldseemüller's Tabula Terre Nove *also known as 'The Admiral's Map', 1513, is one of the earliest printed maps of the New World.*

OPPOSITE: *Map by the navigator Juan de la Cosa, 1500, the earliest representation of the Americas.*

Portrait of a man said to be Christopher Columbus, 1519.

error meant that Columbus estimated the Earth to be 18,765 miles (30,200km) around, almost a quarter less than its actual circumference of 25,000 miles (40,000km). He was also certain that Asia was within only a few thousand nautical miles of Europe. Advisers deemed it unwise to back an expedition founded on such a vast underestimation, but Ferdinand II of Aragon and Isabella I of Castile remained intrigued, and after two years of deliberations Columbus was finally given the sanction of the Spanish court. If successful, he would earn the title of 'Admiral of the Ocean Sea', appointments of viceroy and governor of all new lands discovered, and ten per cent of revenues in perpetuity.

On 3 August 1492 Columbus's expedition of three ships, the *Santa Maria*, *Pinta*, and *Niña*, left the Spanish town of Palos de la Frontera for the Indies, with letters from 'their most Catholic majesties Ferdinand and Isabella' for the Great Khan of the Mongol Yuan Dynasty in China and for the Japanese and Indian princes they would undoubtedly encounter. Their first stop was the Canary Islands to restock and repair the rudder of the *Pinta*, which had broken after only three days, then they headed out into the untravelled Atlantic.

Columbus's journal entries of this journey are short, and reveal little other than the fact that when measuring the leagues travelled he tended to 'count less than the true number, that the crew might not be dismayed if the voyage should prove long', and that he was forced to repeatedly reprimand his sailors, who 'steered badly'. On 11 October, having followed 'an

One of only two known surviving copies of Joan Blaeu's 10ft- (3m-) wide Nova Totius Terrarum Orbis Tabula *(1648). Between the two hemispheres in the lower centre is the world as it was known in 1490, just before the era of oceanic exploration led by Columbus.*

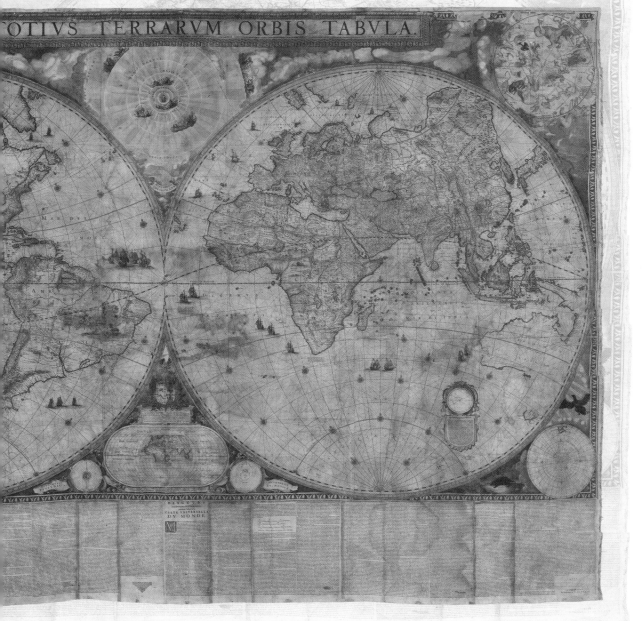

immense flock of birds', a green reed was spotted floating past the ship, and then 'a cane and a stick'. The crew scoured the horizon, eager to win the lifetime pension of 10,000 maravedis (silver and copper coins) promised by King Ferdinand and Queen Isabella to whomever should be first to sight land. After their five weeks' sailing, in the early hours of 12 October, a lookout on the *Pinta*, Rodrigo de Triana, woke the crew with cries of 'land'. His captain, Martín Alonso Pinzón, confirmed the sighting and fired a cannon to alert Columbus. (Triana would not receive the prize, as Columbus would later claim to have seen land before him, and collect the money himself: 'I was on the poop deck at ten o'clock in the evening when I saw a light', he wrote. 'I called Pedro Gutierrez, the Butler of the King's Table … he looked and saw it. I also told Rodrigo Sanchez de Segovia … but he saw nothing because he was standing in the wrong place.')

A painting by John Vanderlyn depicting Christopher Columbus landing in the West Indies on 12 October 1492.

The site of the first European landfall in South America was an island in today's Bahamas, known to its peaceful natives as Guanahani and which Columbus named San Salvador (the exact island has never been identified). 'I could conquer the whole of them with 50 men', noted Columbus of the mild-mannered locals, 'and govern them as I pleased.' The Spaniards left this island to explore five more in the vicinity, and on 28 October landed at Cuba's northeast coast. Thinking this could be the Cathay described by Marco Polo, Rodrigo de Jerez and a talented interpreter named Luis de Torres were sent ashore to find the emperor of China. No imperial palace was found, but they did observe the smoking of tobacco, a habit they immediately adopted.

Columbus moved on to the island of Hispaniola in the Greater Antilles, landing on 5 December. When the *Santa Maria* ran aground on Christmas Day, it was abandoned and the wreck used for target practice to impress the native people. Columbus struck a deal with the local cacique (leader) Guacanagarí, and left thirty-nine of his men behind to establish a colony, including the interpreter de Torres. Columbus, in the *Niña*, then rendezvoused with the *Pinta* on 6 January 1493, and both headed back to Spain, taking with them as many as twenty-five captured members of the hostile Cigüayos tribe encountered in northeast Hispaniola. They entered the harbour of Palos de la Frontera on 15 March 1493, having spent a week in Lisbon after being blown off course by a storm.

When one considers the world-changing significance of this, the first of four voyages made by Columbus, it is strange to think that, in many ways, the mission was ostensibly a failure. He had sworn to establish a route to find the Indies described by Polo, to return laden with the spices, silks and gifts of Eastern kings. None of this he achieved, the most valuable of his cargo being the captured natives of whom only several had survived the crossing. But most remarkably, though Columbus lives on in the modern consciousness as the European who discovered the New World, even after three further voyages (eventually setting foot on mainland South America in the third), Columbus never conceded that what he had found was a new unknown continent – he remained adamant to his death that he had found Asia.

JOHN CABOT JOURNEYS TO NORTH AMERICA 1497-98

'This year, on St John the Baptist's Day, the land of America was found by the Merchants of Bristow.'

ENTRY FOR 24 JUNE 1497, FROM A SIXTEENTH-CENTURY BRISTOL CHRONICLE

Until her death in 2005, the respected British historian Alwyn Ruddock spent the bulk of her academic life researching the Venetian explorer John Cabot, who in 1497 had led an English expedition to North America (the first Europeans to do so successfully since the Vikings 500 years before them). Every so often, rumours that Ruddock had made revolutionary discoveries in the depths of archives around Europe would leak out to great excitement, but then no more would be heard. At one point she completed a draft of a book but, dissatisfied with the result, burnt it. Work began on a second that would – in her words – turn the Cabot story 'upside down', as she claimed to a friend. Ultimately it never materialized. And then came a shocking twist. Shortly after her death, a close friend and trustee of her estate went to Ruddock's house to carry out her posthumous instructions: all of her precious Cabot research – every photocopy, microfiche duplicate and notebook representing decades of groundbreaking investigation – was carefully gathered together, filling seventy-eight large sacks. Then, in accordance with Ruddock's wishes, the entire lot was destroyed.

We will never know for certain why Ruddock concluded with such a perplexing and frustrating act of vandalism of her life's work. But thanks in large part to the efforts of Dr Evan T. Jones and Margaret Condon of the University of Bristol's 'Cabot Project' in the last few years, a number of the documents unearthed by Ruddock have been traced, and we now have a more defined picture than ever of the explorer known as John Cabot, and his remarkable voyage.

The origins of 'Zuan Chabotto' are unknown, but a letter of 1498 refers to him as 'another Genoese like Columbus'. Later he became a Venetian citizen – a record in that city marks him down as a pellizer ('pelt dealer'). By 1483 Cabot was touring

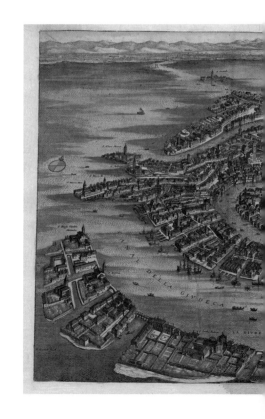

lands of the 'Sultan of Egypt', and claiming to have made a
visit to Mecca, which would have been a dangerous journey
for a Christian to make at the time. One of his merchant deals
must have been less than kosher, as 'letters of justice' were
issued on 4 November 1488, calling for his arrest. He fled to the
Spanish port of Valencia with his wife and three children, to
live under the name 'Juan Caboto de Montecalunya'. There he
worked as a bridge contractor, no doubt drawing on Venetian
knowledge of subaquatic engineering. In Seville he would
have been swept up in the excitement as news of Columbus's
discovery reached Spain, and likely it was this that inspired
his 1495 journey to England with the goal of convincing
Henry VII to authorize a Cabot-led voyage to find the East
described by Marco Polo, via a very different route. Cabot's idea
was to travel across the Atlantic on a more northerly latitude,
which would greatly shorten the distance, and perhaps even
result in beating Columbus to the discovery of China and Japan.

Recognizing its potential to upstage the Spanish, King
Henry approved the mission, granting 'John Cabot, citizen of
Venice' the right by letters patent 'to sail all parts, regions and

Matthäus Merian's finely detailed map of Venice (1636), where John Cabot worked as a pelt dealer before making his voyage to North America.

coasts of the eastern, western and northern sea, under our banners, flags, and ensigns … to find, discover and investigate whatsoever islands, countries, regions or provinces of heathens and infidels …' The letters of patent ensured not only Cabot's claim to any discoveries, but safe passage under the protective banner of the English Crown. As well as a way to the East, it was also hoped the endeavour might result in the discovery of the island of Brasil, a mythical island that lived in rumour, and indeed on maps, for centuries. A mention in the *c.*1471-76 chronicles of the Basque writer Lope Garcia de Salazar gives some idea why merchants sought it so ravenously:

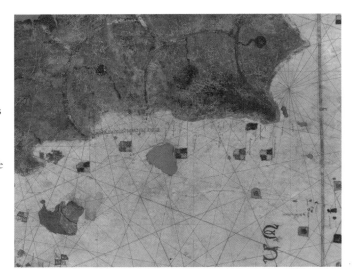

A section of Juan de la Cosa's map (see Christopher Columbus Crosses the Atlantic Ocean entry on page 52 for main image) marking a long stretch of North American coast with five English flags with the note that this was 'the sea discovered by the English'.

A vessel from Bristol found it one dawn and, not knowing that it was it, took on there much wood for firewood, which was all of brazil (brasilwood, an Asiatic timber), took it to their owner and, recognizing it, he became very rich. He and others went in search of it and they could not find it. And sometimes ships saw it but due to a storm could not reach it. And it is round and small and flat.

There is only one known source for Cabot's first and unsuccessful attempt to sail the Atlantic in the summer of 1496, a brief summary in a letter discovered only in the 1950s, written by the Bristol merchant John Day to Christopher Columbus in 1498: 'As regards the first voyage which Your Lordship wished to know about, the fact is that he [Cabot] went in one ship and the people whom he engaged disconcerted him and he went ill provisioned and encountered contrary winds and decided to return.' Cabot returned dejected to Bristol docks and spent eight months planning the second attempt. The 50-ton *Matthew* was secured, and on 2 May 1497 Cabot headed out into the North Atlantic.

Again, no logbook survives (if one was even kept), nor any other record made by Cabot or his crew, and so we rely on references from other contemporary sources to fill in the picture. From the aforementioned John Day letter, written to provide information to a distressed Columbus on the rival expedition, we learn that the crew numbered twenty and included two friends of Cabot, one from Burgundy (The Netherlands) and a 'barber' from Genoa who probably served as ship's surgeon.

Day also describes the course of the *Matthew*, writing that after passing Ireland Cabot's ship sailed north 'for some days' before turning west through waters familiar from Icelandic trading, and onward, farther than any English ship previously travelled, sailing on that course for thirty-five days until finally they sighted land. The location of Cabot's landing has never been conclusively established, but most consider it to be Newfoundland. Most valuably, Day mentions the latitude of Cabot's landing, placing its northernmost point '1800 miles [2900km] west of Cabo Dursal' (Dursey Head, Ireland) and its southernmost point parallel with 'Rio de Burdeos' (the Bordeaux river, France).

De Jode's landmark map of North America, 1593. The first folio-sized atlas map to feature the continent, it is strewn with annotations of explorers' discoveries of the region, including those of Cabot.

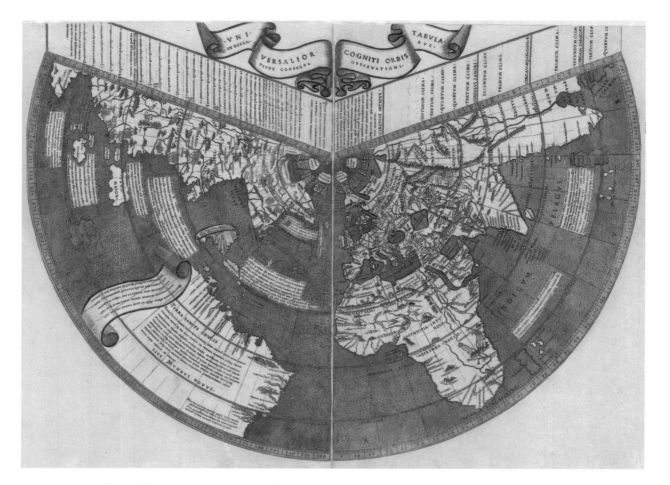

Cabot and his men went ashore with a crucifix and planted 'banners bearing the arms of the Holy Father and the arms of the King of England'. They observed trees large enough for crafting the masts of ships, and a land rich in pasturage. Moving tentatively inland, they came across the remains of a fire set by unknown people, and a whittled and painted stick that suggested the area was inhabited (most likely by the native Beothuk people). Acutely aware of the vulnerability of their small party, the men returned to their ship and sailed along the coastline. 'They saw running ashore two bultos [big objects], one chasing the other, but were unable to tell whether they were men or beasts; and it seemed to them that there were cultivated lands where they thought there might be villages', wrote Day.

After a month of coastal exploration the expedition turned for home, crossing the Atlantic in a mere fifteen

Johannes Ruysch's Universalior Cogniti Orbis Tabula, *showing the extent of European discoveries of America by 1507.*

Herman Moll's map of New Found Land, c.1732, which Cabot claimed for the English.

days and reaching Bristol on 6 August, from where Cabot rode to the king's residence at Woodstock, north of Oxford, to inform him of the news. A note in the king's account books tells us that a reward of £10 was paid to 'hym that founde the new isle'. To the Italians, the idea of this fugitive bankrupt being hailed as the English Columbus was highly comical. On 23 August, Lorenzo Pasqualigo wrote: 'that Venetian of ours [is] called the Great Admiral' – a mockery of the title awarded Columbus – 'and vast honour is paid to him and he goes dressed in silk, and these English run after him like mad'.

Robert Fabyan, author of the sixteenth-century London record *Fabyan's Chronicle*, provides the last mention of John Cabot. Though the explorer could have rested on his laurels, with the success of his voyage affording him favour with Henry VII, Cabot wasted no time in securing funds for another voyage to the new land. The fleet of five ships departed in May 1498, but as they ventured out into the Atlantic ocean they were struck by a violent storm. One ship, half-wrecked, managed to crawl back to Ireland. The rest of the party, including Cabot and his flagship, were never seen again.

VASCO DA GAMA REACHES INDIA 1497-99

*'The heroes and the poets of old have had their day;
another and loftier conception of valour has arisen.'*

FROM THE 1572 PORTUGUESE EPIC *Os Lusíadas*,
WRITTEN IN HONOUR OF VASCO DA GAMA

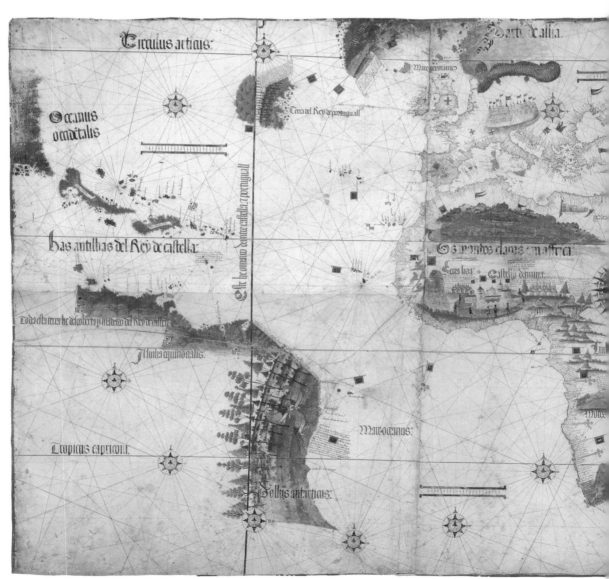

It had been ten years since Bartolomeu Dias had triumphantly rounded the Cape of Good Hope, demonstrating the feasibility of a sea route from Europe to the trading hub of India's Malabar coast, and the Portuguese Crown had been slow on following through. On his return to Europe, Christopher Columbus had stopped at Lisbon, and related to King João II the discoveries he had made for the rival Crown of Castile. An enraged João wrote to the Spanish monarchs, citing the terms of the Treaty of Alcáçovas, which both had signed in 1479, that stated all lands discovered

The Cantino planisphere, or world map, is the earliest existing map displaying Portuguese geographic discoveries. It takes its name from Alberto Cantino, an agent for the Italian Duke of Ferrara, who smuggled it out of Portugal in 1502.

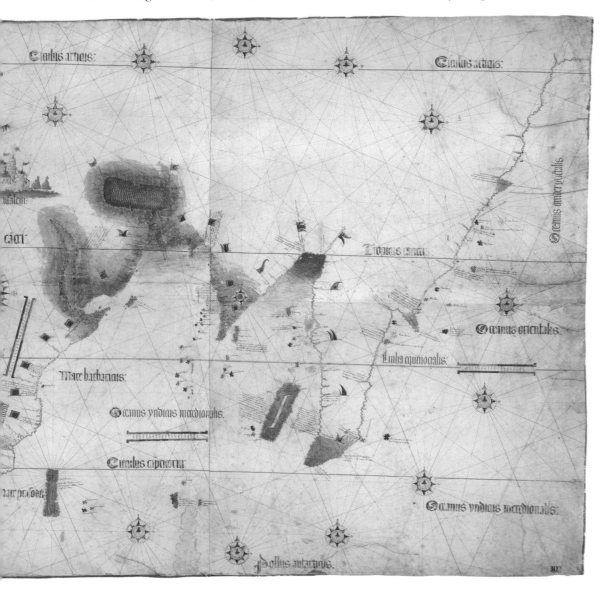

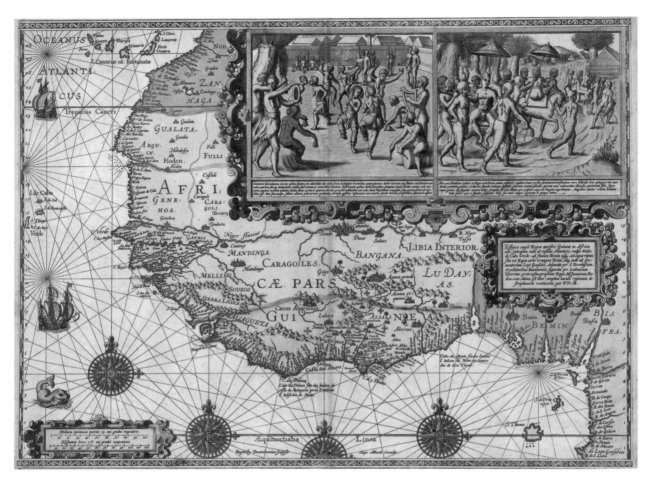

south of the Canary Islands (which in his view included those discovered by Columbus) were in fact the property of Portugal. After negotiation with King Ferdinand and Queen Isabella, a duopoly was agreed with the signing of the Treaty of Tordesillas in 1494, which divided the non-Christian world into two with a meridian line running down through the Atlantic (shown on the Cantino planisphere, vertically bisecting the left-hand third). Discoveries to the west belonged to the Spanish, while those to the east, including Africa's west coast and the route to India, could be claimed by Portugal. (The protracted negotiations of this treaty explains the lull in Portuguese exploration during these years.) Finally, in 1497, with the authorization of King Manuel I of Portugal (a keen emulator of Henry the Navigator), the explorer Vasco da Gama embarked with an armada on the first European sea voyage to India.

A map by Petrus Plancius of the west coast of Africa, based on information from Luís Teixeira, official cartographer to the Portuguese Crown (1660).

A portrait of Vasco da Gama, c.1525.

Four vessels carrying 170 men and loaded with supplies set sail from Lisbon on 8 July, and followed the route established by the earlier pioneers, south along the west African coastline. At Sierra Leone, set at the base of Africa's western prominence, Da Gama abandoned the coast and headed south, searching for the prevailing South Atlantic westerlies that would fill the sails of his ships and sweep his expedition in an easterly direction. This spectacular looping manoeuvre, known as the Volta do Mar ('Turn of the Sea'), saw the Portuguese sailing almost three months without sight of land, an astonishing achievement, and by November 1497 they had 'doubled' (sailed around the headland) of the Cape of Good Hope and landed at Mossel Bay, just as Diogo Cão had done ten years earlier. More than 5000 nautical miles (9260km) had been covered before beginning the next leg of the journey, which involved sailing north along Africa's southeastern coast. On Christmas

Day they sighted the dangerous Natal coast (Natal being the Portuguese word for Christmas), and by March had made it as far up the east African coast as Mozambique island. The local ruler there launched attacks on the visitors on learning they were Christians, and the local pilots Da Gama had hired to steer them through the waters betrayed him and attempted to dash the ships on rocks. Despite losing a ship the expedition survived, and at the port town of Malindi on the Kenyan coast they were able to recruit a skilled pilot from a friendly local chief and, with the navigator's knowledge of the monsoon winds, within twenty-three days they had arrived at Calicut on India's western Malabar coast.

For the Portuguese the landfall was monumental, and the news of Da Gama's achievement shocked Europe to the point of disbelief – the Venetian writer Girolamo Priuli records the distorted rumour that 'three caravels belonging to the king of Portugal have arrived at Aden and Calicut in India and that they have been sent to find out about the spice islands and that their captain is Columbus'. To Priuli this achievement seemed impossible: 'This news affects me greatly, if it's true … However I don't give credence to it.'

To the Indians, though, it was of little significance, at least at first. The token gifts and items of trade Da Gama had brought with him were viewed as worthless trinkets, and the Arab traders of the Malabar coast convinced the Calicut authorities to snub the Portuguese. In August 1498, having unsuccessfully attempted to establish a trading position in the emporia, Da Gama headed for home. Disastrously he ignored the advice of his pilots to wait for the monsoon winds. During the protracted storm-hit crossing back to Malindi about half the crew were lost to scurvy and other ailments, and when, after four months, their two remaining ships pulled into Lisbon, just forty-four men remained. Regardless, for his accomplishment Da Gama was rewarded by King Manuel I with the town of Sines, and the title 'Admiral of the Seas of Arabia, Persia, India and all the Orient', apparently designed to trump the Castilian appointment of Columbus as 'Admiral of the Ocean Seas'. A fitting prize for a voyage that defined the African form on the map, refuting the Ptolemaic assertion that the Atlantic and Indian Oceans were independent of each other, and that brought Western and Eastern races together for the first time since Alexandrian antiquity.

A portolan chart of 1492 by Jorge Aguiar, illustrating contemporary Portuguese knowledge of the Mediterranean.

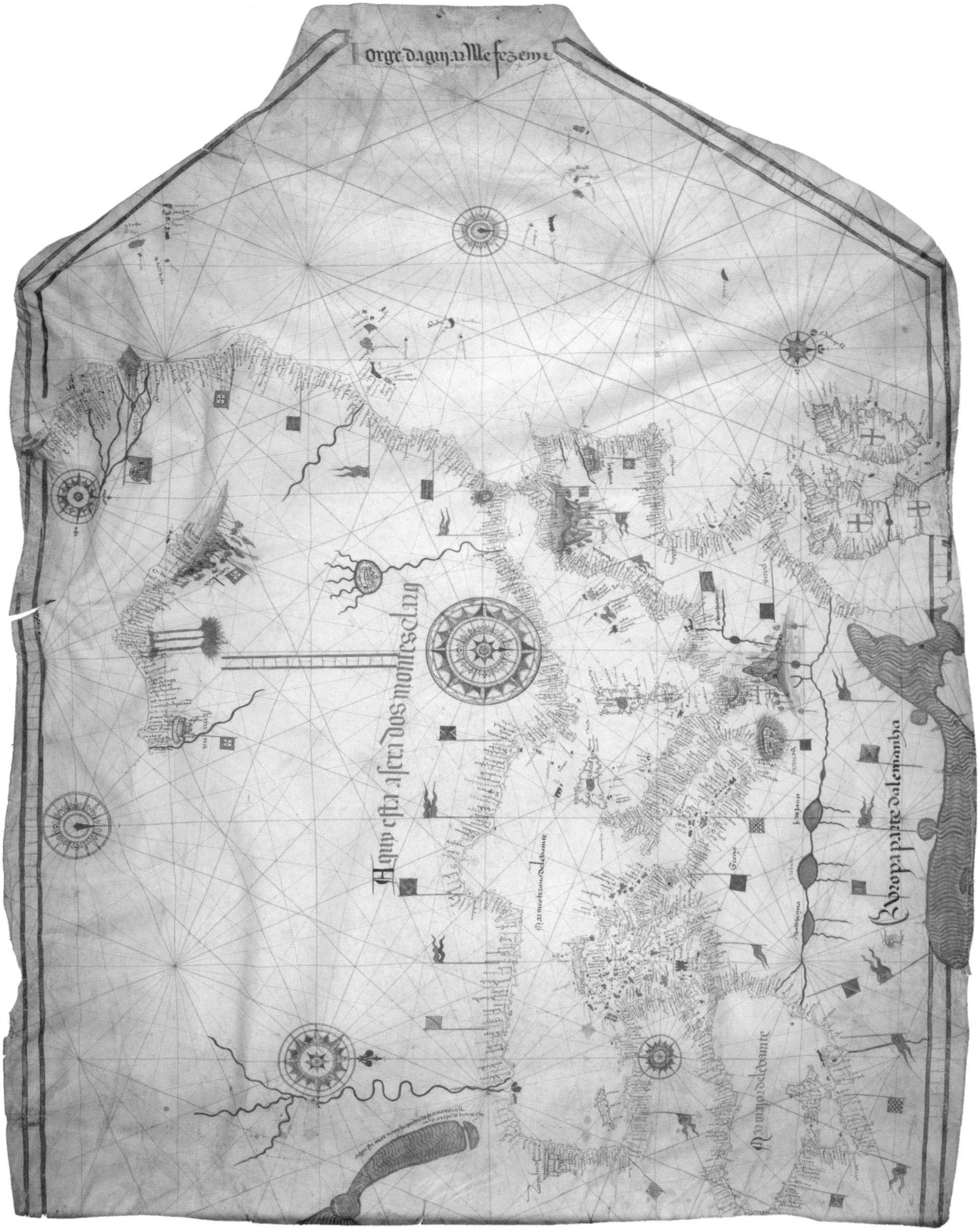

PEDRO CABRAL CRACKS THE ATLANTIC CODE AND DISCOVERS BRAZIL 1500

'One of them gazed at the admiral's golden collar and began to point towards the land and then at the collar, as if he wished to tell us that there was gold in the country.'

FROM A LETTER BY ONE OF CABRAL'S CREW, PÊRO VAZ DE CAMINHA

Terra Brasilis *by Pedro Reinel and Lopo Homem, part of the* Miller Atlas *created for King Manuel I of Portugal of 1519, less than twenty years after Cabral landed.*

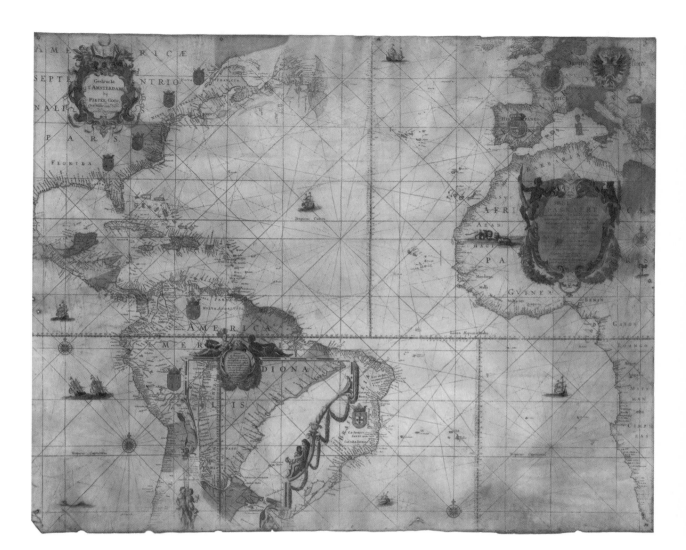

As far as we can tell, the European discovery of Brazil by Pedro Álvares Cabral, one of the major figures of the Age of Discovery, was made entirely by accident. In 1500, just one year after Vasco da Gama's return from his momentous opening of the sea route to India, arrangements for a subsequent mission to exploit the new avenue were well under way. At this time it was the custom of the Portuguese Crown to appoint favoured members of the patrician class to lead new military and naval ventures – irrespective of their experience and qualifications – and to stock the crew with experienced navigators. For reasons undocumented, King Manuel selected Cabral as commander-in-chief for the next mission to India, and on 3 March 1500 the expedition of thirteen ships and 1500 men left Lisbon.

Willem Blaeu's magnificent and exceedingly rare chart of the Atlantic, c.1695, intended for use aboard European ships making the crossing.

The party was charged with spreading Christianity wherever it landed, to continue the search for the mythical kingdom of Prester John and, most importantly, to establish a Portuguese presence in the west African trade in slavery and gold, and an entrepôt (trading post) in India's commercial hive.

By this time the navigational technique known as the Volta do Mar was well known to Portuguese navigators, and after Cabral had reached the island country of Cape Verde on the west African coast the thirteen ships launched into the manoeuvre, which involved sailing to the east by first heading out across the Atlantic to the west, to loop back and capture the westerlies that would sweep them in an easterly direction around the southern cape of Africa. Just a day into the exercise, however, disaster struck – one of the ships, captained by Vasco de Ataíde and carrying 150 men, disappeared without a trace. 'Vasco de Ataíde was lost from the fleet without enough wind to make it happen', wrote Pêro Vaz de Caminha, a Portuguese knight accompanying Cabral as secretary to the royal factory, who chronicled the expedition: 'The captain did his best to find it but it appeared no more.'

De Caminha's account, in a letter to King Manuel, consists of the sole primary source for the remarkable events of the

Oscar Pereira da Silva's depiction of the arrival of the Cabral expedition on Brazilian shores.

Cabral voyage. After crossing the equator on 9 April, a further twelve days of southwestern sailing resulted in a sighting of seaweed, suggesting land proximity. The next day they sighted coastline and anchored off a point that Cabral named Monte Pascoal ('Easter Mount'). The navigators had discovered what is known today as Brazil. In performing the Volta do Mar, the Portuguese ships had travelled so far southwest, searching for the winds that would take them east, that they had unwittingly crossed the entire Atlantic, at roughly its narrowest distance between Africa and South America.

A small landing party led by Nicolau Coelho went ashore to interact with the natives now gathering on the sands. In his letter, which is commonly referred to today as 'Brazil's birth certificate', De Caminha describes how the Mesolithic people 'were dark, entirely naked, without anything to cover their shame. They carried in their hands bows with their arrows. All came boldly towards the boat, and Nicolao Coelho made a sign to them that they should lay down their bows, and they laid them down.' Coelho traded a few items, including a red cap for a hat plumed with long feathers.

The following day the Portuguese again went ashore and erected an enormous wooden cross, kneeling before it and encouraging the natives to do the same in the first Christian mass on that soil. Cabral realized with delight that, despite the new territory being to the west, it just fell on the Portuguese side ('370 leagues west of the Cape Verde Islands') of the global dividing line of the aforementioned Treaty of Tordesillas of 1494. He claimed it for King Manuel, and dispatched a ship to bring the news back to Lisbon. After restocking their ships, the fleet departed its unexpected stopping point to resume the voyage to India, but not before spending two days cruising the coastline, in which time Cabral became convinced the new land was, in fact, a continent. They then headed east for Africa on 5 May, suffering severe storms several weeks later in the South Atlantic and losing four of their ships.

In a year, an expedition led by Gonçalo Coelho and recorded by Amerigo Vespucci (from whom Martin Waldseemüller mistakenly gave the Americas their name for the first time on his 1507 map) would chart in detail 2000 miles (3219km) of the Brazilian coast, but it is Cabral who is credited with opening the way to the ensuing Portuguese colonization – the first man to touch four continents.

FOLLOWING PAGES: *The only surviving copy of Martin Waldseemüller's* Universalis Cosmographia *(1507), incorporating the latest discoveries of South America, including those of Cabral. The first map to name America, in honour of the explorer Amerigo Vespucci (lower leftmost panel), it was bought by the United States Library of Congress in 2003 for $10 million.*

JUAN PONCE DE LEÓN
DISCOVERS FLORIDA 1513

'If it please God's will to settle it ... I shall be able to do so.' JUAN PONCE DE LEÓN, IN A LETTER TO CHARLES V

In 1492, after a series of military campaigns over ten years, Queen Isabella I of Castile and King Ferdinand II of Aragon succeeded in taking Granada, the last state of the Iberian Peninsula under Muslim rule. With the retaking of the peninsula finally complete, peace allowed the Spanish to explore new opportunities, the greatest of which arrived in the form of the New World. When Columbus departed on his second voyage to South America in 1493, he took with him a 1400-strong contingent of men dreaming of making their

Oronce Finé's massively influential double cordiform world map of 1531, incorporating the latest geographic discoveries of the New World.

Map content:

SEPTEMTRIO.

Cum Priuilegio.

OCCIDENS.

Naguater.
Tali.
Coste.
Chiacha.
Canara gay.
Guax ult.
Xuala.
Xuaquile.
Chalaqua.
Aisoona.
Chaque.
Vilbahali.
Lacane.
Chillano.
Quigata.
Tascalisa.
Cafaqui.
Catlachegue.
Ayx.
Xualatino.
Rio del Spirito Santo.
Culuca.
Rio de Cañaueral.
Achusi.
Rio de Flores.
Rio de Nieues.
P. de S. Maria.
Bayia baya.
Baya de s. Iofeph.
Rio Seco.
Aymay.
C. de Cruz.
C. Desterto.
Montañas.
Rio del Oro.
Rio de Pescadores.
Costa Baxa.
Rio Escondido.
Medanos della Magdalena.
Rio de las Palmas.

ORIENS.

C. Gruefo.
Canal de Bahama.
Iucayanoq3.
Bahama.
Abau.
Binini.
C. de Cañareal.
Rio de Corriento.
Baya de Soute.
Iugo de Ponte.
Baya de Cauto.
S. Martyres.
Tortugas.

LA FLORIDA.
Auctore Hieron. Chiaues.

Circulus   Cancri

81   80   79

---

golden fortune – this included a former soldier named Juan Ponce de León.

After arriving in the West Indies on the island of Hispaniola (today divided between the Spanish-speaking Dominican Republic and the French-speaking Haiti) towards the end of the year, Ponce de León was quick to establish himself as instrumental to successful (i.e. brutal) settlement. When the native Tainos assaulted a small Spanish garrison in the province of Higüey on Hispaniola's eastern side, the newly appointed governor, Nicolás de Ovando, ordered Ponce de León to crush the rebellion. The result was a massacre of the natives, and the governorship of the province for Ponce de León.

In 1508, having been granted the governorship of Puerto Rico by King Ferdinand II, Ponce de León continued to look farther afield, ears pricked by rumours of other gold-rich islands just over the horizon to the northwest of Hispaniola. There was also the incentive of beating Diego Columbus (son of Christopher) to a valuable discovery. Columbus was

A 1608 edition of Ortelius's important map of Florida, showing inland details provided by Gonzalo de Oviedo y Valdés, recording the discoveries of Hernando de Soto.

Florida Indians, from Theodore de Bry's Grand Voyages.

battling the Spanish Crown for his right to claim the titles and privileges promised to his father, and having arrived at Hispaniola he was working hard to supplant local Spanish figures, including Ponce de León.

On 4 March 1513, Ponce de León set off with three ships and 200 men to find the 'Islands of Benimy'. The enterprise was self-funded, but if successful he could lay claim to exclusive rights over the island and any neighbouring lands for three years. Heading out of a Puerto Rican port they sailed northwest, following the chain of Bahama Islands then known as the Lucayos. On 27 March, they sighted an unknown island but carried on, farther across open water until sighting another island. It being the Easter season, or Pascua Florida ('Festival of Flowers'), the land was christened La Florida. The precise spot of their landing is disputed – possibly St Augustine; or perhaps what is now called Ponce de León Inlet; but most likely landfall was made even farther south near Melbourne beach.

They stayed for a peaceful five days, and then cruised south to examine the coast, when they encountered something strange: 'All three vessels ... saw such a current', wrote

Antonio de Herrera y Tordesillas in 1615, 'that, although they had a strong wind, they could not go forward, but rather backward … The two vessels that found themselves nearest the land anchored, but … the third vessel … could find no bottom, or did not know of the current, and it was drawn away from land, and lost to their sight, though the day was clear with fair weather.'

This is the first recorded encounter with the Gulf Stream, at its most powerful point (the current would later be exploited by Spanish traffic sailing back to Europe). The Spaniards escaped its grip and hugged the coast as they continued south, reaching Biscayne Bay at Florida's southern tip, and moving along the Florida Keys, which to their captain resembled men in suffering and so were named Los Martires ('The Martyrs'). They fought with natives on the Florida mainland and moved on to the Dry Tortugas islands, where they captured and feasted on giant sea turtles, monk seals and giant flocks of seabirds. After eight months, Ponce de León finally returned to Puerto Rico, though not before a second encounter with powerful currents saw them swept to Cuba, to their utter confusion.

Gold was always the motive for Ponce de León, and indeed for every conquistador hacking their way through the New World and enslaving native populations with forced labour systems known as 'encomiendas'. But it wasn't until after his death that the most popularly known myth was added to his story: the search for the Fountain of Youth. The idea goes back to Antiquity – Herodotus locates the Fountain in Ethiopia, while others pointed to India – but the first to attach the idea to Ponce de León was Gonzalo Fernández de Oviedo y Valdés in *Historia General y Natural de Las Indias* of 1535, in which he states that Ponce de León was driven by the search for a fountain of a paradise region called Bimini that would reverse his aging. Hernando de Escalante Fontaneda, who survived a shipwreck and lived with the Floridian natives for seventeen years, also mentions in his 1575 memoir that the explorer had indeed searched for the rejuvenating waters in that area. The story, fittingly, lives on to this day. The Fountain of Youth National Archaeological Park in Saint Augustine is one of the most popular tourist attractions in the area; as well as featuring a reconstruction of the original native village, visitors flock to drink the water from a nearby spring.

FOLLOWING PAGES: The Fountain of Youth *by Lucas Cranach, 1546.*

THE CIRCUMNAVIGATION OF FERDINAND MAGELLAN 1519-21

'The glory of Magellan will survive him.' Antonio Pigafetta

In 1517 the Crown of Castile was preoccupied with one goal above all others: to find a western route to the fabled Spice Islands (Maluku Islands, or the Moluccas), the Indonesian archipelago bursting with cloves, nutmeg and mace, which for Europeans were treasures as precious as gold. Its location was known – the question was how to get there. Having agreed the Treaty of Tordesillas with the Portuguese in 1494, designating all new discoveries to the east the property of Portugal, the Spanish were prevented from making use of the only known marine routes to Asia. And so their attention switched to the west, with hopes resting on the discovery of a naval route through or around the New World. A five-vessel expedition was assembled to bring this to fruition, and to the consternation of both their countrymen King Charles I of Spain selected a Portuguese to lead it.

The man known today as Magellan was born Fernão de Magalhães to a family of Portuguese nobility with connections that opened doors to the royal court. Despite his labours in battle for the glory of Portugal, Magellan fell out of favour after fighting in Morocco in the two-day Battle of Azemmour against the Islamic Wattasid Dynasty in 1513. Unfounded accusations of illegal trade deals with the Islamic Moors tarred his name, and Magellan found himself shunned in his own country. He therefore renounced his Portuguese nationality and arrived in Spain in 1517 to serve Charles I, changing his name to Fernando de Magallanes. Just one year later, he was named captain of the planned voyage to the west. If successful, he and his partner, Rui Faleiro, were promised a ten-year monopoly on the discovered route, governorships and five per cent of the net gains of any new territories discovered, their own island and a fifth of the total profits of the expedition. They soon set sail from Spain in September 1519.

As they headed out across the Atlantic for the barely charted eastern coastline of South America, Magellan realized that

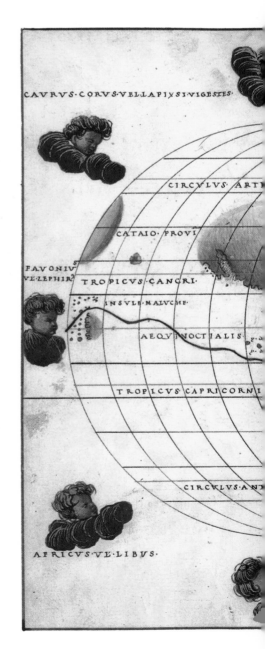

The world map from a 1544 portolan atlas dedicated to Hieronymus Ruffault, Abbot of St Vaast (France), showing the route that Magellan took around the world. The fainter brown line traces the route from Cadiz, Spain, to Peru, via overland trek across the Isthmus of Panama – this was how the huge amounts of silver were transported from Peru to Spain.

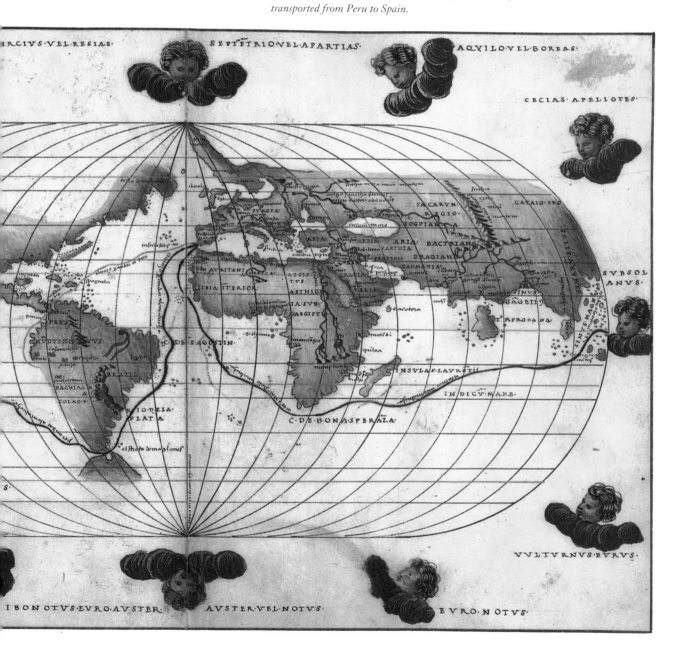

the immediate danger to the mission was not the treachery of
the weather but his own crew. The men were a volatile mix of
Spanish, Portuguese, English, Italian, German and others, with
many resentful of their Portuguese commander and his early
instigation of harsh rationing. By December they had reached
Brazil, but it being a Portuguese territory they continued
cruising south at distance along the coast. Vasco Núñez de
Balboa had glimpsed the Pacific ocean (or the 'Sea of the South'
as it was known) in 1513 after making the overland trek across
the Isthmus of Panama, but it was a maritime route that was
needed, and so Magellan and his men meticulously investigated
every inlet and waterway on their slow way south, sometimes
travelling far inland in the hopes of stumbling on the passage
through to the Pacific. Supplies were dwindling, and in March
1520 they established Patagonia's Puerto San Julián, where
they anchored to replenish and repair. Rations were tightened
further, and on hearing rumours of imminent mutiny
Magellan ordered the killing of Luis Mendoza, captain of the
Victoria, and Gaspar de Quesada of the *Concepción* to make an
example. Some forty other men attempted to take
the ships out in a bid for home, but they were blocked and told
to expect death, though the punishment was de-escalated to
hard labour.

By October the voyage continued with only four ships,
the *Santiago* having been lost during a search mission. Juan
de Cartagena had mutinied and so was left behind, marooned
with the bodies of the executed mutineers (the bones of whom
were discovered years later by Sir Francis Drake). On 21
October 1520, at 52°S latitude, the navigators discovered a
westward passage of deep briny waters which they turned into,
naming it Estrecho de Todos los Santos ('All Saints' Channel').
This we now refer to as the Strait of Magellan.

Despite the breakthrough, the bellyaching among the
ranks continued. The *San Antonio*, commanded by Estêvão
Gomes, fled the company and made a break for Spain. On
28 November 1520, the three remaining Spanish ships emerged
into the southern waters of what Magellan named the Mar
Pacifico (Pacific ocean). For ninety-six days they sailed to
the west, across an ocean more vast than any contemporary
map could illustrate. Their supplies disappeared and they
were forced to subsist off 'old biscuit turned to powder, all
full of worms and stinking of the urine which the rats had

*A later portrait of Magellan
by Nicolas de Larmessin.*

made on it', recorded Antonio Pigafetta, the chronicler of the expedition. 'We drank water impure and yellow.' And then scurvy struck, its cause at that time a mystery. 'This malady was the worst, namely that the gums of most part of our men swelled above and below so that they could not eat. And in this way they died, inasmuch as twenty-nine of us died … I believe that never more will any man undertake to make such a voyage.'

Though diminished, the Spanish sailed on and finally reached Guam and the Mariana Islands, the first Europeans to do so. They filled their ships and bellies with fresh food and water and struck out again, soon landing at the Philippines. Magellan was keen to forge allegiances with the new cultures they encountered, and did so by introducing Christianity and siding with them against their enemies, a technique he had learnt with the Portuguese. He chose the leader of the natives of Cebu Island, Rajah Humabon, who Magellan baptized as Don Carlos. As a gesture of good faith, Magellan agreed to lead a small contingent to the neighbouring island of Mactan,

A world map from 1482 constructed using Ptolemy's system, the kind that Magellan would have consulted, despite the virtual lack of any information on the Pacific ocean.

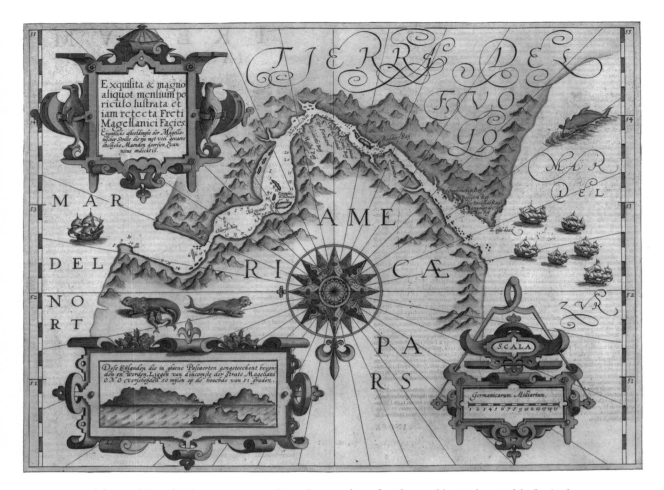

and depose Humabon's sworn enemy, Lapu Lapu, who refused to be converted to Christianity. Expecting little in the way of resistance, Magellan was met instead with a furious force of over 10000 Mactan warriors, and he and eight of his men were swiftly cut down and taken to pieces by the natives. 'All those people threw themselves on him', wrote Pigafetta, 'and one of them with a large javelin thrust it into his left leg, whereby he fell face downward. On this all at once rushed on him with lances of iron and bamboo and with these javelins, so that they slew our mirror, our light, our comfort, and our true guide.'

With only 115 men remaining of the original 270, the *Concepción* was abandoned and Juan Sebastián Elcano took command to complete the mission. The Philippines were left behind, and the two ships finally reached the Spice Islands, where they acquired a huge cargo of cloves. They departed for home, though poor planning again meant that supplies were

Mercator's map of the Strait of Magellan, the earliest to appear in a commercial atlas.

at a miserable low by the time the crew of sixty rounded the Cape of Good Hope. On 10 September 1522, after a torturous journey of starvation, resurging disease and a vessel constantly springing leaks, the *Victoria* crawled into a Spanish harbour with a crew reduced to just eighteen.

The *Victoria*'s cargo of cloves was of such value that its sale not only covered the financial cost of the expedition, but meant it actually made a profit. The discoveries made were of much greater significance: they had proved with their monumental circumnavigation that the world was round, with a circumference greater than maps estimated at more than 24,900 miles (40,000km). And with the discovery of the strait, despite it being a murderous passage that few were keen to reattempt, through one of the greatest voyages of exploration ever made the Spanish were now provided with their own avenue from the Atlantic to the Pacific. Although Magellan himself had not survived the journey, the legacy of his singular resolve would transform Europe.

The first printed map of the Pacific, Ortelius's Maris Pacifici *of 1590, featuring Magellan's ship* Victoria.

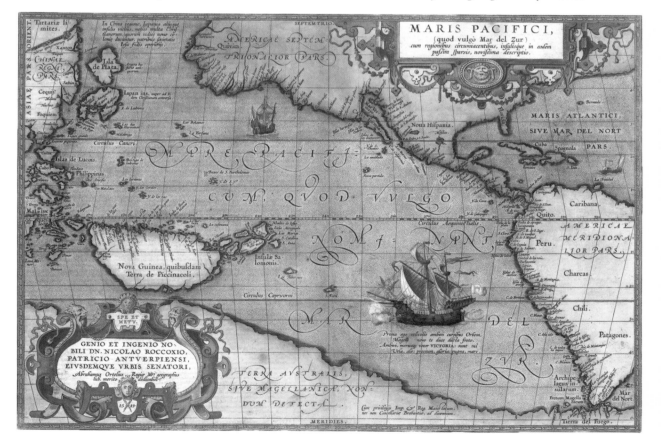

VERRAZZANO TRACES THE EAST COAST OF NORTH AMERICA 1524

'I did not expect to find such an obstacle of new land as I have found.' Giovanni da Verrazzano

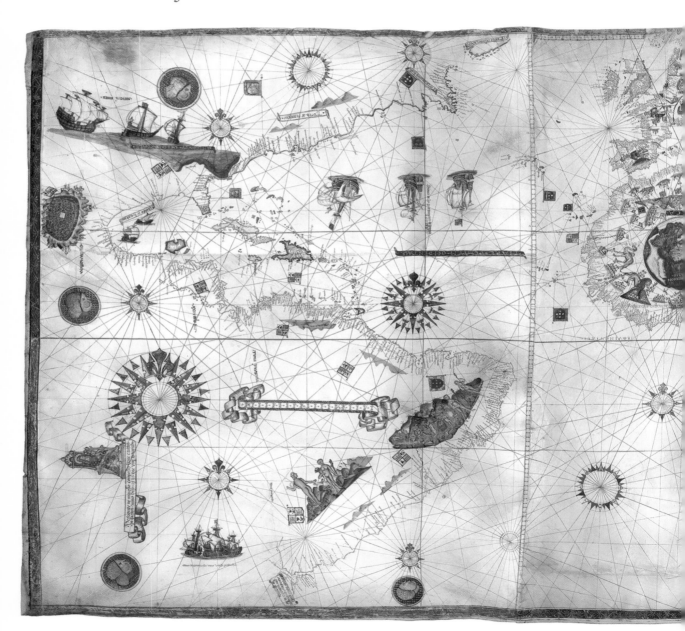

By 1524, with the inking of new discoveries, a full image of the world was taking shape. The Americas, in particular, were blossoming on the map: Pigafetta and the rest of Magellan's crew had returned with data tracing the southernmost coastline, and the confirmation that the 'Sea of the South' sighted on the other side of the continent by Vasco Núñez de Balboa was, in fact, an entirely new ocean – the Pacific. Farther north lay Juan Ponce de León's 1513 discovery of the

A portolan planisphere by Vesconte Maggiolo, 1531, measuring 6.7 × 3ft (2 × 0.9m) and drawn on six goat skins. Valued at $10 million, it shows the mythical 'Sea of Verrazzano' as well as the discoveries of Magellan and others, and is the first depiction of the US eastern seaboard.

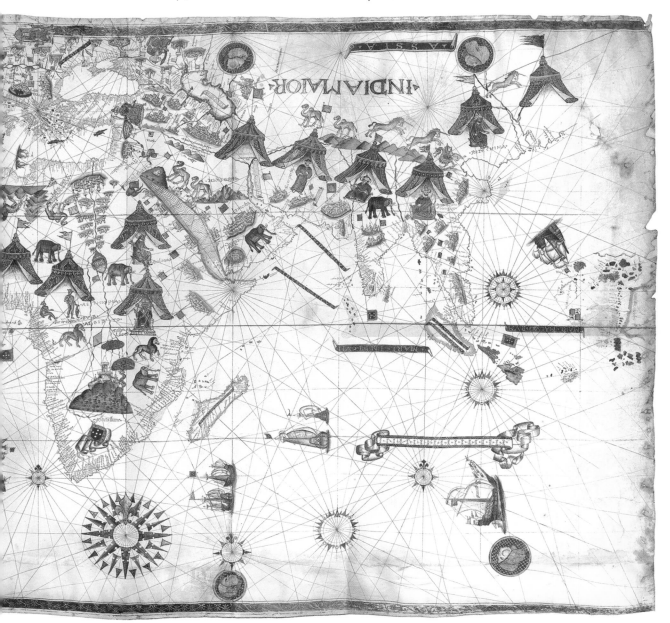

Portrait of Giovanni da Verrazzano.

'island' of La Florida; and to its west, Mexico, first arrived at by the Spanish forces of Hernán Cortés in 1517 and conquered by 1521, felling the Aztec Empire for the rule of Castile. The Spanish explorer and cartographer Alonso Álvarez de Pineda had followed the northern shoreline of the Gulf of Mexico in 1519, searching for a passage through to the Pacific; while to the far north John Cabot had landed in the region of Newfoundland.

This, then, left the vast majority of North America's eastern seaboard – some 1864 miles (3000km) – left for discovery, with the tantalizing possibility of there being a navigable passage through to the Pacific and on to the riches of China. Like others of his profession, the Florentine explorer Giovanni da Verrazzano cared little about the flag his expedition bore, so long as the command was his. For the silk merchants of Lyon (a major economic centre in the sixteenth century, home to 169 of France's 209 major trading companies), the chance of finding a convenient route to the Orient – in a temperate climate, no less – was worth the investment, and so King Francis I was convinced to back the Florentine and throw France into the new land rush.

Verrazzano set off from Madeira with fifty men in January 1524, leaving behind the unready *La Normande*, the ship that was to accompany them. After eight weeks sailing across the Atlantic they neared Cape Fear on the North Carolinian coast and, after a short stay, cruised north so as not to encounter Spanish ships to the south. They arrived at an isthmus, where Verrazzano made the blunder for which he is most famous: spying glittering waters on the other side of the narrow strip

A 1550 hand-painted map by Alonso de Santa Cruz, dedicated to Emperor Charles V, of the Aztec capital city Tenochtitlán before its fall to the Spanish and conversion to Mexico City.

of land, he assumed this to be the narrowest point of the Americas. What he was actually looking at was Pamlico Sound (in North Carolina), the largest lagoon on the North American east coast, but in a letter to King Francis he wrote that he could see the Pacific:

From the ship was seen the oriental sea between the west and north. Which is the one, without doubt, which goes about the extremity of India, China and Cathay. We navigated along the said isthmus with the continual hope of finding some strait or true promontory at which the land would end toward the north in order to be able to penetrate to those blessed shores of Cathay. To which isthmus was given by the discoverer [the name] Verrazzano: as all the land found was named Francesco for our Francis.

'Verrazzano's Sea', as it became known, would lead to a century of confusion for cartographers and navigators.

The German cartographer Sebastian Münster's Tabula Novarum Insularum *(1554), the first printed map of the American continent. North America is wildly distorted at the waist to match Verrazzano's supposed sighting of the Pacific from the Atlantic across a thin belt of land.*

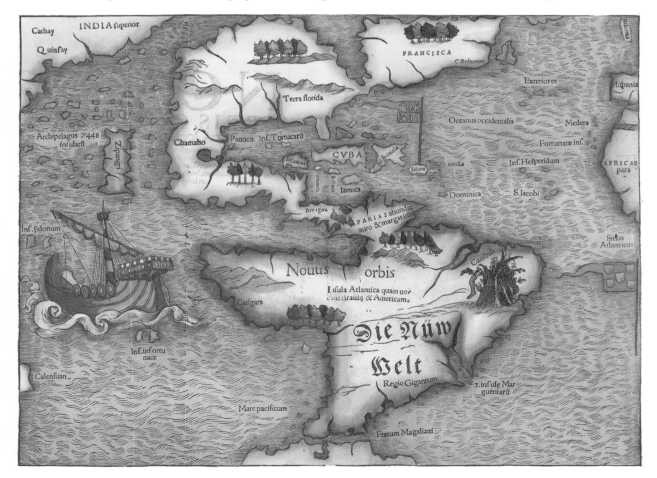

Unable to find any inlet into the Sound (despite there being several) they continued northwards, recording the coastline. Although they missed the openings to Virginia's Chesapeake Bay and the Delaware Bay, the Verrazzano expedition became the first to enter New York Bay and the Hudson River, which they studied in detail, and headed north to Rhode Island's Narragansett Bay. Reaching Nova Scotia meant a re-emergence into charted territory, and Verrazzano plotted a return course to Dieppe, reaching France two months later in early July, 1524.

The failure to find a passage to Cathay did little to diminish the significance of Verrazzano's voyage. His letters to King Francis provided detailed descriptions of encounters with natives along their journey, as well as reports on the flora, fauna and minerals to be found in the region. The mistaken sighting of the Pacific was an anomaly in an otherwise efficient navigation – in fact, one might be forgiven in wondering if it was a deliberate slip, designed to excite the wealthy backers of the mission and mitigate the sting of failure.

What became of Verrazzano himself is a greater mystery as accounts of his fate differ. After a second voyage much farther south (again, it is curious that he didn't follow up on his Pacific sighting if he did indeed believe it to be the ocean that he had seen); and on a third, exploring Florida, the Bahamas and the Lesser Antilles, some reports have it that Verrazzano was executed for piracy by the Spanish, at Puerto del Pico, Spain. Other sources suggest an even bloodier end: it was claimed that, after the explorer landed on the island of Guadeloupe, he was promptly killed, cooked up and devoured by the Carib natives.

FRANCISCO PIZARRO
CONQUERS PERU 1526-33

'There lies Peru with its riches; here, Panama and its poverty. Choose, each man, what best becomes a brave Castilian.' FRANCISCO PIZARRO

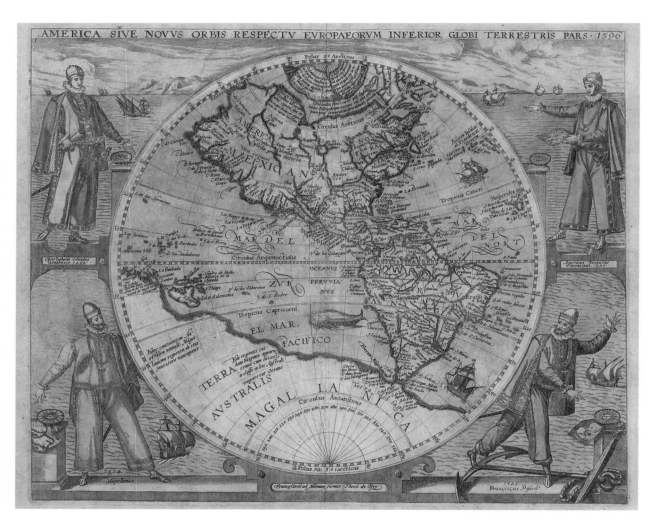

Theodor de Bry's 1596 map of the New World, cornered by Columbus, Vespucci, Magellan and, in the lower right, Pizarro.

By the 1520s whispers of golden cities hidden deep in the mysterious 'green hell' of the New World's jungle had built to a crescendo. In 1527 Sebastian Cabot, son of John Cabot, arrived at the broad mouth of the Rio de la Plata (between Argentina and Uruguay), labelled the 'Mar Dulce' by its discoverer Juan Díaz de Solís in 1516. Cabot was there on behalf of the Spanish searching for a through-passage to Asia in continuance of the work of Solís, whose progress up the Uruguay river had been cut short when he and his landing party were eaten by Indians, as his crew looked on in horror from the ship. Cabot, though, was swayed from his mission by rumours of a 'White King' who lived among the 'Mountains of Silver' (the undiscovered Andes).

Lured by these tales he sailed deep into the mainland along the Paraná river, almost reaching as far as Paraguay's Asunción. Though Cabot himself saw no city of riches, a friar named Francisco César sent west returned with a cargo of gold and silver, engendering the myth of 'the City of the Caesars' that would obsess explorers and haunt maps for 250 years.

For Spanish treasure hunters, a source of particular excitement was the news from the co-founder of the Panamanian settlement, Pascual de Andagoya, who had reported cruising south along the Colombian Pacific coast and stumbling on a gold-rich territory overseen by a native chief named Birú. (This would be corrupted to form Peru, a name originally applied to the vast entirety of southern Spanish settlement.) De Andagoya fell ill and returned to Panama before he could make anything of his findings, but like blood in the water this and other golden rumours drew the most ruthless of sharks from across Europe. Among them was Francisco Pizarro, a vicious soldier of illegitimate birth who had accompanied Vasco Núñez de Balboa in his crossing of the Panamanian Isthmus in 1513. Buoyed by the success of Hernán Cortés in his conquering of Mexico and destruction of the Aztec Empire, Pizarro sought his own triumph, and amid a frenzied rivalry with his fellow conquistadors launched a series of expeditions into dark, uncharted Peru.

The first mission of 1524 in one of the few ships built on the Pacific side of the New World, is remarkable for the swiftness of its failure: after reaching the Colombian coast, Pizarro, his partner Diego de Almagro and their eighty conquistadors were struck by storms, and shortly after, in a hostile encounter with

natives, de Almagro lost an eye to an Indian arrow. The names they gave to their points of landfall, such as Puerto del Hambre ('Port of Hunger') and Punta Quemado ('Burned Port') give some sense of their grim experience. Back they shrank to Panama for two years of planning, before attempting a second voyage in 1526, this time with 160 men.

Pizarro disembarked at the Colombian San Juan river and, while he and a unit of men hacked their way through the density of jungle and mangrove swamps, his pilot Bartolomé Ruiz continued south, capturing a native raft laden with jewels and gold, originating from Tumbes in northwestern Peru. This news reinvigorated an exhausted Pizarro, but after heading south with Ruiz to find the origin of the raft they encountered a bellicose Ecuadorian tribe under Inca rule at Atacames, and Pizarro made the decision to draw his men back to Isla de Gallo off the Colombian coast, refusing to give up the mission. As the Spaniards slowly succumbed to disease and other hostilities of the uninhabited island, they wrote to the governor of Panama begging to be rescued from their commander, 'a crazed slaughterer'. When his men received permission to abandon him, Pizarro drew a line in the beach and promised

OPPOSITE: Diogo Homem's 1588 map of South America draws on Pizarro's explorations, and those of his brother Gonzalo's men along the winding Amazon.

Francisco Pizarro, Diego de Almagro and Hernando de Luque divide up Peru in this 1706 engraving.

a golden reward for those who stayed for a third attempt at investigating further south along the coastline. Just thirteen men, known today as Los Trece de la fama ('the Famous Thirteen') crossed the line to take part in the search.

By April 1528 Pizarro and his men had reached the Peruvian Tumbes region, and were dazzled by the golden and silver decorations adorning the people and their residences. They returned to Panama to plan and restock for the next expedition, and Pizarro went to Spain to report on the riches he had seen. He was granted by King Charles V and Queen Isabel the Capitulación de Toledo, a license that officially authorized him to conquer Peru for the Crown of Castile.

The Codex Quetzalecatzin of 1593. One of the very few Mesoamerican manuscripts to survive from the sixteenth century, made at a time when the Spanish were investigating the human and community resources of the new colonies established by Pizarro and his fellow conquistadors.

In early 1532 Pizarro and his men, replenished with reinforcements brought by Sebastián de Belalcázar, landed at Peru's Tumbes – and to their surprise found the place burnt to the ground. It turned out that they had arrived just as the Incan Empire was riven by civil war between Atahualpa and Huáscar, the two sons of the last paramount emperor. Atahualpa had been victorious, and was on the march with an escort of thousands to the Incan city of Cuzco for his coronation. To Pizarro, this presented opportunity. He and his 185 men made the daring decision to leave the coast behind them (along with any chance of escape) and head deep into the mainland in pursuit of the imperial Incan cavalcade. With essentially no information as to the difficult topography ahead, they struck out across miles of plains and along the treacherous passes of the high Andes, and arrived at the town of Cajamarca to find Atahualpa in residence with forces of such numbers that their fires glowed 'like a brilliantly star-studded sky'.

Atahualpa granted Pizarro an audience the following day in the plaza of his fortress. The Incan leader arrived covered in gold and jewels, carried on a grand litter by eighty men, surrounded by his entourage of troops and a crowd of townspeople. The great chief refused Spanish demands to submit to Charles V, making clear that 'I will be no man's tributary.' At this, Pizarro made his most psychotically audacious decision of all: he attacked the Peruvians. Despite being outnumbered fifteen to one, the Spaniards with their steel swords cut down the Incan forces in a massacre known as the Battle of Cajamarca. Pizarro slaughtered Atahualpa's honour guard and took the Incan captive. Aware of the Spaniards' obsession with gold, Atahualpa offered to fill to the ceiling a room measuring 22 × 17ft (7 × 5.2m) with 'the sweat of the Sun' in exchange for his life. The deal was accepted, and Atahualpa fulfilled his side of the bargain. Regardless, he was then found guilty at an impromptu trial and executed by garrote (the news of which would cause great dismay to King Charles). Still, the bloody-handed Spanish forces were not done. Pizarro led his men on to Cuzco, sacking the city on 15 November 1533 and driving its leadership into scattered exile, effectively sealing the Spanish conquest of Peru and precipitating the extinction of one of the greatest civilizations to ever exist.

SIR FRANCIS DRAKE SAILS AROUND THE WORLD 1577-80

'There must be a beginning of any great matter, but the continuing unto the end until it be thoroughly finished yields the true glory.' FRANCIS DRAKE

One of the most thrilling periods of English history is the age of Drake, when the long night of Spanish New World dominancy was shattered by the exploits of the adventurer, slaver and warrior who harried, captured and robbed Iberian ships and outposts with such astounding success that he earned the nickname of El Draco ('The Dragon') from the fearful Spanish, along with a bounty of about £4 million in today's currency placed on his head by King Philip II, and a knighthood from Elizabeth I. In addition to his remarkable victories along South America's Pacific coast, in 1580 Drake would also become the first captain to complete a circumnavigation of the Earth.

It was in 1517 that the expedition of the conquistador Francisco Hernández and his group of settlers, which had set out from Cuba, discovered the Yucatán Peninsula and glimpsed for the first time a city of the New World and the hint of its wealth (Hernández likened the pyramids he saw to those of Egypt, referring to the structures as mosques, and labelling the entire area 'El Gran Cairo'). Since that time, Spanish steel had cut relentlessly through the land and people of the New World to bleed it dry of its treasure. Matching the enormity of the haul of gold, silver, gems, hides, hardwoods and other treasures were the logistics of transporting the plunder back to Spain. Rather than risk sailing around the southern tip of the continent through Magellan's dangerous strait, the loot was transported across land via mule and llama train, with the Spanish Main (the collective term for the captured coastal territories including Florida, the Gulf of Mexico, Panama and South America's north coast) serving as the point of launch for ships to ferry the goods across the Atlantic to Spanish ports.

Portrait of Francis Drake by Hondius c.1583.

For decades the Spanish maintained this gold harvest with a fiercely guarded hegemony over the South American territories carved out by the conquistadors. The French were focused on colonies in North America, the Portuguese on their discoveries in the eastern regions of the continent, named by them Santa Cruz and Brazil. Rather unexpectedly, between 1528 and 1544 German explorers could be found pushing through the Venezuelan plains and into the highlands of Colombia, only to be forced into withdrawal. Spain dominated – and then came the English.

Francis Drake had seen for himself the elaborate network of the Spanish Main operation, having made several expeditions to the region to relieve them of their gold. He had crossed the Panamanian Isthmus, and on sighting the waters of the Pacific fell to his knees and 'implored Divine assistance that he

The lesser-known cartographer Giovanni Battista Boazio produced this map of Drake's voyage to the New World in 1589.

FOLLOWING PAGES: *The world as Francis Drake knew it, before his great voyages. Pierre Desceliers' manuscript planisphere of 1550 bears the arms of Henry II of France (lower left corner of the map) and the Duc de Montmorency (lower right).*

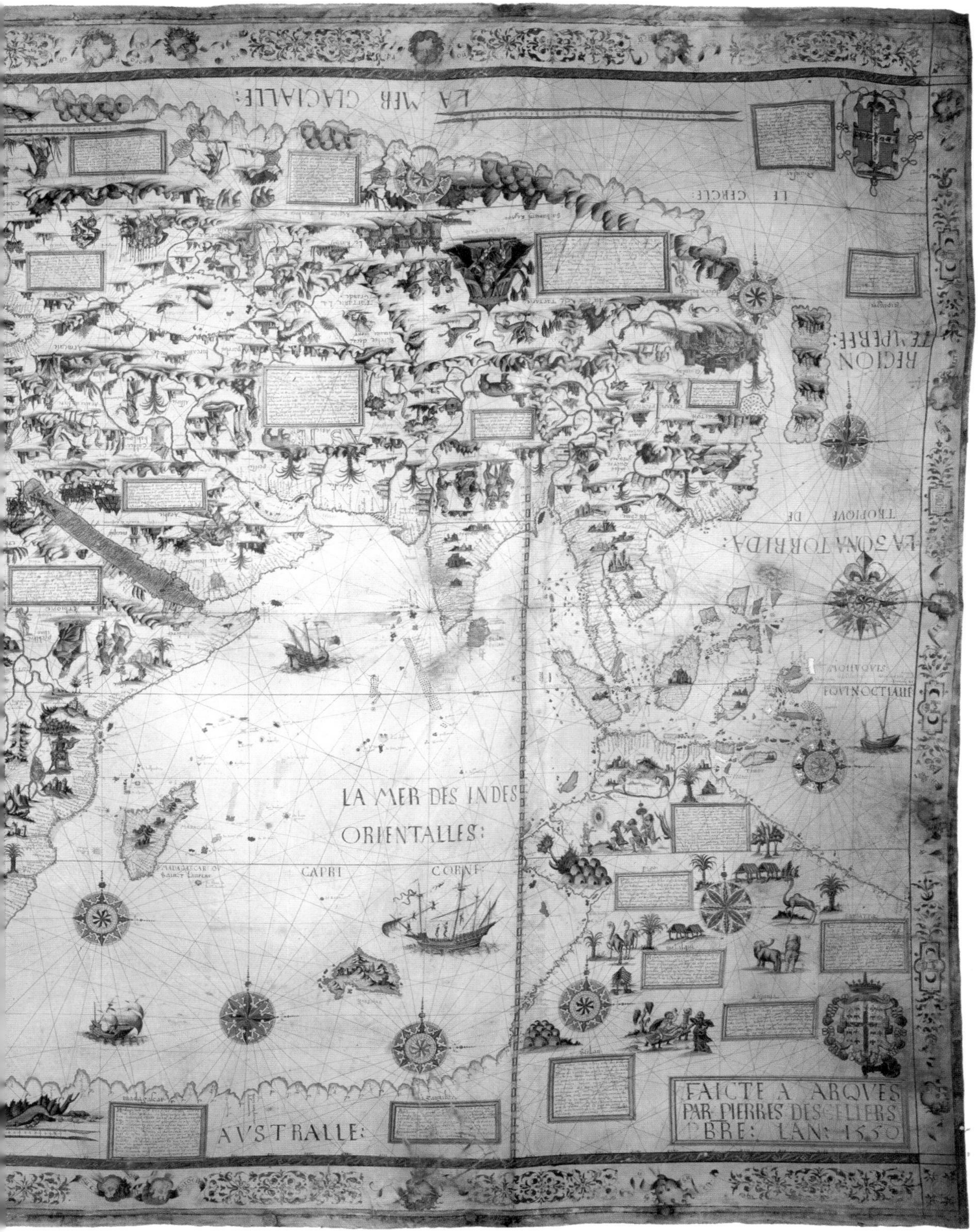

LA MER GLACIALLE

LE CERCLE

REGION TEMPEREE:

LA ZONA TORRIDA:

TROPIQVE DE

EQVINOCTIALE

LA MER DES INDES
ORIENTALLES:

CAPRI   CORNE

MADAGASCAR OV
L'ISLE SAINCT LAVRENS

FAICTE A ARQVES
PAR PIERRES DESCELIERS
P:BRE: LAN: 1550

AVSTRALLE:

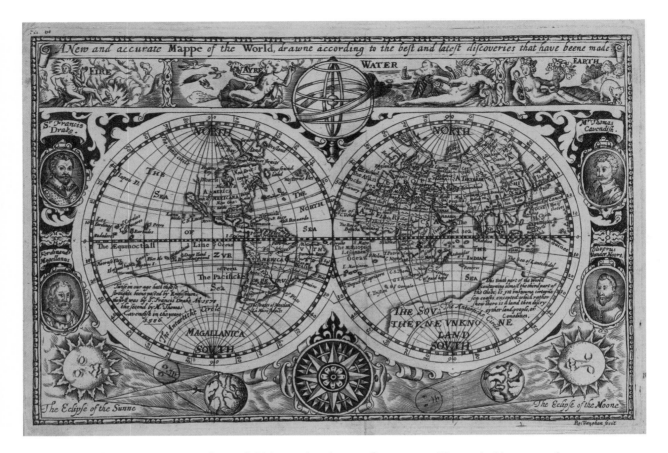

The rare double-page map by Robert Vaughan from The World Encompaffed *(1628), the first full-length account of Drake's circumnavigation of the world.*

might, at some time or other, sail thither and make a perfect discovery of the same'. He got his wish in 1577 when Elizabeth dispatched him aboard the 120-ton, 18-gun *Pelican* with an accompanying four ships, with secret orders. Publicly the mission was to Alexandria, Egypt for trade. In fact Drake was to lead his unsuspecting men into Magellan's wake, south to the bottom of the world, through the southernmost straits to round South America. They would surprise the Spanish on the Pacific, loot their treasure ships and investigate the possibility of a navigable easterly passage through the continent back to the Atlantic at a more convenient parallel. This was the same dangerous route that had led Magellan's exhausted lieutenant and chronicler, Pigafetta, to warn that 'nevermore will any man undertake to make such a voyage'.

Certainly in its initial stages the Drake mission suffered similarly to that of Magellan. After adding a captured vessel named the *Mary* to their fleet, following their Atlantic crossing two of the ships, the *Christopher* and the *Swan*, had to be scuttled after losing men, and when the party pulled into the Argentinian port of San Julián, where Magellan had dealt lethally with his mutineers, Drake also learned of imminent insurrection. The nobleman Thomas Doughty was put on impromptu trial, accused of treason and witchcraft, and with Drake as both prosecutor and judge was soon found guilty. The two men then dined together, 'as cheerfully, in sobriety, as ever in their lives they had done aforetime', wrote the ship's chaplain Francis Fletcher. Doughty was then beheaded and the journey resumed.

The *Mary* was abandoned when it was discovered to be rotting, and with the three remaining ships Drake plunged into the Magellan Strait. (The *Pelican* by now had been renamed *Golden Hind*, perhaps in honour of the Lord Chancellor Christopher Hatton, whose crest was a hind.) The storms of the strait pummelled the English vessels, destroying the *Marigold* and forcing the *Elizabeth* to return to England. But the *Golden Hind* and its captain prevailed for fifty-two days over the roughest seas in the world, and so it was that the first English force to emerge into the Pacific consisted of a single ship, a modesty of size that would prove to be anything but a disadvantage.

In the fresh glow of a Pacific sunrise Drake wasted little time in carrying out the Queen's secret orders. With eighteen cannon and fewer than 100 men, the English flagship sailed north along the Pacific coast of South America, attacking Spanish ports and colonies with relatively little resistance, because the Spanish were scattered in number, and in total shock at seeing an English vessel appear in their waters. With each sacking Drake made sure to seize Spanish maps of the area, and with developing intelligence the victories continued. The Chilean port of Valparaíso was seized with little difficulty, and yielded a great haul of Chilean wine; while as they approached Peru an essentially defenceless Spanish ship (for on the Pacific few Spanish ships needed guns) was captured with 25,000 Peruvian pesos (about £7 million today) in its hold. Of greater interest was the information that an immensely loaded treasure ship named *Nuestra Señora de la Concepción* (known to sailors as the *Cacafuego*, or 'fire-shitter') was in the area, on its way to Manila. Drake soon caught up with the galleon, thanks in part to it being weighed down with 26 tons of silver and thirteen chests of assorted treasure.

The next six days were spent transferring the *Cacafuego*'s goods to fill the hold, and even the bilge, of the *Hind*. Not a Spaniard was killed – the *Cacafuego*'s crew were even gifted forty pesos each as a token.

The issue now for Drake was how to return to London with his overstuffed ship. There was little possibility of seizing Panama and traversing the isthmus, and considerable reluctance to submit the overweight *Hind* to the Magellan Strait for a second time (a good thing, it turned out, for the Spanish had sent an interception force there). Instead Drake headed north, first to Vancouver and then returning south to the warmer climes of California (which he called 'New Albion'), where he spent a month attending to his ship.

With only one option, on 23 July 1579 Drake led the *Golden Hind* out across the Pacific, sailing for sixty-eight days with

The extremely rare Wright-Molyneux map (the only one in private hands), found in only a few copies of Richard Hakluyt's Principal Navigations ..., *detailing Drake's discoveries. Unlike other contemporary charts, the map draws only on verified information, leaving blank the areas where geographic information was lacking.*

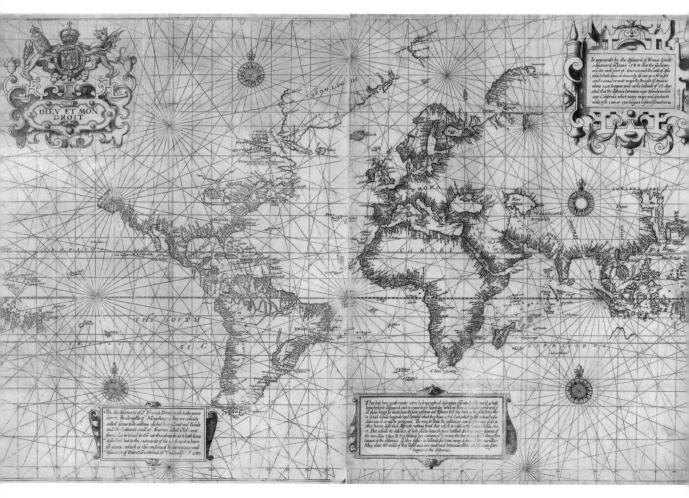

Drake attacking the Caca Fuego,
by Levinus Hulsius, 1626.

relative ease before reaching the goal of all previous European
Pacific explorers: the Spice Islands. Their stay was brief,
though long enough to load 6 tons of cloves. Home was the
pressing objective. They continued westwards, affording a
short call on Java and its five rajahs. On 18 June 1580 they
passed the Cape of Good Hope, 'the fairest Cape in all the
circumference of the earth', reaching Sierra Leone by 22 July
and finally pulling into Plymouth docks on 26 September 1580,
with fifty-nine men remaining, and a hold of treasure and
precious cargo of which the queen would claim half (a prize
that eclipsed the rest of the Crown's entire income for that
year). Drake received his knighthood aboard the *Hind* in April
1581, and the records and descriptions of the *Hind*'s encounters,
along with their cartographic intelligence, were pored over
with fascination. Drake had torn the binds of Spanish Pacific
supremacy and shown with spectacular flair that nowhere was
safe from English reach, and the sea fire of its dragon.

MATTEO RICCI AND THE JESUIT MISSIONARIES IN CHINA 1582-1610

'Therefore go and make disciples of all nations, baptizing them in the name of the Father.' MATTHEW 28:19

After the death of the Yongle emperor in 1424, for more than 130 years China turned away from any ambition of global discovery in favour of isolationism and an internal focus.

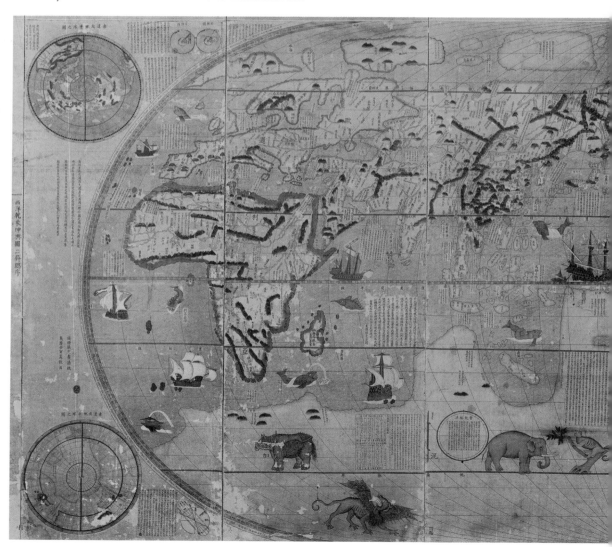

Chinese maps of this time consist almost entirely of China, its fifteen imperial provinces dwarfing the rest of the world, which takes the form of a few islands on the outermost fringes beyond the sea. Europe's merchants spent decades attempting to make inroads, but Chinese hostility to outsiders barred any progress. A shift in this attitude eventually came in 1557 when the Portuguese were able to establish a trading post at Macau in the Pearl estuary on the South China Sea. This vibrant merchant hub would also become a base for a separate set of Western visitors with a more divine mandate: Jesuit missionaries, sent by the Catholic Church to bring the word of God to the Taoist–Confucian–Buddhist Chinese.

A Korean copy of Matteo Ricci's A Map of the Myriad Countries of the World, *otherwise known as 'The Impossible Black Tulip of Cartography'. It shows the world as it was known in the early seventeenth century, with the 'Middle Kingdom' (as China called itself) at the centre.*

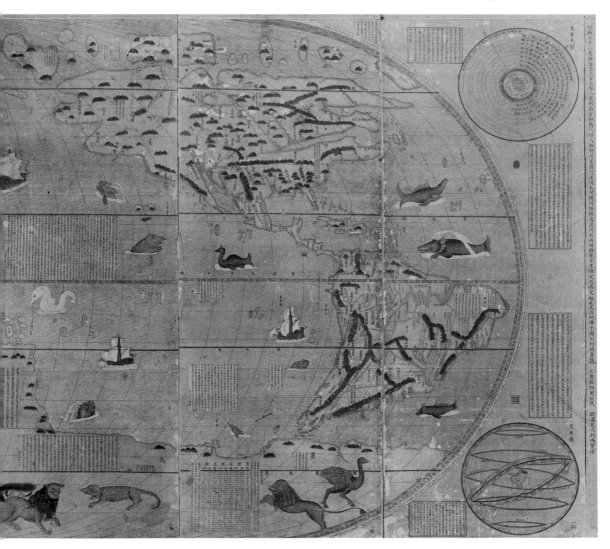

De Jode's map of China, 1593, with corner vignettes showing how Europeans imagined day-to-day life in the mysterious East (which includes sailing in land yachts, lower right).

The most remarkable of these travelling scholars was Matteo Ricci, who was inspired to volunteer for the Far East by the missionary triumphs of the co-founder of the Society of Jesus, Francis Xavier. Xavier had successfully converted thousands around the world to Catholicism, but had never achieved Chinese entry. Ricci, a skilled mathematician and cartographer, arrived in Macau in 1582 determined to break the anti-foreigner seal placed around the port city. He devoted himself to the study of Chinese language and customs, becoming one of the first to master Chinese script and Classical Chinese. With a fellow Jesuit, Michele Ruggieri, Ricci left Macau and travelled through the Guangdong province, visiting first the city of Canton and then Zhaoqing, where on the invitation of the governor, Wang Pan, they settled.

P.MATTHEVS RICCIVS MACERATENSIS, QVI PRIMVS F SOCIETAE
IESV E VANGELIVM IN SINAS INVEXIT OBII V [˙] .LVTIS
1610 ÆTATIS. 60.

Matteo Ricci, 1610.

Missionary work was a delicate diplomatic operation.
Overt proselytizing and lectures of Western knowledge at
odds with contemporary Chinese understanding were likely
to offend, with lethal consequences. Ricci operated with great
intelligence, deftly engaging with his audience's inquisitiveness
by demonstrating Western curiosities like mechanical clocks,
oil paintings and finely bound books. To nurture the cultural
exchange he translated Euclid into Chinese, transliterated
Chinese using the Latin alphabet and shared memorization
techniques; but perhaps his most effective tool was cartography.

A Map of the Myriad Countries of the World (see pages
108-9), sometimes referred to as 'The Impossible Black Tulip
of Cartography' (named in awe of its survival), is an enormous
world map produced by Ricci and his Chinese collaborators
Mandarin Zhong Wentao and Li Zhizao, drawing on both
Western and Eastern cartographic sources to create a visual
fusion of contemporary understanding. Carved onto six large
wood blocks to form a total measurement of 5ft (1.52m) by 12ft

(3.66m), the map was designed to be placed in six standing screens, immersing its viewer in the glory of creation. Bought by the US Library of Congress for $1 million in 2010, the map is covered in Ricci's commentaries in Chinese. Just south of the Tropic of Capricorn, he notes, he is 'filled with admiration for the great Chinese Empire', which has treated him 'with friendly hospitality far above my deserts'. Elsewhere he writes that: 'The Middle Kingdom is renowned for the greatness of its civilization.' These extolments helped ease the transition of Chinese geographical understanding, for the world of 'barbarian' lands illustrated by Ricci's map was far vaster than imagined. The map is also devoid of the kinds of artistic and mythological flourishes one finds on European maps at that time. There is no hypothetical Terra Australis, for example, it

The first map of China printed in English and the first incorporating the work of Matteo Ricci in print, by Samuel Purchas, 1625. The band of black in the top-left corner represents the Gobi Desert; below it runs the Great Wall.

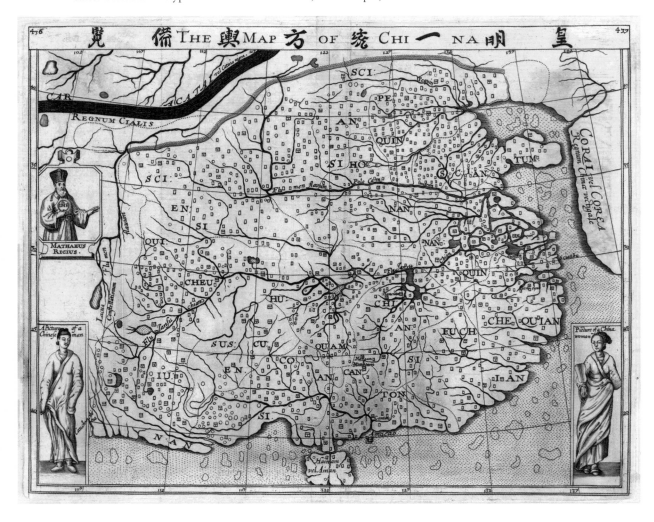

being an instrument purely of science, to respectfully educate with the known facts of global geography. Other scientific notions are introduced too: the annotations break down the idea of parallels and meridians, explaining the evidence for the sun being larger than the moon, and they present a chart of day and night lengths. *A Map of the Myriad Countries of the World* was, in Ricci's opinion, 'the most useful work that was done to dispose China to give credence to the things of our holy Faith'.

For nine years until his death he travelled throughout China, sharing Western mathematics, astronomy and geodesy, which would lead to his becoming the first Westerner to be invited inside the Forbidden City, the Chinese imperial palace in the centre of Beijing. For more than a century after Ricci, Jesuit travellers and their scientific expertise would be welcomed in China.

A typically decorative map by Vincenzo Coronelli of Asia from 1695, dedicated to the explorative work of missionaries on the continent.

WILLEM BARENTSZ, HENRY HUDSON AND THE QUEST FOR AN ARCTIC PASSAGE 1594-1611

'This land may be profitable to those that will adventure it.' HENRY HUDSON

While Europe's missionaries were driven by Asia's potential for proselytization, its merchants remained obsessed with its potential profit. The European fixation on reaching the resources of Asia, which in part had driven Drake on his southwesterly journey around South America to play merry hell with the Spanish, was being explored with a northerly focus too. The existence of such a navigable avenue was wholly theoretical, yet never did faith in its existence waver – the political and financial advantages it offered meant it simply had to be there. This conviction was steeled with contemporary misconceptions: that water of great depth and energy could not be frozen; that the Midnight Sun at the top of the world shone with such unbroken intensity that an uncongealed sea must await beyond a peripheral belt of ice. While cartographers seized on rumours and myths to manifest this transcontinental passage on maps in various unfounded forms like the 'Strait of Anian' and the 'Great Sea of the West', some of the greatest names in the history of European exploration made their reputations in the Arctic Ocean pursuing every inlet, bay and local rumour to exhaustion, navigating every channel with no promise of success, on the chance it betrayed an eventual thoroughfare to the glittering waters of the Pacific.

The first major expedition to find the Northwest Passage was made by Martin Frobisher in June 1576, backed by the merchant consortium the Muscovy Company and with the endorsement of Queen Elizabeth I. After sailing into Frobisher Bay in Canada's Nunavut region (opposite Greenland's west coast) on his first voyage, the story takes a bizarre turn with Frobisher's discovery of a clod of black earth 'as great as a half-penny loaf'. On his return to England three of four assayers dismissed it as worthless, while a fourth declared it to be gold-rich. This ensured the green light for a second, larger expedition in which all intention of finding a passage was dropped in favour of mining more of the golden ore. Frobisher returned triumphantly to London with 200 tons of the stuff in his hold; a third voyage would yield an equally large haul. However the material was later proven to be iron pyrite – with zero gold content, it was worthless.

By 1596 the Dutch explorer Willem Barentsz had led two unsuccessful voyages in search of a 'Northeast' passage around the northern coast of Siberia. The first had taken him as far as the curved shoehorn of Novaya Zemlya, a giant island group

OPPOSITE: *The Arctic according to Mercator, the first to map the region in 1569. Largely mythical, before exploration this was the first map specifically of the North Pole. In the centre can be found 'Rupes nigra et altissima', the mythical black magnetic mountain believed to exist at the top of world, helping to explain the attraction of the compass needle.*

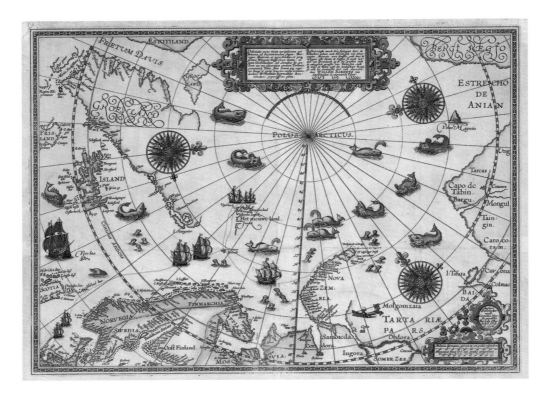

just above northern Russia; but a polar bear attack on board their ship (the sailors had wrestled it on deck to take it home as a prize) and an onslaught of icebergs had forced a return to the Netherlands. During the second voyage the ship again reached Novaya Zemlya and, despite suffering another polar bear attack that claimed two crew, successfully passed the southern tip of the archipelago to enter the Kara Sea north of Siberia. This was discovered to be frozen solid, and so the journey was halted once more.

Then came Barentsz' third attempt, a voyage considered one of the greatest in the history of Polar exploration. Again the plan was to round Novaya Zemlya, but this time Barentsz was to lead his men north, up its west coast and over its northern headland, high into the Arctic. The rounding they achieved, discovering Bjørnøya (Bear Island) and beyond it Spitsbergen. But then the ice sheets closed swiftly around the ships, crushing them to splinters and stranding the Dutchmen in the bleakest of environments. The sixteen men were forced to overwinter in the bitter Arctic, the first attempt of this kind, and from the ships' timber built a cabin which they named Het Behouden Huys (The Saved House). With average temperatures of

Willem Barentsz's landmark 1598 map of the Arctic region, drawn from his observations made during his 1596 voyage. It shows the newly discovered Bjørnøya (Bear Island) and Spitsbergen.

-22°F (30°C) (and virtual darkness between mid-October to the end of February), comfort was with impromptu measures like using heated cannonballs to thaw their frozen beds, but by June supplies had run out and the desperate decision was made to take two small boats and head for Russia's Kola Peninsula. Barentsz died in the attempt, but thirteen of his men, beset by scurvy, somehow survived the 1500-mile (2400km) southwesterly journey, and were rescued by Russian merchants.

Dutch sailors on the Barentsz expedition fend off a polar bear approaching the ship, while in the background two bears are about to help themselves to meat soaking in water; dated 15 September 1596, from Gerrit de Veer's journal of the expedition.

Possessed of similar grit to Barentsz was Henry Hudson, an English explorer who appears on record for the first time in 1607, the year he headed a new northerly Muscovy Company mission to Asia. The plan was to sail directly across the North Pole, which was assumed to be unfrozen. The expedition made it as far as Spitsbergen off northern Norway, by their estimation reaching a latitude of 80°N, a new record. Beyond this point the ice was impenetrable and forced the navigators to turn back, but a year later the Muscovy Company again sent Hudson on the passage's trail, this time via northern Russia. He reached Novaya Zemlya, but was forced back by the ice.

A third voyage in 1609 saw Hudson now sailing for England's chief rival at the time, the Dutch East India Company, with orders to find an eastern passage. Ice in the Barents Sea north of Norway obstructed his path and he was forced to turn back a third time. Clearly frustrated, instead of returning to dock Hudson improvised and headed west to find a way through North America. After reaching Newfoundland, damage to his ship forced him south, and after a month the Englishman had entered New York harbour and sailed up what is now known as the Hudson river as far as Albany in search of the Pacific, claiming the area for the Netherlands. (This journey would be used by the Dutch to establish a trading post at this point, and whose presence just ten years later would expand to the founding of 'New Amsterdam', better known today as New York City, on Manhattan Island.)

Though Hudson had irked English authorities with his
work for the Netherlands (his logbook had to be smuggled out
to the Dutch ambassador), the value of his experience ensured
he had the opportunity for redemption with a fourth voyage
under an English banner in 1610. Aboard the optimistically
named *Discovery*, the voyagers rounded the southern tip of
Greenland, entered the Hudson Strait (originally discovered by
Martin Frobisher who named it 'Mistaken Strait', as he felt it
held no promise to a Northwest Passage), and with tremendous
excitement entered the wide and seemingly endless Hudson
Bay of northeastern Canada. They spent the autumn mapping
its eastern shores, but by November had become trapped in
the ice at James Bay and were forced ashore. When the ice
released their ship in the spring of 1611, Hudson ordered that
the mission resume to find the passage. However, for all his

*1601 map of the northern region
and the discoveries made by the
Barentsz expedition, from the
journal of one of the party, Jan
Huyghen van Linschoten.*

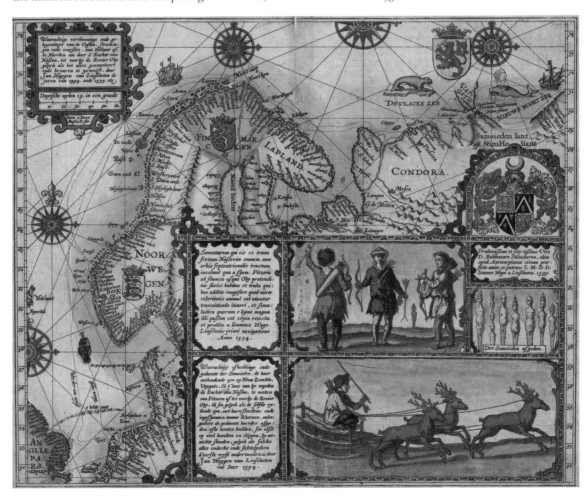

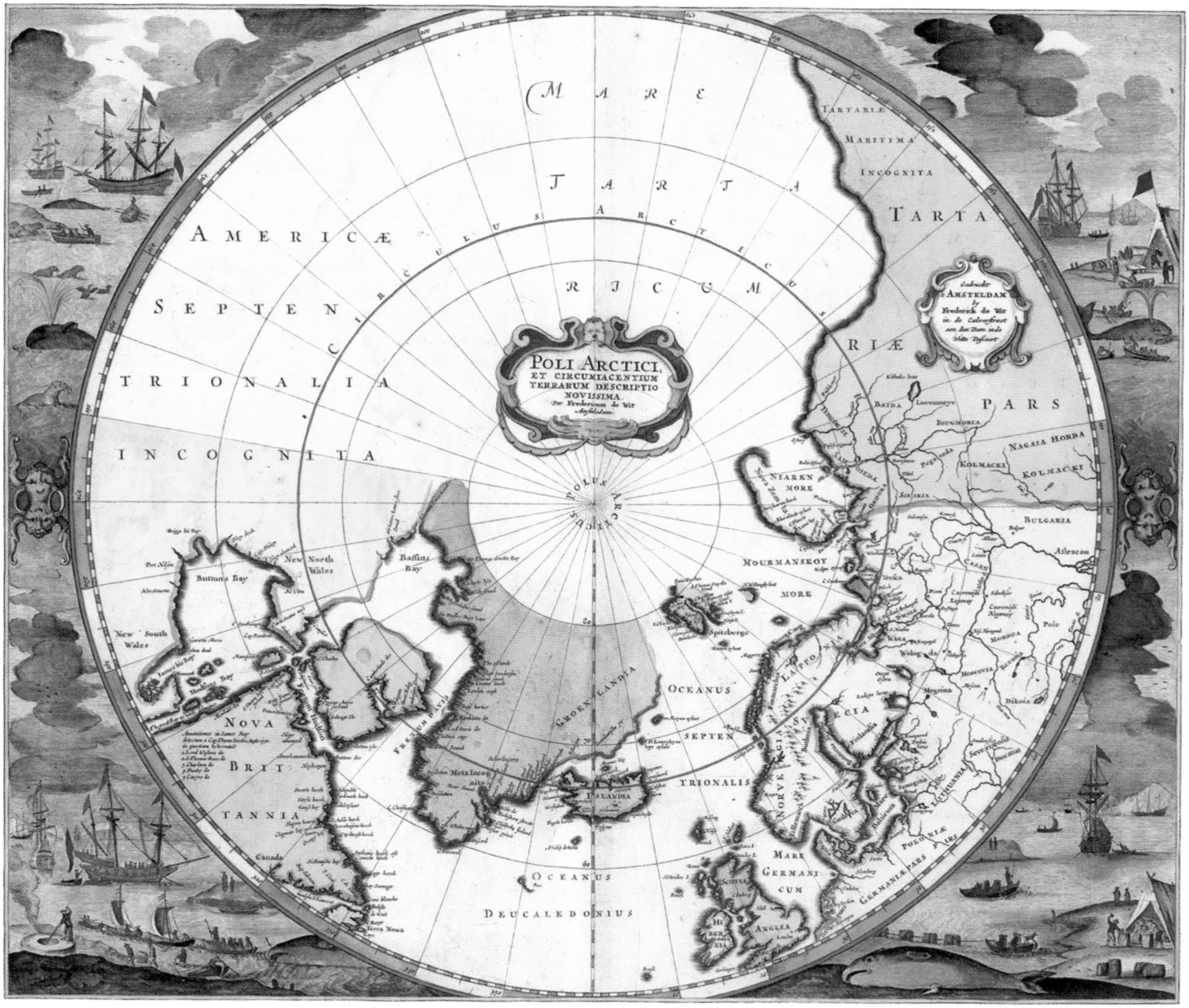

enthusiasm, his skills at reading his men were severely lacking. Riddled with scurvy and frostbite, and facing the prospect of months more of frozen hell, the crew mutinied and cast adrift Hudson, his son John and seven loyal crew in a small boat. The mutineers eventually made it home to England where they were arrested, but perhaps, because of the value of their knowledge, suffered no punishment. Hudson and his castaways were never seen again.

The Poli Arctici *c.1715, by Jan Jansson, revised by Frederick de Wit, showing the progress in charting the Arctic region.*

SIR WALTER RALEGH SEARCHES FOR EL DORADO 1595-1617

'For whoeever commands the sea commands the trade; whosoever commands the trade of the world commands the riches of the world, and consequently the world itself.' WALTER RALEGH

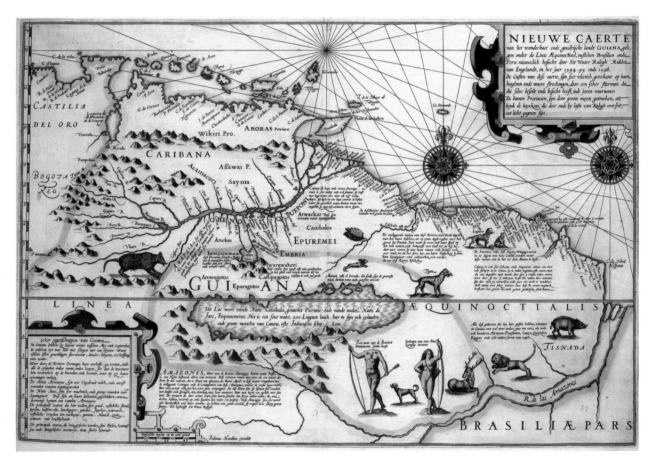

Hondius's map of the region now known as French Guiana (1598).
The central feature is the mythical Lake Parime, marked as the site
of the lost city of Manoa, or El Dorado, so keenly searched for by
Sir Walter Ralegh. Below are equally fantastic illustrations of the
Blemmye (headless men) and the Amazons.

The trouble with rumour, especially of the geographical strain, is its talent for adaptation. The twelfth-century tale of Prester John, for example, mentioned previously as a motivator for early Portuguese exploration (see The Portuguese Explore the African Tropics entry on pages 48-51), told of a fabulously wealthy Nestorian Christian monarch whose vast resources could be a valuable ally for the Crusaders mourning the shock loss of the county of Edessa to Saracen forces in 1144. But where precisely was this kingdom? Otto, bishop of Freising in Germany, writes in his contemporary chronicle of it being in 'the extreme orient, beyond Persia and Armenia', but no trace was ever found. The search for this 'lost' priest–king gripped Europe for five hundred years. Mongolia was considered an option in the thirteenth century until the Empire collapsed. Then, Africa – Ethiopia perhaps. (Certainly this was the conviction of Ortelius, who shows the glittering kingdom on his 1573 map *A Description of the Empire of Prester John or of the Abyssinians*.)

And then there is the most elusive of legends: El Dorado. Meaning 'the gilded one', the fantasy originates from a native coronation ceremony in which the chieftain covered himself in gold dust to form a living idol, and hurled great quantities of gold and jewels into a lake to appease a water demon. Spanish conquistadors picked up hearsay of it in Ecuador in 1535. The custom was extinct before the Spanish arrived, but the story was passed around so often that El Dorado no longer referred to a figure but an entire city of gold, a utopia somewhere among the Andes, or the llanos (plains) of Venezuela, or amid the broadleaved forest of the Amazon biome, or in the land of 'Guiana' somewhere beyond eastern Peru.

The last iteration reached the attention of Sir Walter Ralegh, a knighted favourite of Queen Elizabeth I. Few men have paid a greater price for the pursuit of rumour than Ralegh, who learnt of the El Dorado myth from a Spanish letter captured by the colonist George Popham. Its writer conflated the story with the equally mythical 'golden city of Manoa', said to lie on the shore of a 'Lake Parima' (also non-existent), awaiting discovery. Ralegh left Plymouth on 6 February 1595 to find it, arriving off Trinidad on 22 March. Easily seizing the Spanish town of San José de Oruña, he captured the governor, Antonio de Berrio, who saved himself by claiming to be an expert on the Orinoco river. With Berrio's

Sir Walter Ralegh, 1650.

piloting, Ralegh led his men up this labyrinthine Venezuelan river, one of the longest in South America. The Englishmen became hopelessly lost, and were forced to return to the coast and eventually Britain, on 5 September, with little to show for the effort.

Ralegh compensated for the failure with an exaggerated account of the adventure, published as *The Discovery of Guiana* (1595), which was rightly regarded with scepticism and remains a colourful example of myth propagation. Ralegh's faith in the golden city remained undaunted: 'I have been assured by such of the Spaniards as have seen Manoa, the imperial city of Guiana, which the Spaniards call El Dorado', he writes in the journal, 'that for the greatness, for the riches, and for the excellent seat, it far exceedeth any of the world, at least of so much of the world as is known to the Spanish nation.'

Before he could consider returning, however, more pressing matters presented themselves. When Elizabeth I died in 1603 her successor, James VI and I, had Ralegh arrested for his alleged involvement in the Main Plot, a rumbled conspiracy

Sir Walter Ralegh encountering the natives of Guiana, by Theodore de Bry, 1599.

against the new monarch. After defending himself in court Ralegh was found guilty, but his life was spared by King James and instead he was imprisoned in the Tower on a thirteen-year sentence. By 1616, though, James was low on funds and in need of a cash injection, and so a freshly pardoned Ralegh emerged blinking in the daylight to find himself granted royal permission to lead a second expedition to find the 'mountain of gold' he had claimed to have glimpsed on his first voyage.

The mission was blighted with misfortune from the start. Chaotic weather scattered the ten-strong fleet, and on their arrival at Venezuela in November 1617 a portion of the crew, including Ralegh, were enfeebled by a violent illness. As Ralegh was incapacitated his devoted deputy and friend Lawrence Keymis led an expedition up the Orinoco, taking with him Ralegh's son Wat. For three weeks the party navigated the river inland, entering the Caroni river. On 12 January 1618 the English flotilla attacked a Spanish outpost called San Thomé, believing it to be the site of a goldmine. After taking the fort in a bloody assault no gold mine was found, and a distraught Keymis learnt that young Wat had been killed in the melee.

They returned to Ralegh in Trinidad to break the news of his son's death, and their contravention of his order to not engage the Spanish, for this had been an express condition agreed with King James to maintain the fragile post-bellum peace of the Anglo-Spanish. Devastated, Ralegh refused Keymis his forgiveness, and the lieutenant shot himself.

On his return to England on 21 July 1618 Ralegh was arrested, and on the demands of the Spanish ambassador was beheaded in the Old Palace Yard at the Palace of Westminster on 29 October 1618, officially decried for betraying his king, but lauded as a hero by a public still highly charged with anti-Spanish sentiment.

The 'Ditchley' portrait of Queen Elizabeth I, c.1592.

THE DUTCH EAST INDIA COMPANY AND THE EUROPEAN DISCOVERY OF AUSTRALIA 1606-29

'Small things grow great in unity.'

MOTTO OF THE DUTCH EAST INDIA COMPANY

Arguably one of the most beautiful maps ever produced, the majestic *Leo Belgicus* (shown here in rare sitting form by Claes Janszoon Visscher) gathers the Low Countries – modern Netherlands, Luxembourg and Belgium – in defiant and powerful form. The cartographer Micha'l Eytzinger had the idea in 1583, adapting the traditional Dutch heraldic lion to produce a map of fierce patriotism at a time when the Netherlands was engaged in the Dutch War of Independence from Philip II of Spain between 1568 and 1648.

In fact Visscher's proud and magnificent *Leo* is a fitting gatekeeper to the history of early European contact with Australia, for it was produced at a time when global trade was dominated by the Dutch East India Company (VOC), which was established in 1602 to regulate the Dutch trading ships now trafficking regularly with the East. It is almost impossible to overstate the size, power and wealth of this chartered company, which grew swiftly to become the first multinational corporation, the first to issue stock, and to this day by far the most

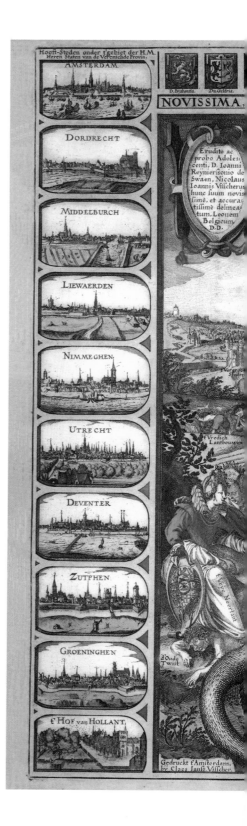

ABOVE: *The supremely powerful VOC minted a range of its own currency in bronze, silver and gold for use in its Far Eastern territories.*

RIGHT: *The Sitting Leo Belgicus, 1611, by the Dutch mapmaker Claes Janszoon Visscher. Only two copies are known of this map – one of the rarest and most beautiful of the seventeenth century.*

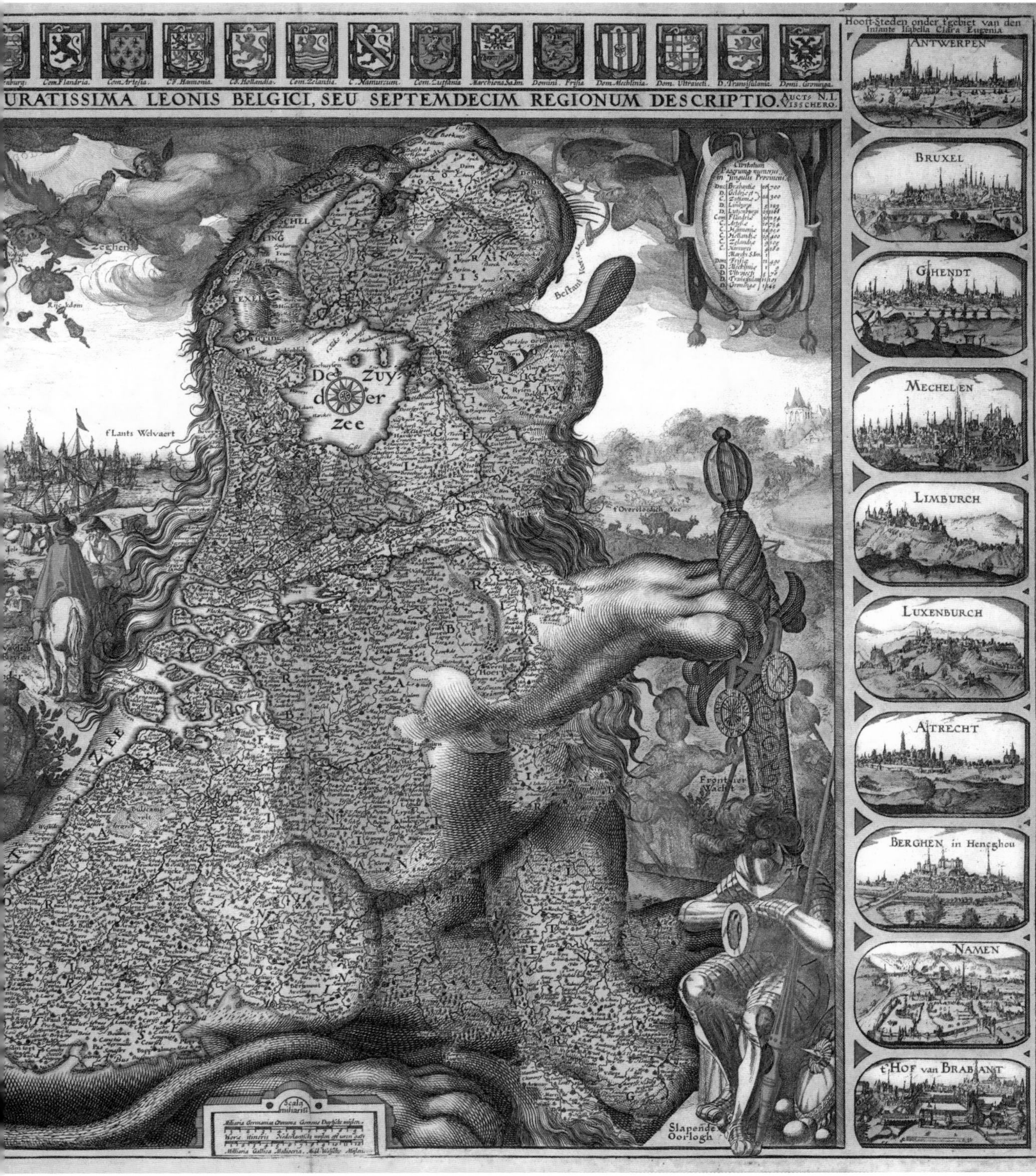

Hoon-Steden onder 't gebiet van den Infante Isabella Clara Eugenia

Com.Flandria. Com.Artesia. Cõ.Hannonia. Cõ.Hollandia. Com.Zelandia. C.Namurcum. Com.Lussania. Marchiona.Sa.Im. Domini. Frisia Dom.Mechlinia. Dom. Ultraieti. D.Transisulania. Domi.Groninga.

...URATISSIMA LEONIS BELGICI, SEU SEPTEMDECIM REGIONUM DESCRIPTIO.

ANTWERPEN

BRUXEL

G'HENDT

MECHELEN

LIMBURCH

LUXENBURCH

ATRECHT

BERGHEN in Heneghou

NAMEN

t'Hof van BRABANT

De ZUY der zee

f Lants Welvaert

f'Overtlodach Ver

Slapende Oorlogh

Scala

valuable company in history. Through its aggressive monopoly of trade and colonial activity in Asia, driven by a voracious mercenary appetite, the VOC endowed itself with the power of nations, able to operate with its own currency, declare war and colonize new lands. Some of the greatest explorers in history sailed under its banner, and with cartographers a staple of the crew, its discoveries formed much of the basis of European understanding of Asian geography and beyond. Between 1602 and 1796 almost one million men were dispatched by the VOC to sail their secret spice routes to the Indies, harvesting a total haulage of about 2.5 million tons of Asian goods. (For comparison, their main competitors, the British East India Company, managed only one-fifth of this amount.)

The Dutch explorer Hendrik Brouwer helped to catalyze this prosperity in 1611, by reinventing the route taken to the East. The established way was a taxing voyage, necessitating the rounding of the violent Cape of Good Hope and later crossing the treacherous reefs of the Bay of Bengal. Added to this were the vicissitudes of tropical weather systems, and hostile encounters with Portuguese and English shipping. The journey usually took a year to complete, but the Brouwer route halved this time with an ingenious exploitation of the 'Roaring Forties', the powerful unbroken westerly winds between the southern hemisphere latitudes of 40 and 50 degrees. The winds blasted Brouwer's three-ship party across the Indian Ocean, after which the west Australian current swept them north to Java. This would become the default route for all VOC expeditions.

It was another VOC captain, Willem Janszoon, who unwittingly made one of the most significant discoveries of the company: the first documented sighting of the Australian coast. As master of the yacht *Duyfken* ('Little Dove'), on 18 November 1605 Janszoon set sail from the small port town of Bantam, Java, with company orders to explore the coast of New Guinea. Though the original logs of the *Duyfken* are lost, copies of its map survive and show the first tracing of part of the Australian coastline. Janszoon, however, failed to notice the Torres Strait, which divides Australia from New Guinea, and so after entering the Gulf of Carpentaria assumed the land he arrived at, which would later be known as the western coast of Queensland's Cape York Peninsula, to be a continuation of New Guinean territory. (By sheer coincidence, only seven

Jan Jansson's map of the East Indies,
Indiae Orientalis Nova Descriptio, *was first published c.1630. In the southeast corner can be found 'Duyfkens Eyland', the earliest printed charting of Australia.*

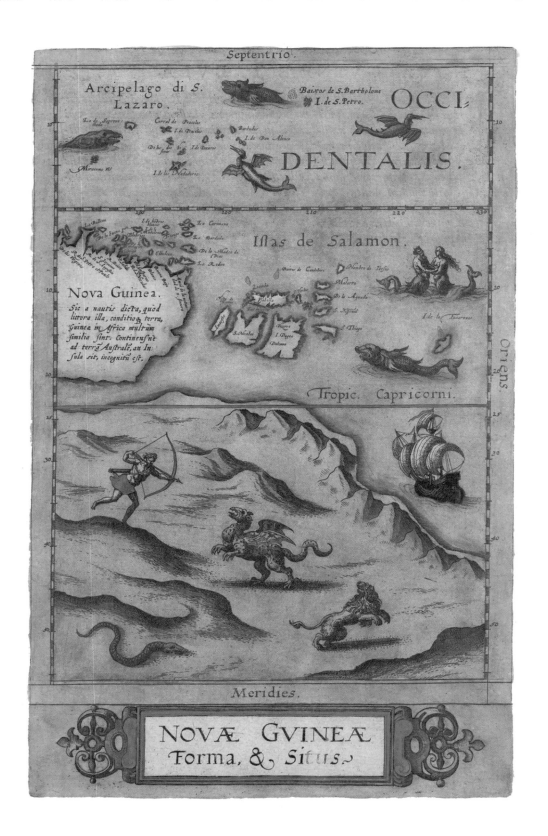

months later the Spanish explorer Luis Váez de Torres would sail this strait that would later be given his name, entirely unaware that an entire unexplored continent lay only a few miles south.)

Janszoon made landfall at the Pennefather river on the western shore of Cape York, the first recorded instance of European feet hitting Australian soil. It was not a particularly joyful discovery for Janszoon, however. The land was swampy and the natives hostile – ten of the crew were lost in skirmishes during the expedition. At a spot that would later be called Cape Keerweer (Dutch for 'turnabout'), Janszoon decided to end the mission and return to Bantam, reaching port in June 1606, with stories of the land he named 'Nieu Zeland', after the Dutch province of Zeeland. (This, of course, would not be adopted until later by Abel Tasman, for his discovery of a separate country.)

All new navigational data and discoveries were carefully recorded by the VOC but kept hidden in their private Zee-Fakel ('Sea Torch') atlases, successfully protected from theft and leaks, on the whole, for around 150 years, maintaining Dutch hegemony of the spice trade. Cartographers were placed under strict orders to never reveal or publish the information, as such; it wasn't until years later that the discoveries of the *Duyfken* would emerge on maps.

One surprising cartographic leak from this veil of secrecy is a map first published in 1630 by the Dutch cartographer Jan Jansson, who somehow got hold of the *Duyfken* data and included it on his map of the East Indies, marking 'Duyfkens Eyland' beneath New Guinea. This was a particular triumph for Janssonius over his rival Blaeu, who, being the official cartographer of the VOC, was bound to secrecy and unable to print his maps for the public. Along with the Duyfken's map and a chart of the Pacific by Hessel Gerritsz, this map by Jan Jansson serves as one of the earliest first mappings of Australia.

OPPOSITE: *The first printed map of a part of Australia, by Cornelis De Jode. The lower section of this map shows the territory of what is now Queensland, complete with mermen, sea monsters, dragons and lions. This map is also rare in that it depicts the continent as separate from New Guinea, which later cartographers would join.*

FOLLOWING PAGES: Nova Totius Terrarum Orbis, *the magnificent world map, first issued in 1606, of Willem Blaeu, official cartographer of the VOC, incorporating data from its explorations.*

QUATUOR
ELEMENTA

IGNIS

AER

AQUA

TERRA

LUNA

MERCURIUS

VENUS

ZONA FRIGIDA

ZONA TEMPERATA

ZONA TORRIDA

ZONA TEMPERATA

ZONA FRIGIDA

NOVA TOTIUS TERRARUM ORBIS GEOGRAP

ULTERIUS SEPTENTROVEM
AMERICA ADHUC IN
NITI EST

AMERICA
Anno Domini 1492 a Christopho-
re Columbo nomine Regis Castel-
læ primum detecta, et ab Ameri-
co Vespucio nomen sortita 1499.

Circulus Arcticus

Anian
Regnum

Quivira
Regnum

El Streto d'Anian

Ceterorum hic homines
per campos ferinato vita
in tentoriis, Tartarorum
more, agrestem vitam degit

AM ERICA SEPTEN

TRIO NALIS

Totuna
gay

Chilaga
Avanares
Albardos
Capaschi
Calicuas

Nievada

NovA
FRANCIA

Sierra

Tropicus Cancri

FLORIDA

MAR
D

Ilhas de
Ladrones

Sinus
Mexicanus

NO

Nova Guinea

MAR DEL

Circulus Æquinoctialis

Insulæ
Salomonis

ZUR

AME

RI
BR

MERI

DIO NA

CHILIS

MARE

Tropicus Capricorni

PACIFICUM

Fretum Magalanicum

Terra del
Fuego

AMERICA
SEPTENTRI
ONALIS

EVROPA

Excudebat
Guilielmus Blaeuw
Amsterodami sub signo
Solarii deaurati.

MA

GAL

Circulus Antarcticus

Cum ob terrestrem sphaeram
hic modo in planum redactam finum
prope polos adumbrarere necessimum
Borealiorem et Australiorem partem a
quinquagesimo parallelo duobus cir-
culis hic delineatis conclusimus
vale et fruere.

TERRA AUSTRA

ZONA
FRIGIDA

MURUS BABYLONIS

COLOSSUS

PYRA MIDES

ACAU

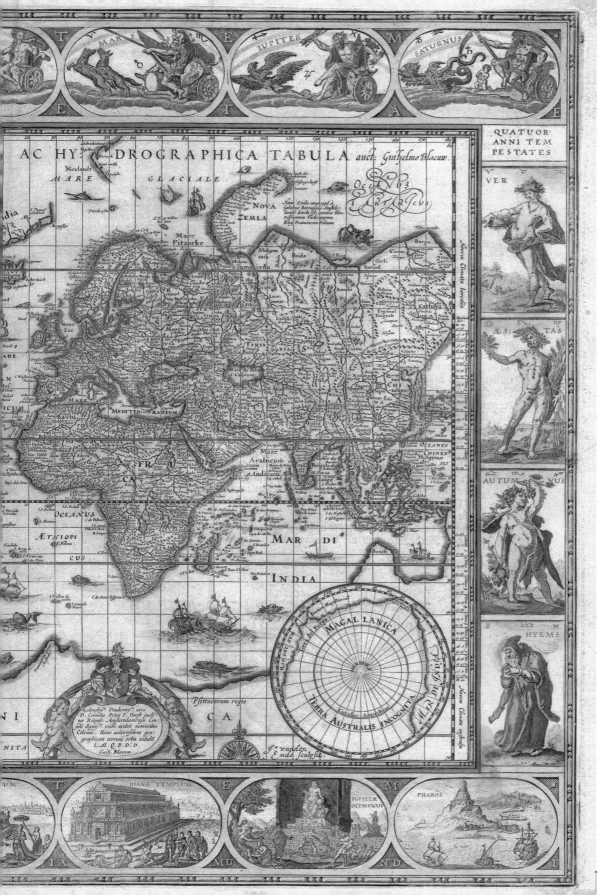

ABEL TASMAN FINDS NEW ZEALAND 1642-44

'In the afternoon, about 4 o'clock … we saw …
the first land we have met with in the South Sea …
very high … and not known to any European nation.'

ABEL TASMAN'S DIARY ENTRY OF 24 NOVEMBER 1642

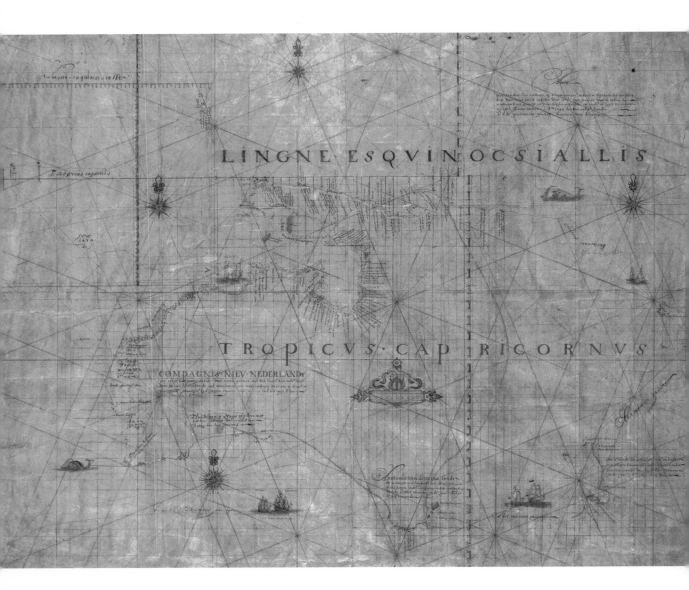

By the mid-seventeenth century the Dutch East India Company (VOC) had successfully maintained its monopoly on trade throughout the entire East with a robust network of outposts everywhere from Iran to Japan, safeguarded with a powerful naval presence. While a doctrine of perpetual expansion was the core of its constitution, under the governorship of Anthony Van Diemen, the period of 1636-45 saw an explosion in VOC exploratory missions, masterminded from Batavia (Jakarta), the VOC capital established in 1611.

Van Diemen was particularly keen to find two islands first reported in 1584, when a Spanish navigator repeated a rumour he'd heard of a ship headed for Japan, carrying a Portuguese and an Armenian, that was blown wildly off course and found an unrecorded pair of islands rich in silver, known to the Japanese. These were given the irresistible names Rica de Plata ('Silver') and Rica de Oro ('Gold') – despite there being no mention of gold in the original story. Van Diemen dispatched the Dutch navigators Matthijs Quast and Maarten Vries to the north Pacific to find these piles of treasure in island form. Quast took steps to ensure his men kept the horizon under close scrutiny for signs of the Ricas – any man caught sleeping while on watch was fined a month's pay and given fifty lashes. If it happened again this was doubled, a third offence would see him hanged. Unsurprisingly the five-month mission turned up numerous unchartered islands, yet none were the fabled lands of gold and silver.

Van Diemen's ambitions took in fields far farther than Japan and her secret phantom islands. It was in 1642 that the governor-general turned his attention to the South Pacific, commanding a preferred captain from the Ricas mission, Abel Janszoon Tasman, to lead a two-ship expedition that would be considerably more successful.

Tasman's orders were to scour the ocean for the Solomon Islands, again based on Spanish reports, to find and explore the great unknown southern continent Terra Australis and to investigate the possibility of an eastern trade route with Chile, circumventing Spanish lanes. On 14 August 1642 Tasman and the vessels *Heemskerck* and *Zeehaen* launched from Batavia, heading to Mauritius to capture the

OPPOSITE: *The Tasman map of 1644, based on the observations of the eponymous explorer, shows parts of Australia's western and northern coastlines with remarkable accuracy. Over the next 100 years it would be the foundation for maps of the region until Captain James Cook charted the east coast of Australia in 1770.*

BELOW: A view of the Murderers' Bay...(1642). This is the first European impression of Māori people, drawn by Tasman's artist Isaack Gilsemans, after a skirmish between the Dutch explorers and Māori people at what is now called Golden Bay, New Zealand.

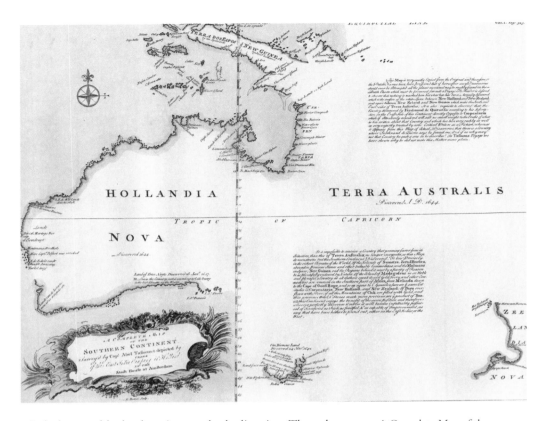

winds that would take them in a southerly direction. These they found, and though the intention had been to reach a record-breaking latitude of 54°S, at 42°S they were swamped with thick mist and spun eastwards. They continued on this course, unknowingly sailing below Australia, until on 24 November land was sighted – the first European observation of Tasmania. Despite the roughness of the waters, the ship's carpenter was ordered to swim ashore and plant the Dutch flag. From the deck, Tasman claimed the island for the Netherlands and the VOC, and dutifully named it Van Diemen's Land in honour of 'our illustrious master, who sent us to make this discovery'.

After naming Mounts Heemskerck and Zeehaen, the Dutch proceeded on their easterly course, with the aim of finding the Solomon Islands. Instead they made the second of their historic discoveries, sighting the west coast of the South Island of New Zealand. They cruised north along the island's coast, anchoring so that the men might go ashore at what is known today as Golden Bay. Tasman's original name for it, however, was Moordenaars Baej ('Murderers' Bay'), after a force of Māori warriors attacked the landing party and killed four Dutch sailors.

A Complete Map of the Southern Continent. Survey'd by Capt. Abel Tasman & depicted by Order of the East India, *Emanuel Bowen 1744.*

The Dutchmen headed north again, mistaking the Cook Strait as an inlet and therefore wrongly assuming the two islands of New Zealand to be one long landmass, the 'Staten Landt' discovered off the southern coast of South America by their countrymen Jacques Le Maire and Willem Corneliszoon Schouten in 1616.

By now Tasman and his crew were in dire need of fresh water. Unable to land on the North Island they made the decision to head northwest, where they glimpsed the eastern Fiji Islands. Again, due to hazardous conditions, they were unable to go ashore, and so continued on their return journey to Batavia. They arrived on 15 June 1643 to share the news of their findings, having covered more than 5000 miles (8000km) of unmapped water, completely unaware that they had achieved something extraordinary: a circumnavigation of Australia.

Pieter Goos's New World Map … *(1666), drawing on the discoveries of Tasman's voyages. This map remained unchanged through twenty editions of Goos's atlas until his death in 1675.*

THE EDUCATED PIRATE:
THE ADVENTURES OF
WILLIAM DAMPIER 1683-1711

*'The world is apt to judge of everything by the success;
and whoever has ill fortune will hardly be allowed a
good name.'* WILLIAM DAMPIER

William Dampier.

Compiling the achievements of the seaman described by
Samuel Taylor Coleridge as 'a man of exquisite mind' serves
as a reminder of just how extraordinary it is that the name
William Dampier is not better known. Born in East Coker,
Somerset, Dampier was the first person to circumnavigate the
globe three times and the first Englishman to step foot on and
explore parts of Australia; and for making notes on its flora,

fauna and indigenous people, he is considered its first natural historian. The account of his travels, *A New Voyage Round the World* (1697), was a new melding of maritime adventure and natural history that made him England's first best-selling travel writer. His second work, *Voyages and Descriptions*, contained 'A Discourse of Trade-Winds, Breezes, Storms, Tides and Currents', the first maps of the wind systems found across all the world's oceans, collected from his first-hand experience.

Dampier is cited in the *Oxford English Dictionary* more than 1000 times for introducing words to the English language including avocado, barbecue, breadfruit, the verb caress, cashew, catamaran, chopsticks, posse, settlement, snapper, soy sauce, stilts (as house supports), subsistence (in farming), subspecies, swampy, thundercloud, snug and tortilla. Taking place after Francis Drake and before Captain Cook, his story represents the transition of European exploration from adventures of plundering buccaneers to missions of more scientific inquiry, because it possesses both elements. For Dampier, a man of science, was also a pirate.

He had gone to sea at the age of eighteen, working as a sugar planter in Jamaica and a woodcutter in Mexico, until in 1679 he joined the crew of the buccaneer Captain Bartholomew Sharp in their ransacking of the Spanish Main.

Map engraved by Herman Moll showing part of Dampier's first circumnavigation voyage in the 1680s, from A New Voyage Round the World … *(1697).*

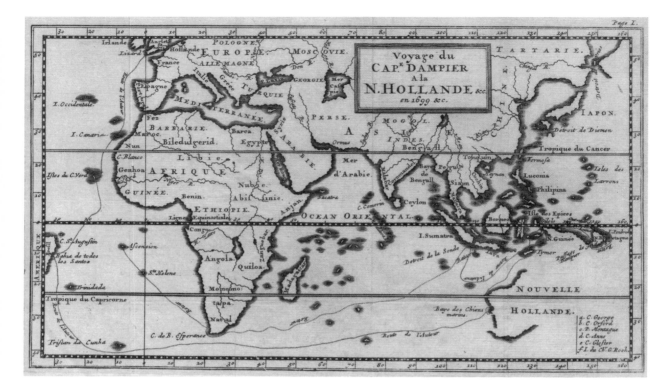

Dampier's route to New Holland (Australia), 1699.

He took part in a raid across the Isthmus of Darién in Panama, capturing Spanish ships in the Pacific and looting Spanish colonies in Peru. This was the beginning of a ramshackle first circumnavigation, as he transferred between various privateer vessels, joining Charles Swan's *Cygnet* in 1686. (On his later return to the relative sanity of London, Dampier would claim not to have participated in any piracy, but there are records of him taking command of a Spanish ship taken by the *Cygnet* in 1687 off Manila.)

It was aboard the *Cygnet* that Dampier first glimpsed the northwest coast of Australia, near King's Sound, on 5 January 1688. Shortly after, he and two crewmen were abandoned on the Nicobar Islands in the eastern Indian Ocean, but the men modified a small canoe and paddled 80 nautical miles (150km) north through a crashing storm to reach Sumatra. Dampier finally made it back to England in 1691 with little more than his journals and a tattooed Indonesian slave named Prince Jeoly (sometimes Giolo), whom he exhibited in London as a publicity stunt for the publication of his book.

A New Voyage Round the World brought Dampier's name not just to the attention of the public, but also to the Admiralty.

Pa. 412.

Dampier & his Companions in their Canoe, overtaken by a dreadfull Storm.

In 1699 he was commissioned by King William III to sail to New Holland (Australia) via Cape Horn, in search of the as-yet-undiscovered Terra Australis. Dampier asked for the two best ships and crews available – instead he was given the dilapidated HMS *Roebuck* and a mutinous group resentful of the non-navy man. They set out on 14 January, choosing to go via the Cape of Good Hope to avoid the seasonal storms that swirled about South America's southern coast. The *Roebuck* was in a rotten, worm-riddled state, but the Englishmen managed to reach Australia's west coast, pulling into Shark Bay on 6 August 1699 and spending time exploring and recording the wildlife. They left Australia in September, sailing to Timor and around the northern coast of New Guinea. Though they were less than 100 miles (160km) from the shore of Western Australia, the *Roebuck* was now deteriorating at an alarming rate, and Dampier decided to turn for home. After rounding the Cape of Good Hope the ship began to founder, and in desperation they ran aground on the remote Ascension Island in the South Atlantic. For five weeks Dampier was marooned there with his mutinous crew, until a passing East India ship brought them back to London.

Dampier was court-martialled for having had his lieutenant, George Fisher, thrown into a Brazilian jail on the outward journey. Though he was found guilty and dismissed from the

Dampier and his companions in their canoe, overtaken by a dreadfull storm. *From David Henry's* An Historical Account of All the Voyages Round the World … *(1773).*

navy, Dampier would complete two further circumnavigations.

The second, launched in 1703, was to serve English interests off the Pacific South American coast – which is to say, to work against the interests of the Spanish and French. Captaining 120 men aboard the *St George*, Dampier captured a number of Spanish ships off the coast of Peru and launched a failed attack on Santa María, a town on the Gulf of Panama. In May 1704, one of the crew, Alexander Selkirk, was dumped on the uninhabited Juan Fernández archipelago in the South Pacific for complaining about the leaking state of his vessel.

In 1709, when Dampier was completing his third circumnavigation, he sailed the privateering ship *Duke* via Juan Fernández, rescuing Selkirk after four years and four months

Prince Jeoly, the tattooed Indonesian slave Dampier brought back to London. 'This famous Painted Prince is the just Wonder of ye Age.'

A Map of the Discoveries made by Captⁿ Willⁿ Dampier in the Roebuck in 1699

The Equinoctial Line

PART OF GILOLO

TERRA de PAPOS

CERAM
Amboina
Banda Isles

NOVA GUINEA

NOVA BRITANNIA

TIMOR I.

English Leagues

This Country was first discovered by Saavedra a Spaniard in 1529 who called it Terra de Papuas, but the Dutch Discoverer Schouten, imposed on it the Name of New Guinea. It is the least known to Europe of any of the Eastern Countries. The Inhabitants are generally speaking Blacks, but there is a Nation of Whites seated in one part of it whom some have suspected to be a Remnant of ye Ten Tribes of Israel, who were carried into Captivity by the Assyrians. The Kings of the Moluccas were formerly wont to have a Guard of these Papuas about their Persons, esteeming them the bravest and most faithful Soldiers in the Indies. They have hitherto defended their Country against all Invaders.
It is very difficult to say Positively what are the Produce of New Guinea, because no Europeans have penetrated beyond the Coasts; however, the Inhabitants of the Moluccas, are known to trade with the People of this Country for Gold and Spices which Sufficiently demonstrates that it is well worth the discovering.
This Discovery of Captain Dampier that the Country he named New Britain was an Island, is of very great importance, since it lessons the Difficulties of settling a Colony in this part of the World that might probably be attended with great Advantages, as well with respect to ye profits drawn from the Plantations as from the Commerce of the neighbouring Countries. In our Twentieth Section the Reader will meet with the latest Discoveries that have been since Capt. Dampier's Voyage.

E. Bowen Sc.

completely alone. (The story was one of several true accounts of marooned buccaneers that inspired Daniel Defoe's novel *Robinson Crusoe*.)

Dampier returned to England with loot valued at £147,975 (about £19.9 million today), most of which had been seized from a Spanish galleon, *Nuestra Señora de la Encarnación y Desengaño*, along the coast of Mexico in December 1709. Dampier, however, never got to enjoy the fruits of his privateering. He died almost £2000 in debt in 1715, and was buried in an unmarked grave. Selkirk, meanwhile, never quite recovered from his hermetic ordeal. He spent his later years living alone in a cave built in the grounds of his father's estate.

A 1745 map by Emanuel Bowen of a portion of Dampier's discoveries aboard the Roebuck, *showing his route through the Timors, around New Guinea and the discovery of 'New Britain'.*

VITUS BERING'S EXPEDITION INTO THE GREAT FROZEN NORTH 1725-41

*'We should bring glory through the arts and sciences.
In our search for a route, we will be more successful
than the Dutch and English.'*

PETER THE GREAT, IN HIS DIRECTIONS FOR BERING'S EXPEDITION

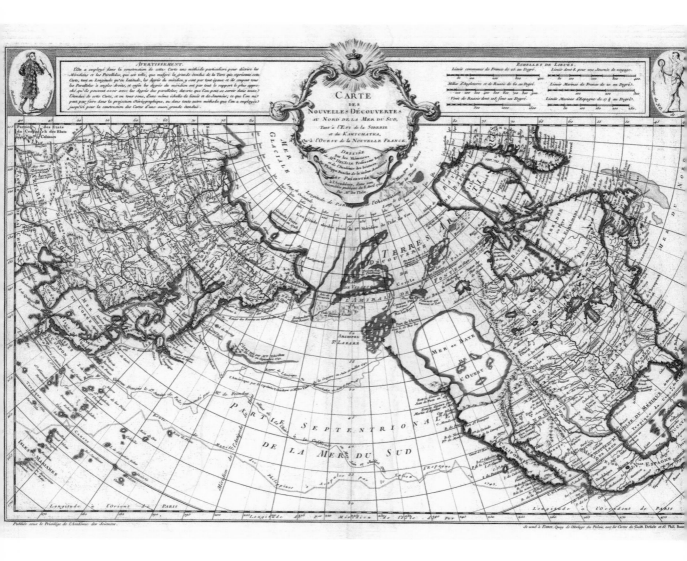

While European sailors like William Dampier were reaching and exploring ever more distant and exotic lands and cultures, there remained unsolved mysteries closer to home. The geography of Russian territory in the far northeast, thousands of miles from St Petersburg across the severity of Siberia, was a total enigma. Could there be, somewhere amid this blank space in the upper-right corner of the national map, some vast promontory, a land bridge connecting the country with North America? Or was it divided by water and, if so, by what distance?

In 1724, Peter the Great was in poor health. Surgeons had operated on the troublesome imperial bladder and he'd spent much of the year bedridden. His realm, however, was flourishing. Under his modernist rule the Russian Empire had grown powerfully and culturally, undergoing a philosophical revolution of a more scientific and reasoned thinking inspired by the Western Enlightenment. In this year, though, the last before his death (after the bladder turned gangrenous), Peter still held one last ambition for himself and his country: to discover its true extent. Peter delegated the challenge to Vitus Jonassen Bering, an experienced Dane serving as a first captain in the Russian navy. Bering had briefly retired from service after twenty years, feeling he'd shamed his wife by not progressing past his low rank, and so readily accepted the prestigious role and the huge logistical issues involved. The mission, known as the First Kamchatka Expedition, would be a gruelling undertaking. There was no chance of reaching the eastern coast by sailing along Russia's northern coast, because of the inevitable obstruction by Arctic ice. Instead, in January 1725, Bering and his thirty-four men set off from St Petersburg for Okhotsk on the Pacific coast on a mammoth 3500 mile- (5633km-) land crossing of some of the world's most brutal terrain.

By February they had travelled the 400 or-so miles (644km) to the city of Vologda, then out across the Ural Mountains, arriving in Tobolsk on 16 March having covered more than 1750 miles (2816km). Thirty-nine men joined the mission from the local garrison at Bering's request, and by the spring of 1726 they had left Ust-Kut on the Lena river, picking up men along the way, though according to Bering 'few were suitable'. A party of this size had never before travelled this undeveloped route, and quite often they built the roads as they needed them. At each town they caused great resentment, as the drain on local resources reduced supplies to dangerously

OPPOSITE: *Map by Guillaume de l'Isle and Philippe Buache showing the latest discoveries in the northern Pacific. While the eye might initially be drawn to the 'Mer de Ouest', the mapmakers' mistaken belief in a giant inland sea in North America, one can also find the tracks of the two expeditions of 'Cap.ne Beering'.*

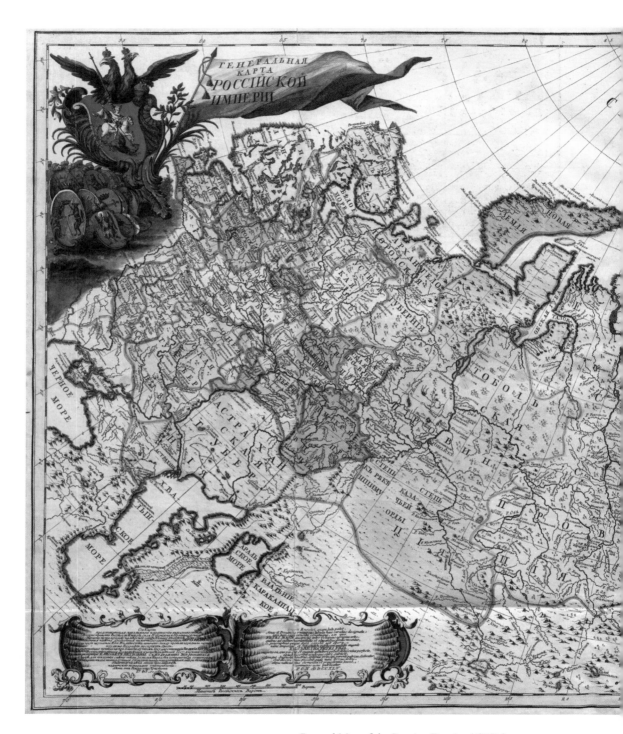

General Map of the Russian Empire *(1745) by an*
unknown cartographer, drawn with the information
collected by the second Kamchatka expedition.

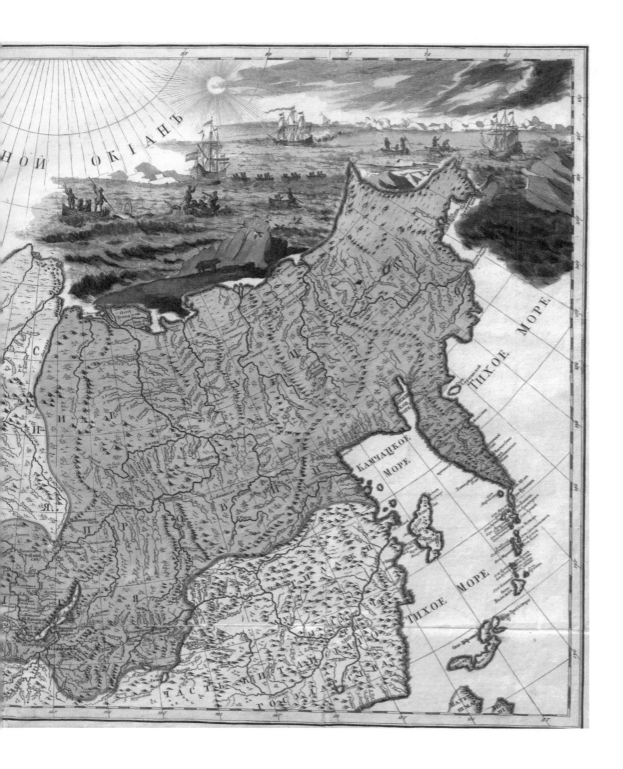

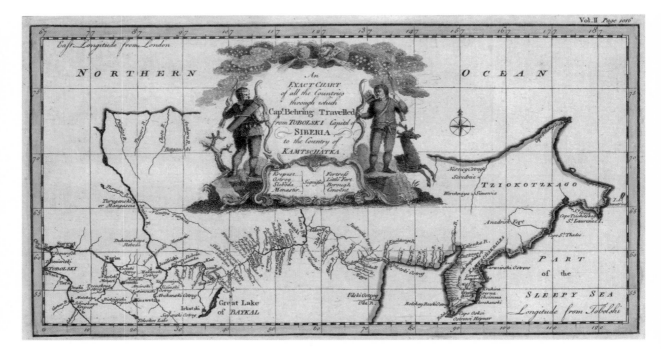

An Exact Chart of all the Countries through which Capt. Behring Travelled from Tobolsk, Capital of Siberia to the Country of Kamtschatka *by Emanuel Bowen, 1744.*

low levels. By the time they reached Okhotsk in June, forty-six men had deserted and several others had died, but they pushed on undaunted to the next stage: to sail to the Kamchatka Peninsula. A 66ft-(20m-) long ship, the *Vostok*, had been constructed in preparation of their arrival, and another, the *Fortuna*, was hastily built – for, in addition to the other demands of their great journey, the men had also dragged along boat-building equipment with them the entire way.

On reaching their Kamchatka outpost another ship was constructed, the *Archangel Gabriel*, and in July 1728 they set off up the eastern Russian coast. Sailing north, Bering passed unaware through the strait between Russia and North America (only 51 miles/82km wide at its narrowest point) that would come to bear his name. Poor visibility meant that he failed to sight Alaska across the water, and after a few days' sailing along the Pacific coast as it turned westwards, and with ice approaching from the north, Bering decided to turn for home. By 28 February they were back in St Petersburg, just over three years since his departure and at the cost of fifteen lives.

Russia had changed in his absence. Peter had died, leaving his niece Anna to reign. Possessed of the same expansionist spirit, Empress Anna ordered a second Kamchatka expedition in 1732. The scale of this endeavour was greater than any other

of its kind. The estimated timetable of two years to complete
a crossing of the Pacific to North America ballooned into a
ten-year myriad of journeys by various groups across Siberia's
entirety. Involving more than 3000 people, and racking up
an enormous cost of 1.5 million roubles (about a sixth of the
annual income of the Russian state), much of Siberia's Arctic
and northeastern coast was delineated, while Bering himself
sighted Alaska's Mount Saint Elias on 16 July 1741. After nine
years away he was keen to return to his family, and after a brief
stop at Kayak Island he turned his ship for Kamchatka. Storms
wrecked his ship on the shore of an island, and the exhausted
explorer finally succumbed to an illness thought to be scurvy.
Bering was buried by his men, there on the island amid the sea
that would both come to bear his name.

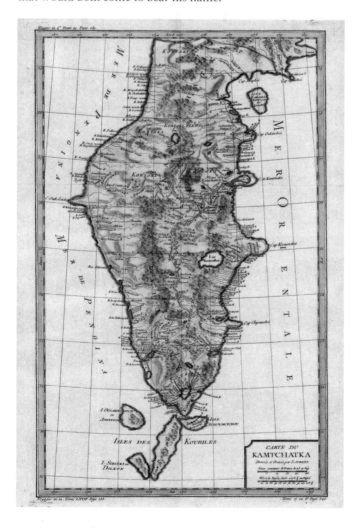

*Bering's men hauled boat-
building materials from
St Petersburg to Okhotsk
to construct a vessel at the
Kamchatka Peninsula, which
is shown here in a 1757 map by
Jacques Nicholas Bellin.*

BOUGAINVILLE'S SCIENTIFIC CIRCUMNAVIGATION OF THE GLOBE 1766-69

'But geography is a science of facts: one cannot speculate from an armchair without the risk of making mistakes which are often corrected only at the expense of the sailors.' LOUIS-ANTOINE DE BOUGAINVILLE

On 10 February 1763 the kingdoms of Great Britain, France and Spain, with Portugal in agreement, came together to sign the Treaty of Paris, thereby formally ending the Seven Years' War. Involving all the great powers of Europe, this, the first global war, was a fusion of various struggles that exploded across continents, with the two sides essentially consisting of France, Austria, Saxony, Sweden and Russia aligned against Prussia, Hanover and Great Britain. A pivotal flurry of blows against France had come in 1759 in an episode known as the French and Indian War, in which attention was focused on the North American theatre of battle, and the colonial territories of New France (Canada, Hudson's Bay, Nova Scotia, Newfoundland), which were besieged victoriously by the British.

'It is an abominable kind of war', wrote one French officer in his journal. 'The very air we breathe is contagious of insensibility and hardness.' The author was Louis-Antoine

Monsieur Bougainville Hoisting the French Colours on a Small Rock Near Cape Forward in the Streights of Magellan. *From David Henry's* An Historical Account of All the Voyages Round the World, Performed by English Navigators ... *(London, 1773).*

de Bougainville, an intelligent and highly educated captain of dragoons and aide-de-camp to the Marquis de Montcalm, with six years' experience of military service and two published mathematical works of integral calculus (which had, among other honours, seen him elected to the British Royal Society). Bougainville had fought in vain to defend Québec City, to prevent the death of the marquis and stop the Colony of Canada falling under British control. Now, as the signatures dried on the treaty, French humiliations were sealed, funds depleted and national pride brought to a dismal nadir. Bougainville, though, had concocted a remedy, and in an extraordinary turn of circumstance the venture would also be the setting for the story of the first woman to circumnavigate the globe.

On 15 September 1763, Bougainville departed from France on a self-funded mission of glory to found the first colony on the little-known Iles Malouines (Falkland Islands). The passengers and future colonists aboard his frigate *L'Aigle* were a group of Acadians (a colony in what is now known as Nova Scotia), who had refused to acquiesce to British rule and had been forced to leave their home in New France. Bougainville's colony numbered as few as 150 so as not to seem to the Spanish as being a base of operations positioned to pillage Peruvian gold. However, having returned to France, Bougainville was ordered by King Louis XV to travel back to the Iles Malouines to evacuate the French settlers and sell the territory to the Spanish, in order to secure their allegiance in the fight against the British.

Far from chastened, Bougainville submitted a proposal to King Louis for a mission for which his return to the islands would be just the first leg: the first French circumnavigation of the world. The king, as eager as Bougainville to realize the dream of French maritime supremacy and restore national honour, agreed, and in 1767, after completing the transfer of the Iles Malouines to the Spanish, Bougainville took the frigates *Boudeuse* and *Etoile* into the roiling waters of the Strait of Magellan.

It was an expedition notable for the unprecedented emphasis on its scientific nature. On board were a multidisciplinary team of scholars that included Count Jean-François de Galaup de La Pérouse (whose own later voyage is covered in The Vanishing of the La Pérouse

FOLLOWING PAGES: Carte Generale de la Terre ou Mappe Monde (1785), one of the most decorative maps of the eighteenth century, by Jean Baptiste Louis Clouet. The routes of Bougainville, Magellan, Tasman, Edmond Halley and Captain James Cook are marked in red.

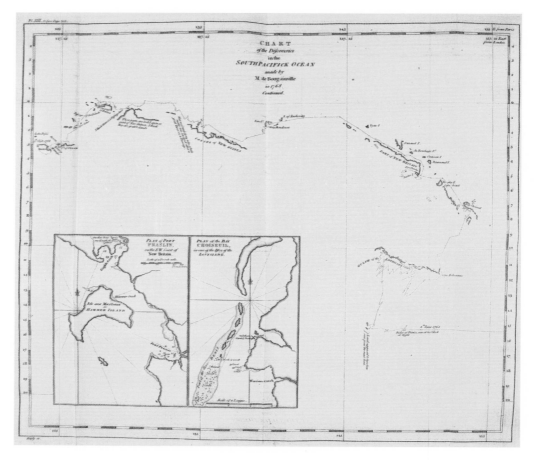

Second chart of Bougainville's discoveries in the South Pacific, 1772.

Expedition entry on pages 162-7), the astronomer Pierre-Antoine Véron, the engineer and cartographer Charles Routier de Romainville, the historian Louis-Antoine Starot de Saint-Germain, and the botanist Philibert Commerçon, who gave the flower bougainvillea its name during the journey and was accompanied by his personal valet.

Such was the turbulence of the passage that it was fifty-two days until the French ships emerged from the strait. Along the way they had encountered the natives of Tierra del Fuego and Patagonia, although this had been of limited use. After one of the sailors presented a local youngster with a piece of glass as a gift, the child ate it and died shortly after, causing local wariness of the strangers. As the ships broke out into the Pacific their sails were filled with powerful southeasterly winds that took them north to the Tropic of Capricorn, and then west. Soon they encountered the Tuamotu Islands (first settled by the Polynesians), which Bougainville named the Dangerous

Archipelago because of the crew's inability to navigate the treacherous surrounding reefs.

In April 1768 they reached the paradise of Tahiti. Unaware that the British sailor Samuel Wallis had made the first European landfall on its black sands just a few months before, Bougainville claimed the island for King Louis, and named it New Cythera, after the Greek island Kythira, mythological home to Aphrodite, the goddess of love. Bougainville marvelled at the Eden he had found. 'The climate on the whole is so healthy that … though our men were continually … exposed to the meridian sun, though they slept on bare soil and in the open air, none of them fell sick there.' *

After nine days the Frenchmen continued westward on their circumnavigation, naming the 'Navigators Islands' (Samoa), skirmishing with the bellicose natives of the 'Great Cyclades' (Vanuatu), and continuing west. A few days later breakers were spotted, a warning they heeded in time to avoid a field of particularly fierce reefs. From the mastheads there were cries of land but the risk was too great, and so their course was changed to northwest, on to the Solomon Islands and past New Guinea – again, Australia's boundless eastern coast, mere miles away, remained undiscovered for now. After stops at Mauritius and the Cape of Good Hope, Bougainville arrived in Saint-Malo on 16 March 1769, the first Frenchman (and only the fourteenth man) to successfully sail around the world. With both ships in good condition and a crew of 330 diminished only by seven, an unusually low loss, it was deemed an unmitigated triumph.

Despite all the wonders encountered along the journey, one of the strangest findings had been made not outside the ship, but on board. For during their time at New Cythera, the ship's surgeon revealed the true identity of Commerçon's valet to be not a boy, but his female partner and assistant, a woman named Jeanne Baret. An expert botanist, she had disguised herself to join the mission, for women were strictly forbidden from being aboard ship or taking part in any exploration, an historically standard proscription that would continue into the next

* It was later found that several of the men did, however, contract syphilis from the 'personal favours' of the Tahitian women offered in exchange for alien objects of fascination, the most demanded of which were iron nails. Bougainville and Wallis blamed each other for bringing the disease to the islands.

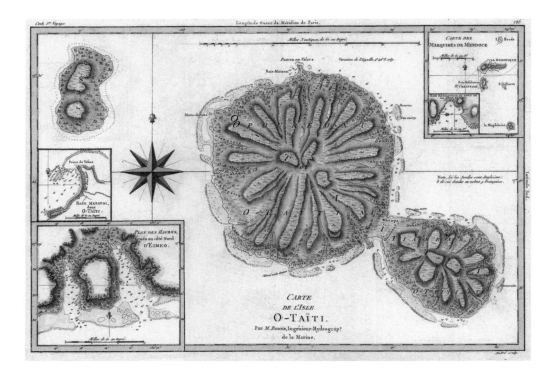

Map of the Island O-Taiti, 1788, by Rigobert Bonne. The centre-left insert shows Matavai Bay, where Samuel Wallis first anchored.

century. (See The Age of the Female Traveller Begins entry on pages 206-15 for more.)

It is extraordinary that the name of Jeanne Baret is not better known, for the levels of courage required to perpetrate such a deception, and the skills and expertise to perform such a role reserved strictly for men, are remarkable. It is clear that Baret was literate, but how and where she received her education – another thing commonly denied women – is unknown. Commerçon was often in poor health, and had hesitated in accepting Bougainville's invitation to join the expedition, but with Baret's company and care on board the ship he was able to carry out his work with her help. Their large private cabin, provided to house their large amount of equipment, ensured a level of privacy that helped sustain the deceit. Despite this, rumours circulated among the crew about Baret's gender, which she tried to stem by claiming to be a eunuch when confronted by the ship's captain, François Chenard de la Giraudais.

According to the accounts of Captain Cook's later voyage to Tahiti, he was told the story of the French expedition's arrival, and how the Tahitian natives had instantly recognized Baret as being female, suggesting that by this time her crewmates

Navig. di Cook - Bougainville T. II. pag. 204.

Dall'Acqua inc.

MAD.ᴸᴸᴬ BARÉ.

An imagined portrait of Jeanne Baret (1816).

would have known the truth. Perhaps, then, this is why Bougainville was happy to be rid of Baret and Commerçon when they chose to remain behind in Mauritius as the expedition returned to France. When Commerçon died in 1773 Baret was initially unable to afford the journey home to France, but by April 1776 she had returned to Paris, finding herself the beneficiary of Commerçon's last will and testament; and in finally completing the last leg of the journey, she became the first woman to have circumnavigated the globe.

CAPTAIN COOK MAPS THE PACIFIC AND SOUTHERN OCEANS 1768-78

'Was it not for the pleasure which naturly results to a Man from being the first discoverer, even was it nothing more than sands and Shoals, this service would be insupportable.' JAMES COOK, 17 AUGUST 1770

A decorative, double-hemisphere map by Louis Brion de la Tour, 1783, tracking the voyages around the world of Captain James Cook.

There is arguably no modern figure popularly regarded with quite the same level of admiration as Captain Cook in the eighteenth century. Take, for example, the third edition of the *Encyclopedia Britannica* (1797). Sir Walter Ralegh's entry runs to two pages; Christopher Columbus, three. Magellan enjoys a mere two paragraphs, if one includes the details of the Magellan Strait. Captain James Cook is dedicated thirty-nine double-column pages.

In 1766 the British Admiralty gave Cook the command of the *Endeavour* for a scientific voyage to the Pacific ocean. Ostensibly the mission was to document the transit of Venus across the face of the Sun. This, it was hoped by the Royal Society, would enable the measurement of the Earth's distance from the Sun, and allow more accurate nautical navigation. On 26 August 1768, 39-year-old Lieutenant Cook left Plymouth with a motley complement including the scientist Joseph Banks, Swedish botanist Daniel Solander, the artist Sydney Parkinson and two greyhounds. To provide milk, there was the most experienced voyager of them all, a goat that had previously circumnavigated the globe with Samuel Wallis.

After stopping at Madeira for supplies (somehow making room on board for 3000 gallons/13,638 litres of wine), they rounded Cape Horn with surprising ease and made their way to Tahiti, the optimal point for observing Venus cross in front of the Sun, arriving 13 April 1769 in time to conduct the cosmic survey. Cloudy weather conditions obscured their view, however, and the meagre data collected was disappointing.

And so Cook turned to a secret second set of instructions, to be opened on completion of the primary mission. His orders now were to search for Terra Australis, the giant continent thought to lie at the base of the southern hemisphere (as shown on Mercator's world map on page 158). Cook headed as far south as the forty parallel (roughly the same latitude as Wellington, New Zealand), the limit permitted by the Admiralty, but found no sign of the vast theoretical southern land. Instead he headed

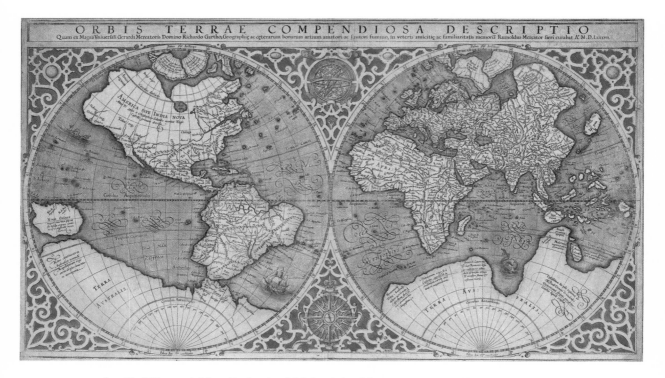

ORBIS TERRAE COMPENDIOSA DESCRIPTIO
Quam ex Magna Vniuersali Gerardi Mercatoris Domino Richardo Gartho, Geographiæ ac cæterarum bonarum artium amatori ac fautori summo, in veteris amicitiæ ac familiaritatis memoriä Rumoldus Mercator fieri curabat Aº. M.D.Lxxxvii.

west for Abel Tasman's New Zealand, which he sighted in
early October 1769. The encounters between the crew of the
Endeavour and the Māori quickly turned violent, and unable to
make peace with the natives the British sailed on, recording the
New Zealand coastline in detail.

Cook then headed west, and on 19 April 1770 he and the
crew of the *Endeavour* became the first Europeans to reach the
eastern Australian coastline, which until that time had been
drawn on maps as a blank space, fading into the theoretical
Terra Australis. On 29 April Cook and crew made their
historic landfall on the Australian mainland, christening the
area 'Stingray Bay', but later changing this to Botany Bay after
Joseph Banks and Daniel Solander returned with a wealth
of exotic samples. They continued north, but with their ship
being damaged on the Great Barrier Reef they eventually
returned home via the Cape of Good Hope.

Despite charting the coasts of New Zealand and Australia
and proving them to be independent landmasses, the Royal
Society's determination to uncover the Terra Australis
persisted, and so in 1772 Captain Cook was commissioned
to lead a second voyage farther south to find it. He set off in
the *Resolution* from Plymouth on 13 July 1772, having been

*Rumold Mercator's 1616 world
map, showing Terra Australis,
the mysterious southern continent
supposedly in existence to
counterbalance the weight of the
lands in the northern hemisphere.*

*A 1788 print of Captain
James Cook.*

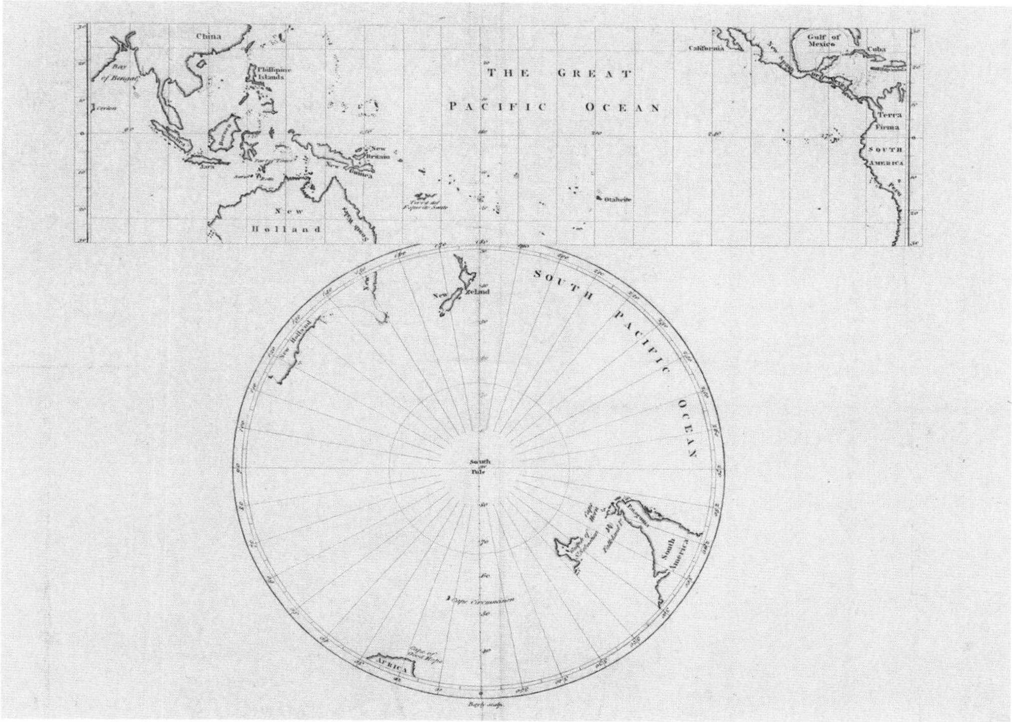

delayed by an imperious Banks, who angrily quit the mission when his demands of a larger ship were not satisfied.

Accompanied by the *Adventure*, captained by Tobias Furneaux, Cook headed for New Zealand again, sailing more than 10,000 nautical miles (18,520km) in four months; at one point he was unaware that they were passing just 75 nautical miles (139km) from the coast of undiscovered Antarctica. Realizing the likelihood of weather separating the ships, Cook and Furneaux made a rendezvous plan for New Zealand's Queen Charlotte Sound. Sure enough, in October the vessels were separated by a gale. Furneaux was delayed by a month, and when he arrived he found a letter left for him under a stump marked 'Look Underneath' by Cook (who had left only a week earlier), in which he explained his schedule for the next four months, allowing Furneaux to make his own plans, including heading home if necessary. This Furneaux leapt at, no doubt encouraged by a recent encounter with Māoris in which ten of his men were attacked and cannibalized.

Cook, meanwhile, pushed farther south, reaching an unprecedented southern position of 71°10'S on 31 January 1774. Enduring the hostility of Antarctic temperatures, and

Untitled chart of 'The Great Pacific Ocean' and 'South Pacific Ocean' (1772), the exceedingly rare first printed map of Cook's explorations of New Zealand and Australia on his first voyage. It's also the first printed map of the east coast of Australia, the first to name New South Wales, and the first of a continental Australia and both islands of New Zealand. This is one of only three known copies.

barely escaping the crush of pack ice and the
threat of icebergs, it became clear that the
hope of a hospitable southern continent was ill
founded. For the next seven months he and his
men toured the warmer parallels of the South
Pacific, testing a model of the inventor John
Harrison's marine chronometer, a timepiece
which proved to be extraordinarily accurate
in facilitating the measurement of longitude.
When they eventually arrived back in England
at Spithead on 30 July 1775, Cook had lost
only four of his men, and none to scurvy, a
remarkably low figure.

The voyage had put an end to the myth of
Terra Australis, earning Cook an honorary
retirement, which he accepted on the condition
he could return should there be a mission to
lead. This came in 1776 with a clandestine
purpose. The public was told the aim was to return home
a Tahitian named Omai brought back with the previous
voyage, but, in fact, Cook – the Admiralty's most proven
way finder – was to lead the *Resolution*, along with Captain
Charles Clerke commanding the *Discovery*, on a search for
the Northwest Passage.

On 12 July 1776 the ships left to deliver Omai back to Tahiti.
This was achieved swiftly and without incident, and so they
proceeded in a northerly direction visiting the Friendly Islands
(Tonga), Bora-Bora and Christmas Island (Kiritimati). They
then became the first Europeans to lay eyes on the Sandwich
Islands, as Cook named them. They had discovered Hawaii.
Anchoring at Kauai, they began trading with the natives and
found that their iron nails were of such fascination that they
were readily swapped for enough pork to feed Clerke's entire
crew. The mission to find the Northwest Passage was ever-
pressing, however (the British government's reward of £20,000
a constant on the commanders' minds), as was the limited
seasonal window to explore the Arctic.

After two weeks, the beaches of Hawaii were left behind
for the west coast of North America. Cook and his crew
mapped much of the Pacific shoreline for the first time, and
pressed on with their northward journey through the Bering
Strait between Russia and Alaska, and passed into the Chukchi

*A unique contemporary pen-and-
ink drawing of Cook's encounter
with the Māori: 'They make a
most frightful appearance', writes
Cook in his journal, of the Māori
tattoos. '[W]e could not but
admire the dexterity and art with
which they were impressed.'*

Sea. They reached as far north as 70°44'N, but were met with a wall of ice 12ft (3.6m) high that stretched across the horizon. With no obvious thoroughfare, the expedition was brought to an end.

The decision was made to return to the Hawaiian sunshine, and on 26 November 1778 they arrived at Maui. Cook circled the island looking for a suitable point of shelter, and put in at Kealakekua Bay, where they were met with a rapturous welcome by the natives. By coincidence, Cook's arrival fitted perfectly with a traditional Hawaiian myth, in which Lono-makua, the god of plenty, once circled the island and arrived in a giant canoe in the same bay. The Englishmen were showered with gifts by the king of Hawaii, Kalei'opu'u, and in early February they left with their ships laden. However, just a few days later their ships were lashed with storms. The mast of the *Resolution* was fractured, and Cook was forced to return to Kealakekua Bay. This time, the natives greeted them in silence and grew increasingly hostile as the crew carried out their repairs. When it was discovered one of their small boats had been stolen, Cook angrily ordered a blockade of the bay and the kidnap of a local chief until the property was returned. He went ashore to resolve the matter with the native leader, but tempers on both sides exploded when the captured chief was shot. At some point, Cook made a signal to his ship offshore, which triggered a mob reaction. He was stoned, clubbed and then cut down by a dagger blow to the back of the head. Four other marines were killed, with his men on the ship powerless to help. Contrary to popular belief Cook was not eaten by the natives, but part of his body was baked to allow easy removal of the bones, a respectful tradition of worship, for despite the circumstances of his death he was held in high esteem by the Hawaiians.

The expedition returned to England without their captain, but in possession of a treasure trove of pioneering navigational data that would greatly advance European knowledge and mapping, gathered by a man who lived up to his vow of sailing 'not only farther than any other man has been before me, but as far as I think it possible for man to go'.

… and her male counterpart, in a traditional mask. Both engravings are based on the artwork of John Webber, the official artist on Cook's final voyage through the Pacific. From A Voyage to the Pacific, *published in 1784.*

THE VANISHING OF THE LA PÉROUSE EXPEDITION 1785-88

'My story is a romance.' Jean-François de Galaup de La Pérouse

As he was bundled through the jeering armed mob filling Paris's newly renamed Place de la Révolution on his way to the guillotine in 1793, you would have thought there to be more sharply pressing matters occupying the mind of the condemned Louis XVI. But as the desacralized 'Citizen Louis Capet' stood on the scaffold in the dark company of his hangmen, he is said to have turned and asked hopefully: 'Is there any news of La Pérouse?'

In 1785 it had been seven years since James Cook's fateful third voyage, and the Englishman's work delineating and detailing the unexplored parts of the South Atlantic and Pacific – though extensive – was far from complete. The French navy had by then recovered from the losses suffered during the Seven Years' War, and with interest kindled by an earlier proposal by a Dutch merchant named William Bolts to explore the North American coast for lucrative fur trading, King Louis had consulted with his Secretary of State of the Navy, the Marquis de Castries, to launch a French mission to build on Cook's progress.

The man given command of the expedition was 44-year-old Jean-François de Galaup de La Pérouse, who had first joined the naval college at fifteen and proven himself a useful navigator and commander in battles with the British. The voyage was to be a circumnavigation of the globe which would, in true Enlightenment fashion, feature a largely scientific contingent. This included the astronomer and mathematician Joseph Lepaute Dagelet, the geologist Robert de Lamanon and the botanist Joseph La Martinière; as well as a physicist, three naturalists and three illustrators. In total the two ships *La Boussole* and *L'Astrolabe* would carry 225 crew, officers and scientists on a voyage predicted to last four years. La Pérouse was an admirer of Cook, and emulated his meticulous approach to charting his progress and devotion to the safety of the crew. In preparation he sent his chief engineer, Paul

Monneron, to London to learn about Cook's pioneering scurvy-prevention methods and to procure navigational equipment – including two inclining compasses from the Royal Society – used on Cook's voyages.

The expedition departed from France on 1 August 1785. The ships rounded Cape Horn with little difficulty, and emerging into the Pacific headed north to Chile. The objectives of the mission were manifold, but the principal ambition was to fill in the blanks of Cook's maps, particularly the northwest coast of America, the Pacific coast of Russia north of the Strait of Tartary (which no European had accurately traced), as well as Melanesia and the general Oceania region northeast of Australia. But, of course, there were also the motives of trade and political expansion – fur trapping and whaling contacts were to be made, scientific collections enriched and allies for future colonial cooperation secured.

After Chile La Pérouse and his men made for Easter Island and then Hawaii, where they became the first Europeans to

Louis XVI giving final instructions to the Comte de La Pérouse, 1785, *painted by Edouard Nuel.*

The Calao de l'Ile de
Waigiou, *recorded during
the La Pérouse expedition.*

set foot on the island of Maui. Next they went to Alaska, from
where they launched a nearly four-month journey carefully
recording the North American coastline on their journey
south to California. As the first non-Spanish visitors to the
region since Francis Drake in 1579, they noted critically the
treatment of the natives at the hands of Spanish missionaries
and conclusively dispelled, among other misconceptions, the
persistent European belief that California was an island,
which had been marked as such on maps from the early
seventeenth century.

From there they sailed across the Pacific in a hundred days,
landing at Macau in east Asia, where they traded Alaskan furs,
before visiting Manila on their way to the uncharted coast of
Korea. From the Kamchatka Peninsula in the Russian Far East
they dispatched their logs, letters and maps back to France, and
on new instructions soon left to head south for Australia's New
South Wales, to investigate the British settlements.

Within the map (title cartouche):

LA CALIFORNIE ou NOUVELLE CAROLINE,
TEATRO DE LOS TRABAJOS, APOSTOLICOS DE
LA COMPA. E. JESUS EN LA AMERICA, SEPT.

GRAN TEGUAIO

GRAN QUIVIRA   MOQUI

MAR DE LAS CALIFORNAS Ó CAROLINAS

CALIFORNAS Ó CAROLINAS

NUEVO MEXICO

MAR DEL SUR

Tropique de Cancer.

It was a weakened French party that drew into Botany
Bay in late January 1788 (coincidentally just four days after
the first group of British convicts had arrived). A stop in the
Navigator Islands (Samoa) had seen them attacked by natives –
twelve of La Pérouse's men had been killed, with twenty more
wounded. The British offered a courteous reception, and the
French spent six weeks recuperating at the colony. In March
1788, having sent the latest batch of records home to France, La
Pérouse and his men refreshed their water supplies, weighed
anchor and headed for a tour of Oceania. This was the last that
was ever seen of them.

When La Pérouse failed to return to France in June as
he had confidently predicted, the tardiness seemed out of
character but not a cause for concern. But, gradually, the alarm
began to build. Finally on 25 September 1791 Rear Admiral
Joseph-Antoine d'Entrecasteaux left France on a search-and-

For much of the seventeenth and eighteenth centuries, European maps such as this by Nicolas de Fer, c.1720, showed California as an island, a misbelief that was definitively disproved by the methodical mapping of La Pérouse.

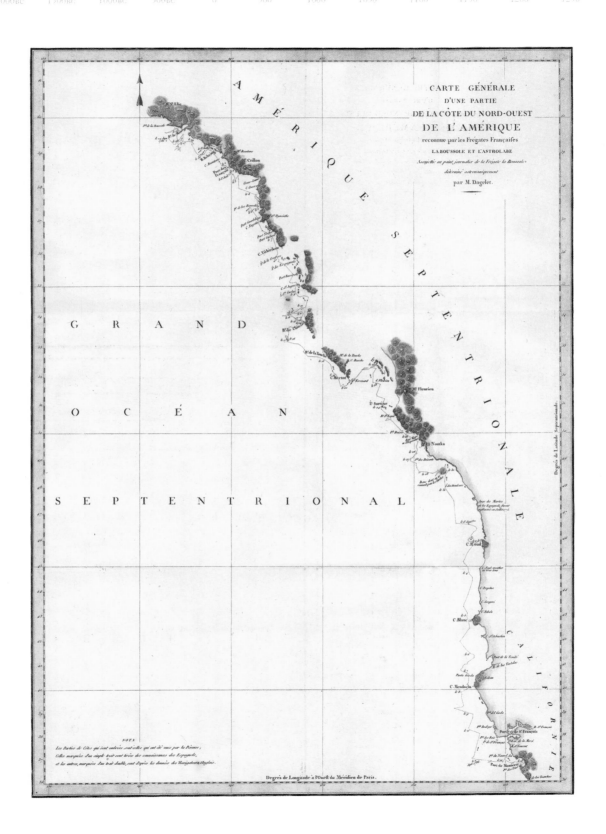

*The La Pérouse expedition
on Easter Island.*

rescue mission, arriving in the region of what is now known as the Solomon Islands in May 1793, but failed to find a trace of the men. In fact it was not until 1826 that an Irish sea merchant named Peter Dillon first found solid clues to their fate in the form of wreckage later identified as that of *L'Astrolabe*; and not until 2008, after nearly two centuries of piecing clues together, when two French navy vessels set out to recreate the final leg of La Pérouse's voyage that the events were finally understood.

It emerged that a powerful cyclone had swept up the ships off the coast of the Santa Cruz Islands, and hurled them against the reefs, wrecking both ships. Some members of crew managed to survive the initial destruction and make it to the Vanikoro, the nearest island, where they were slaughtered by the natives. A few others managed to piece together a raft from the remains of *L'Astrolabe* and set off in a westerly direction, but what happened to them is not known. The bulk of La Pérouse's work, however, survived, thanks to his discipline of routinely sending home what discoveries they had at each point of rest. The ethnographic descriptions, zoological specimens, journals and detailed cartographic illuminations of the expedition saw the men celebrated as national heroes, and were proudly published by the French government as *Voyage de La Pérouse autour du monde* (La Pérouse's Voyage Around the World), copies of which were snapped up by a fascinated international readership.

OPPOSITE: *Map meticulously tracking the progress of La Pérouse's exploration of the northwestern coast of North America, taken from* Atlas du Voyage de La Pérouse *(1797).*

GEORGE VANCOUVER REVEALS AMERICA'S NORTHWEST COAST 1791-95

'We are unavoidably led to observe, with admiration, that active spirit of discovery.'

GEORGE VANCOUVER, *A VOYAGE OF DISCOVERY* (1798)

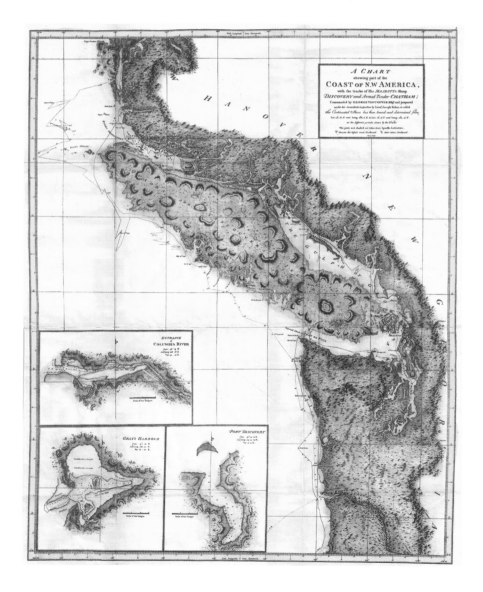

With the Age of Discovery having given way to the Age
of Enlightenment, a transition marked by Cook's voyages,
scientific explorations reached a new level of precision with
the surveying of the British naval officer George Vancouver,
who had sailed at the age of thirteen-and-a-half with Captain
Cook on his second and third voyages. By the age of twenty-
three, when Cook's expedition had returned, Vancouver
had seen New Zealand, the Society Isles, the New Hebrides
and New Caledonia; he had rounded Cape Horn, ranged
nearly the entire length of the North American seaboard and
circumnavigated the Sandwich Islands (Hawaii). He had also
developed the skills of his mentor. Vancouver was possessed of
such precision that his maps would startle Charles Wilkes with
their accuracy when he examined Puget Sound more than forty
years later; while Vancouver's chart of the Alaskan coastline
remained the standard well into the 1880s.

OPPOSITE: *Vancouver's 1798
map ranges from Cape Lookout
(in modern-day Oregon)
northwards past the Columbia
river, the Strait of Juan de
Fuca, Vancouver Island, Queen
Charlotte Sound, to Cape Swaine
(British Columbia).*

The catalyst for Vancouver's three seasonal surveys of
America's northwest coast was the Nootka Crisis, when Spain
and Britain almost came to blows in a dispute over a network of
inlets key to the fur trade on the west coast of Vancouver Island.
The profitability of the sea-otter trade was, of course, neither here
nor there – the claim to Nootka Sound was for sovereignty
over the entire northern Pacific seaboard. The argument over
ownership and colonization rights concluded with Spain
retreating from British threats of war, and, when this was
formalized in the Nootka Sound Conventions of 1790, Vancouver
was handed command of the *Discovery* to take possession of
Nootka Sound and survey the coastlines in the region.

Vancouver sailed from Falmouth in April 1791, rounding
the Cape of Good Hope and continuing east until he sighted
the southwest coast of Australia, of which he formally took
possession for Britain. He and his crew spent December in
Tahiti, before sailing north to the Sandwich Islands (where
he had witnessed the killing of Cook) to stock up on fresh
supplies. From the Sandwich Islands, which would be their
overwintering base for the next few years, they made for the
Pacific American coast, arriving at California's Cape Cabrillo.

They cruised north along the coast, tracing the shores
of California then Oregon and Washington, until reaching
the giant island that would later carry Vancouver's name.
As they entered the Strait of Juan de Fuca, which separates
the southern coast of the island from Washington's northern

Robert Wilkinson's 1804 map of North America, illustrating George Vancouver's discoveries and the first to show the Louisiana Purchase (see Lewis and Clark Hunt for a Route to the Pacific entry on pages 184-189).

coastline, it was obvious that their ships were too large to navigate the intricate scattering of islands, coves, sounds and channels that existed there. Unfazed, Vancouver ordered the launch of the smaller craft, barely larger than rowing boats (indeed in calmer conditions they were frequently forced to propel themselves by oar), and under the observation of other crew members on the shore Vancouver and his lieutenants traced every strait and island coastline in the small vessels, which were stocked with supplies for two weeks at a time. Slowly, over three seasons of exhausting and painstaking procedure between 1792 and 1794, an accurate hydrographic picture of the Pacific northwest was collected.

It did not come without cost, however. Vancouver had become increasingly ill and developed a fearsome mercurial temperament. It's thought he might have been suffering from Graves' disease or myxoedema, thyroid conditions which would have been exacerbated by the physical demands and intolerable weather conditions of the mission. Despite this, the total data accumulated by the Vancouver mission is astounding – in their minor craft they covered more than 10,000 miles (16,000km), recording more than 1700 miles (2700km) of coastline, as well as exploring the Columbia river, circling Vancouver Island and probing every littoral nook and cranny of island-studded British Columbia. The exactitude of his charts would also put to rest the idea of a Northwest Passage at these latitudes.

By October 1798 Vancouver was back in London, dying in obscurity only two-and-a-half years later from the illness that had taken hold during the Nootka surveys. As well as leaving behind a 500,000-word record of his expedition just 100 pages short of completion, the man considered first among the scientific explorers of the eighteenth century had added 388 place names to the world map, with islands, peninsulas, mountains and bays around the world still bearing his name.

FOLLOWING PAGES: *The majestic wall map* Nova Totius Americae Tabula Emendata *by the Dutch cartographer Frederick de Wit, published in 1672. The northwest coast of North America was essentially a giant blank on maps until the meticulous surveying of Vancouver and his men between 1792 and 1794.*

MUNGO PARK EXPLORES NORTH AFRICA 1795-1806

'My hope is now approaching to a certainty. If I be deceived, may God alone put me right, for I would rather die in the delusion than wake to all the joys of earth.' Mungo Park, in a letter to his friend Alexander Anderson, 1793

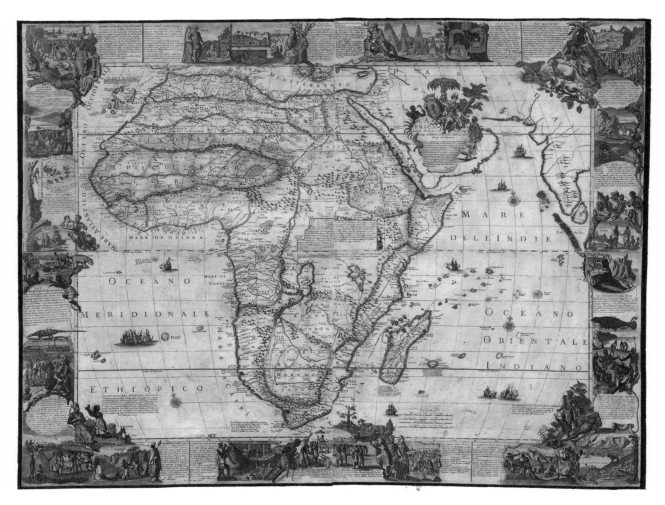

Paolo Petrini's spectacular
African wall map of 1700.

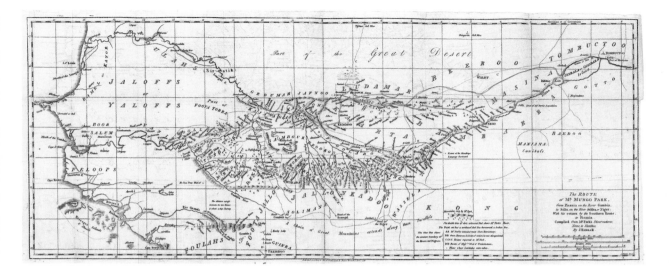

The Route of Mr Mungo Park,
by James Rennell.

By the late eighteenth century Africa remained, to Europeans, a continent of secrets. Though its coastlines had been delineated and trade long established with its west coast, barely any headway had been made in penetrating the hinterland. Knowledge was limited to the western Senegal and Gambia rivers, and Christian Abyssinia to the east. After Captain Cook's Pacific discoveries effectively put an end to the obsession with finding the mysterious southern continent Terra Australis, the great age of sea exploration was coming to an end and attention, both scientific and strategic, turned to Africa.

Contemporary maps of the continent were 'still but a wide extended blank on which the Geographer … has traced with a hesitating hand a few names of unexplored rivers and of uncertain nations', wrote Henry Beaufoy, secretary of the Association for Promoting the Discovery of the Interior Parts of Africa, or the African Association, which had been founded by Joseph Banks, together with eight other wealthy patrons with scientific interests, in 1788. In drawing up plans for an expedition to investigate the continent, the African Association prioritized the solving of an old riddle: the course and termination of the Niger river. From a meeting with Joseph Banks to discuss his zoological discoveries in Sumatra, the Scotsman Mungo Park learnt of the planned African journey and volunteered to lead it. Despite being aged only twenty-three, Park's application was approved and he set sail from Portsmouth on 22 May 1795.

The plan was to sail up the Gambia river, cross overland to the Niger, and reach Timbuktu. The African Association had lost men to the cause before: the first man sent, an American named John Ledyard, set out to find Timbuktu from the Blue Nile but swallowed a fatal dose of emetic in an attempt to cure his dysentery. Another, Major Daniel Houghton, disappeared on his way from the Gambia. (Park later discovered in 1796 that Houghton had been robbed and stripped by Moors, who left him to die of thirst and exposure.) It seemed Park too was destined for failure when, on his arrival, he immediately contracted malaria, but this turned out to be something of a blessing in disguise, as his recuperation helped him acclimatize before his departure and to pick up the basics of the Sudanese Mandingo language.

At first Park made good progress, but by January 1796 three-quarters of his possessions had been forfeited as tributes to native leaders encountered and he was forced to rely on the charity of villagers for provisions. Local conflict then forced a detour to the north into the domain of Ali, nomadic King of Ludamar. Park was held captive at a camp at Benowm for more than three months, to satisfy – he was told – the curiosity of Ali's wife at seeing a European for the first time. He eventually escaped and continued on his journey heading southeast, at one point participating in a local wedding in which an elderly woman cheerfully threw a bowl of the bride's urine in his face. A sign of distinction, he was told. 'This being the case, I wiped my face and sent my acknowledgements to the lady.' He finally reached the Niger, the first European to do so, and described a river flowing eastwards, 'as broad as the Thames at Westminster'. At Ségou (south central Mali), he was informed by locals that, even if he were to survive the few days journey to Timbuktu, he would certainly be killed on arrival, and so despite being frustratingly close to his goal he made the decision to turn for home. Park had been assumed dead by his countrymen, and so his return to England on Christmas Day 1797 was celebrated as something of a seasonal miracle. His *Travels into the Interior of Africa* (1798) was a success with the reading public despite the relatively modest achievements of the expedition, and he returned home to set up a medical practice in Scotland.

The British government soon renewed their interest in West Africa, in part to prevent French expansion. The War Office

Mungo Park, from Travels into the Interior of Africa, *1798.*

drew up a plan to send a unit of men to travel from Pisania on the Gambia river to Bamako on the Niger, where they would construct two 40ft- (12m-) boats and sail down the Niger, establishing trade outposts. This would be a vital test as to the ease with which goods could be transported from the Gambia to the Niger. The newly married Park was asked to lead the mission, to which he readily agreed, bringing with him his brother-in-law, Alexander Anderson.

This time greater preparations were made: the group were heavily equipped with tributes for kings, including 460 yards (420m) of cloth, as well as rifles and a tremendous amount of ammunition. But there was little that could be done about the most lethal of African inhospitalities: disease. Of the forty-five men that left Pisania on 4 May 1805, only eleven arrived at Bamako on 19 August. Most were claimed by dysentery, yellow fever and malaria; the survivors managing to overcome these and the violent onslaught of weather, insects and native robbers they were too weak to fight off. They made their way to Sansanding, just south of Ségou, where they worked on their vessel. The men with the ship-building skills were among the dead, as was Anderson, but they managed to fashion a craft. By the time it was fit for launch the exhausted party were down to five men, with three slaves and a native guide named Amadi Fatouma.

From this point, all that is known about the fate of these men is from a deposition given in 1810 by Fatouma, the sole survivor. On a journey that involved some 1000 miles (1600km), the men sailed down the Niger, passing the port of Timbuktu and pushing on to find the river's end. At the Bussa Rapids their boat became lodged, leaving them exposed to the arrows and spears from a native party on the shore. Park and his men were killed, some drowning after leaping into the water, their remains believed to be buried somewhere on the banks nearby.

Park had suspected that such a fate awaited him. Before leaving Sansanding, he entrusted his journal and letters home to a trader, Isaaco, who brought them back to the west coast. 'I shall set sail for the east', wrote Park in a letter to the head of the Colonial Office, 'with the fixed resolution to discover the termination of the Niger or perish in the attempt. Though all the Europeans who are with me should die, and though I were myself half dead, I would still persevere, and if I could not succeed in the object of my journey, I would at least die on the Niger.'

The Chaetodon trifasciatus, *discovered by a young Mungo Park in Sumatra before he left on his African adventures.*

ALEXANDER VON HUMBOLDT AND AIMÉ BONPLAND EXPLORE SOUTH AMERICA 1799-1802

'There is a drive in me that often makes me feel as if I'm losing my mind.' ALEXANDER VON HUMBOLDT

In 2016 Dr Ken Catania of Nashville's Vanderbilt University decided to see what would happen when he plunged his hand into a tank of electric eels. To his surprise, the 6½ft- (2m-) long creatures (strictly speaking not eels but rather a kind of knifefish) leapt right out of the water and clamped down on his hand to deliver multiple 600-volt pulses capable of stunning a large mammal. 'Despite wearing a glove, it was pretty intimidating', reported Catania. 'I made a little note to myself to come back and study this.'

Until Catania's modern study the electric fish's ability to attack out of water had not been recorded – at least, not since 1807, when the German ecologist and explorer Alexander von

The Heart of the Andes, by Frederic Edwin Church, 1859.

Humboldt witnessed the 'picturesque spectacle' of natives using live horses to provoke the creatures to attack in the pools of the Venezuelan Los Llanos region. Humboldt's story was presumed to be apocryphal. In 1881, a German critic dismissed it as 'poetically transfigured'. *The Atlantic* called it 'tommyrot'. Though it has been more than 150 years since his death in 1859, we are still learning from Alexander von Humboldt.

Humboldt and his companion, the botanist Aimé Bonpland, had come to find themselves in Venezuela through a set of circumstances more whimsical than those of most great explorations. After his mother died and left him a fortune, Humboldt ditched his career as a mine inspector ('a man can't just sit down and cry, he's got to do something'), and with a much remarked-on curiosity and natural energy, spent time in Paris with Bonpland planning a North African expedition, to end with a desert crossing between Tripoli and Cairo. Then reports came in of French arrivals to Algiers being welcomed with accommodation of the dungeon variety, and so instead they decided to walk to Madrid. There they were introduced to Mariano Luis de Urquijo, the minister of state, and a deal was struck: if the explorers agreed to report back on the mineral deposits of South America, they would be granted Spanish authority to wander through the continent as they wished (at their own expense), something never before granted to non-Spaniards. Space on the ship *Pizarro* was found, and on 5 June 1799, after slipping through an English blockade, the men were on their way to South America.

After a stop at the Canary Islands an outbreak of typhus (which both Humboldt and Bonpland managed to avoid) struck the crew and the course was changed to Cumaná, Venezuela, farther north than intended, where they arrived on 16 July 1799. The city (250 miles/400km east of Caracas) afforded so many splendours that the two adventurers abandoned the plan to take a second ship south, and instead decided to explore the region. This was 'a land I had been dreaming about since I was a boy', wrote Humboldt, whose diaries are filled with breathless descriptions of natural wonders: 'Naked Indians, electric eels, parrots, monkeys, armadillos, crocodiles, amazing plants, reading my sextant at night by the light of Venus.'

After nearly two months in Cumaná they left for Caracas, where Humboldt and Bonpland, both keen climbers, made

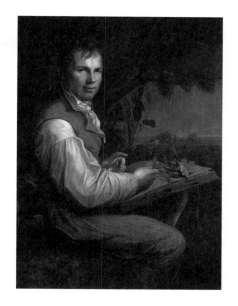

Alexander von Humboldt, *by Friedrich Georg Weitsch, 1859.*

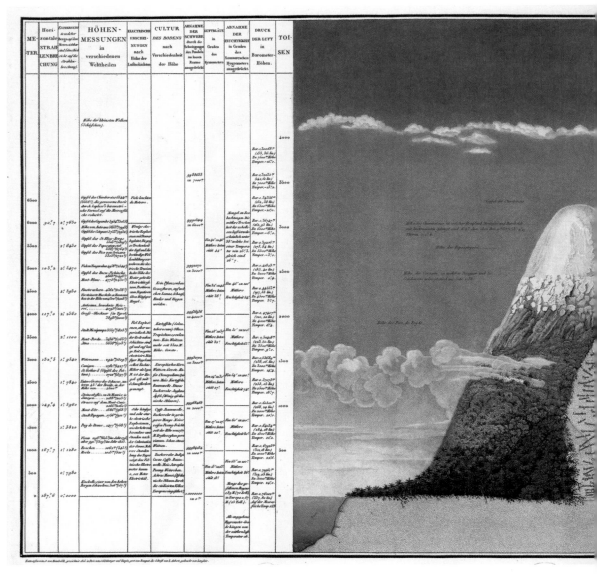

the first recorded ascent of the 7595ft- (2315m-) high Silla of Caracas. They travelled further inland, reaching the Los Llanos region (that 'fills the mind with the feeling of infinity') and its pools of electric eels. They then undertook to map the Orinoco river, a massive task for which they hiked through 1725 miles (2776km) of wild countryside, enduring incessant insect bites and surviving encounters with animals and purportedly cannibalistic tribes. All the while, the pair were diligently, obsessively, collecting and classifying new plant, animal and human skeletal specimens, accumulating some

Humboldt's Naturgemälde, *also known as the* Chimborazo Map, *a giant cross-section of the active volcano Humboldt and Bonpland attempted to scale, with details of surrounding plant geography. From* The Geography of Plants, *1807.*

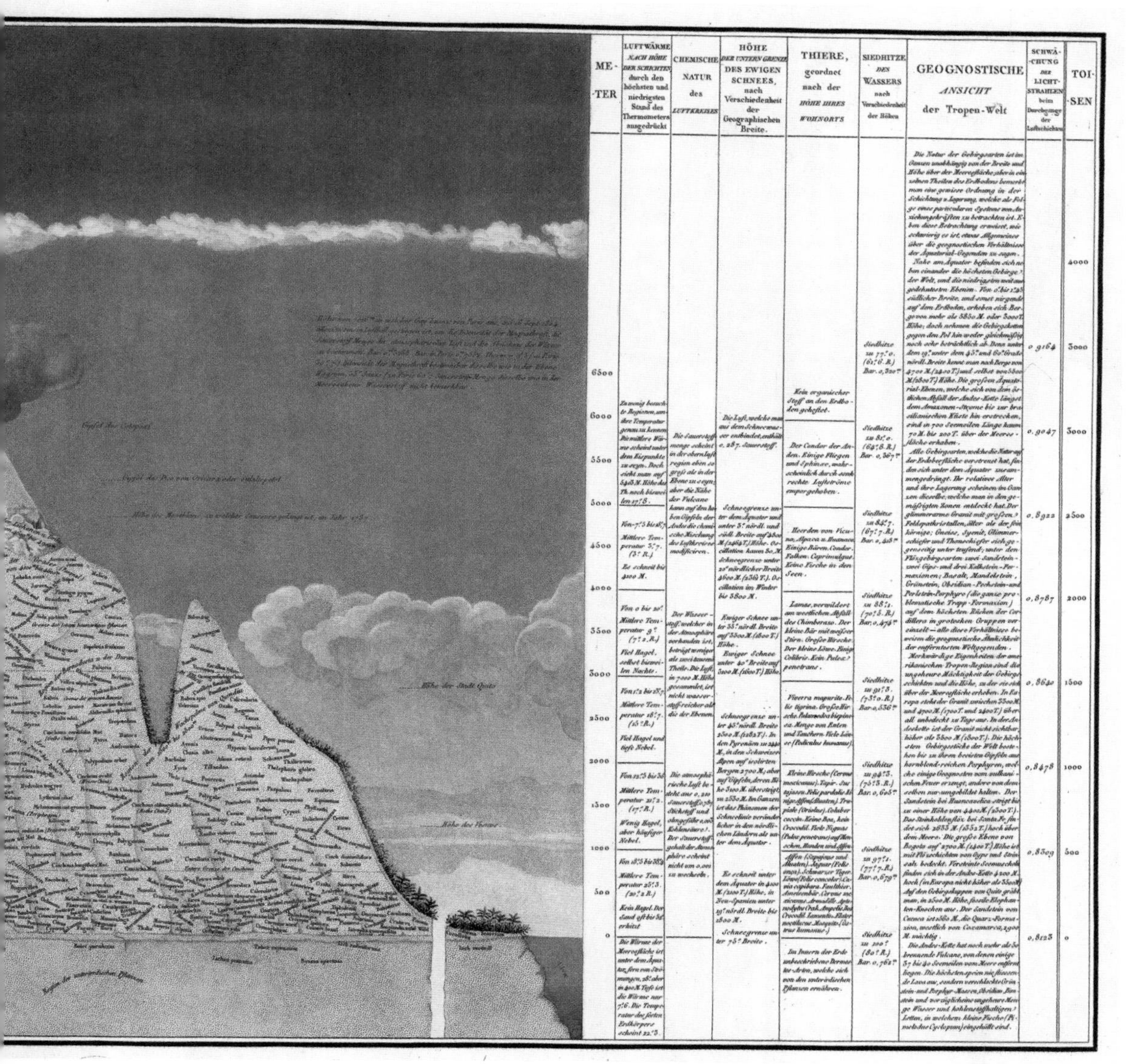

12,000, many of which would be ruined by the humidity. Two months later they explored the territory of the recently extinct Aturès Indians, and debunked Walter Ralegh's mythical Lake Parime, which the Englishman had believed to be the site of El Dorado. Humboldt suggested the seasonal flooding of the Rupununi savannah would have led to rumours of a lake that no one was able to find.

In November 1800 Humboldt and Bonpland sailed for Cuba for a brief visit, before returning to the mainland for another river survey, this time 500 miles (800km) of the Magdalena

River. The inexhaustible pair followed this with a study of Ecuador's volcanoes, scaling the 15,500ft- (4724m-) high active stratovolcano Pichincha on the second attempt, after a mysterious illness (altitude sickness) initially caused Humboldt to pass out. In 1802 they then made their famous attempt on Chimborazo (the highest mountain on Earth if one measures from the centre of the planet rather sea level), but were forced to turn back at 19,286ft (5878m), a world record at the time. The disappointment was soon forgotten when they reached Callao, the main port of Peru, where Humboldt observed the transit of Mercury; and on 9 November he recorded the properties of nitrogen-rich guano, which would introduce the idea of its use as a fertilizer to Europe for the first time.

As 1802 drew to a close Humboldt headed for Mexico, along the way measuring water temperatures and discovering the Peru Current, known also as the Humboldt Current System,

Alexander von Humboldt and Aimé Bonpland at the foot of the Chimborazo volcano. Friedrich Georg Weitsch, 1810.

which flows north along the western coast of South America. After reaching Acapulco, Humboldt and Bonpland spent a year travelling around 'New Spain', touring cities, mines, volcanoes and studying the relics of Aztec culture. Their final stop, before returning to Bordeaux, was a visit to the United States and a meeting with Thomas Jefferson, secured by letter in advance by Humboldt knowing of the president's enthusiasm for science, where they discussed, among other things, their shared passion for the woolly mammoth.

The accumulations of the South American adventure were staggering: a princely collection of 60,000 specimens, a sizeable chunk of his fortune sacrificed, and a lifetime's worth of data to process, which would emerge thirty years later in Humboldt's work *Kosmos*, his comprehensive treatise on the natural world and the connections between all things found in it. Today, the Humboldt legacy is unparalleled in its extent, his name given to animal species, plant species, minerals, currents, parks, peaks, marshes, four Humboldt counties and thirteen Humboldt towns just in North America; lunar craters, lunar seas and even an asteroid. More things have been named after him than any other person in history – this Prussian naturalist and former mine assessor, now known as the 'father of ecology', a man who changed our understanding of our living world and continues to inspire its study.

LEWIS AND CLARK HUNT FOR A ROUTE TO THE PACIFIC 1803-06

'I could but esteem this moment of my departure as among the most happy of my life.'

MERIWETHER LEWIS, APRIL 1805

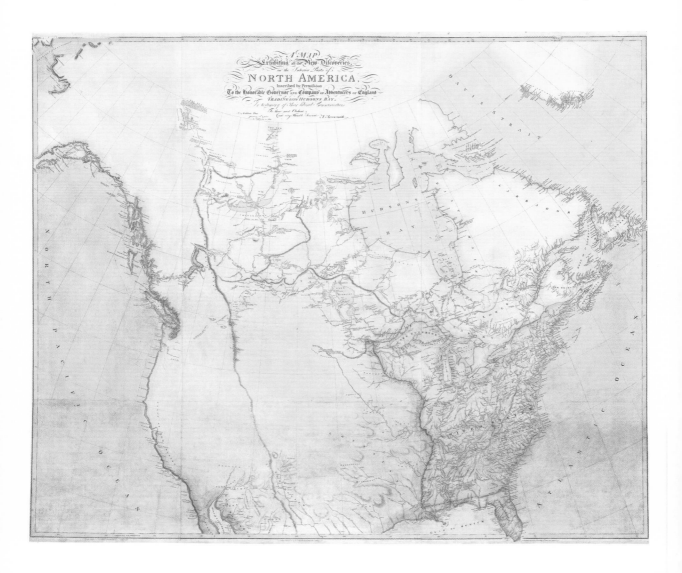

Meriwether Lewis and William Clark's original hand-drawn map of 1810.

Just a year before Humboldt's visit to North America, the United States was less than half its size. In May 1803, for the bargain price of $15 million (around $309 million today), the United States more than doubled its territory with the Louisiana Purchase. Thomas Jefferson secured the 828,000 sq. miles (2,145,000 sq. km) of Louisiana territory from Napoleon, having initially only set sights on the port city of New Orleans and its surrounding coast. To Jefferson and the Republic of the East this central swathe of the North American continent (made up of modern Arkansas, Missouri, Iowa, Oklahoma, Kansas and Nebraska, as well as parts of North and South Dakota and other adjacent states), and indeed the rest of the west, was a wilderness of potentially rich natural resources. French possession had been one of two obstacles to westward expansion – the other being the native inhabitants, who controlled their territory regardless of whichever European nation laid claim, and to whom the United States had recently suffered disastrous losses in battle.

Time was a factor in the realization of Jefferson's dream of consolidation, with the Spanish in the south, the British in the north and the French developing interest in the northwest. And so he created the Corps of Discovery, an expeditionary

Opposite: Aaron Arrowsmith's map of North America, the only map brought by Meriwether Lewis and William Clark on their expedition, shows the vastness of the great unexplored West.

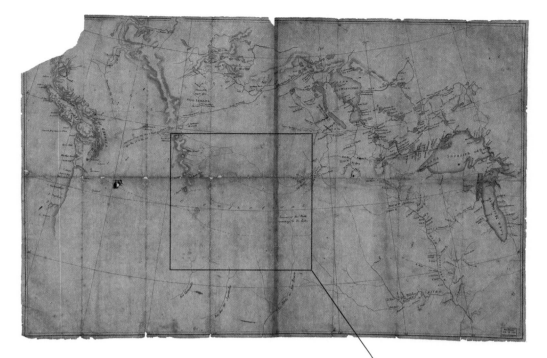

force to navigate the landscape with scientific skill and its people with diplomacy; to map the territory marked as 'Conjectural' by cartographers; and to discover a Northwest Passage to the Pacific – in Jefferson's words: 'the most direct and practicable water communication across this continent, for the purposes of commerce'. A relatively paltry $2500 in funding was obtained from Congress, and unable to find a scientist with 'the firmness of constitution & character, prudence, habits adapted to the woods & a familiarity with the Indian manners and character', Jefferson appointed US army Captain Meriwether Lewis leader of the party, who in turn offered co-captaincy to William Clark. Their differences in personality dovetailed to form a perfect partnership tethered by friendship, with Lewis's enthusiasm and natural leadership qualities working well with Clark's more introverted artistic focus on recording the wildlife of their journey.

The Corps of Discovery set off on their two-year expedition in May 1804, ascending the eastward-flowing Missouri river with a 55ft- (17m-) keelboat and two pirogues (long canoes) with a crew of soldiers, frontiersmen and a dog named Seaman. The keelboat was soon found to be too unwieldy for the meandering

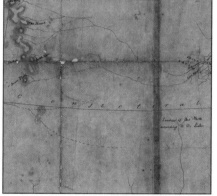

Meriwether Lewis and William Clark's copy of Nicholas King's 1803 Map of the American West, *featuring their annotations. It shows the Missouri river to the Rocky Mountains all far from certain, with the region marked with the giant disclaimer 'Conjectural'.*

Missouri and often had to be dragged across land during the first 1000 miles (1600km), so it was abandoned for the canoes.

After two months of journeying the landscape opened up into the prairies of the Great Plains. The men were met with the full richness of American fauna, encountering herds of elk, antelope and buffalo so numerous that a journal entry records them having to 'club them out of the way'; and surviving attacks from grizzly bears that could withstand several rifle shots. They also captured a 'barking squirrel', or black-tailed prairie dog, which was one of five live specimens sent back to Jefferson (who kept it to entertain visitors to the White House).

This was Sioux (the Lakȟóta people) country. Tempers flared when the Corps refused to pay tributes to the Sioux leaders, and at the last moment a fight was narrowly averted by the intervention of an elder member of the tribe. As they moved into modern North Dakota, relationships were more smoothly established with the Mandan tribe, where they built a fort and overwintered as temperatures sank as low as -40°F (-40°C). A rather disreputable French-Canadian fur trapper introduced himself as Toussaint Charbonneau, 'who Speaks the Big Belley language [of the Hidatsa people]', wrote Clark on 4 November 1804, '& informed us his 2 [squaws] were Snake Indians, we [engaged] him to go on with us and take one of his wives to interpret the Snake language …' The 'Snake language' was that of the Shoshone people, and it was these services of Charbonneau's native teenage wife Sacagawea that Lewis and

A Minitaree Warrior in the Costume of the Dog Dance, 1905, by Karl Bodmer.

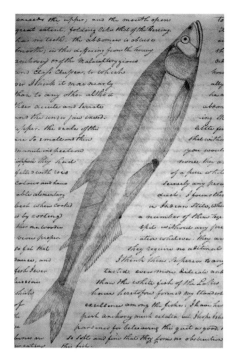

Clark really desired. In April 1805 they continued up the Missouri, and by August were nearing the Rocky Mountains and the Shoshone people. Sixty Shoshone warriors rode out to meet the intruders, and Lewis, who was out in advance, invited their leader to visit their camp. Sacagawea recognized the Shoshone warrior as her brother, Cameahwait. 'She instantly jumped up, and ran and embraced him, throwing over him her blanket, and weeping profusely', reported Clark.

The crossing of the snow-thick Rockies was almost disastrous, with the men resorting at one point to eating their horses and tallow candles to survive. But despite the sub-zero weather not a man was lost, and they descended into the temperate climes beyond the mountains, finding the Clearwater river and canoeing downstream for the first time to meet the Columbia river. This took them through the territory of the Chinookan people, who from their dealings with merchants were noted to have developed a distrust of white men, and an adeptness with tea kettles and English phrases like 'son of a bitch'. Then, as the party moved on,

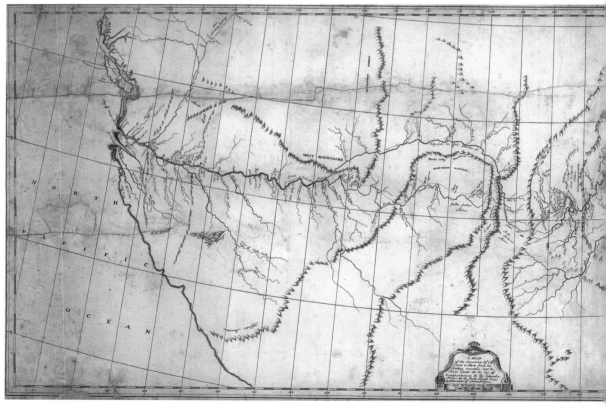

finally 'Ocian in view', recorded Clark. 'O! the joy'. There by the Pacific they built a fort, and waited for a passing ship. They waited through the winter, but no vessel appeared, and so supplies were gathered and the Discovery Corps headed back the way they had come, with Sacagawea's presence helping to convey their peaceful intentions to encountered tribes. On 23 September 1806 the Lewis and Clark expedition arrived in St Louis, ending their journey after two years and four months.* Though no transoceanic passage had been discovered, much of the mysterious country had been charted, its wildlife documented and overtures made with native tribes. From a nebulous morass of cartographers' 'conjecture', a great stride had been taken in the transformation to a land of united states.

*While the party's mapping was extensive, sections of their route were unrecorded. Only recently did researchers realize they could trace this missing data by following their latrines. The expedition lived off a diet of local game birds and as such were frequently constipated – for relief they took pills of mercury chloride, which would pass right through their systems, leaving deposits that are detectable. The best known of these is at Traveler's Rest, in Montana.

OPPOSITE: *'The mouth opens to a great extent ...' William Clark's notebook drawing of the 'Eulachon [Thaleichthys pacificus]'.*

A map of the discoveries of Capt. Lewis & Clark from the Rockey Mountain and the River Lewis to the Cap of Disappointement or the Coloumbia River at the north Pacific Ocean, *1807*.

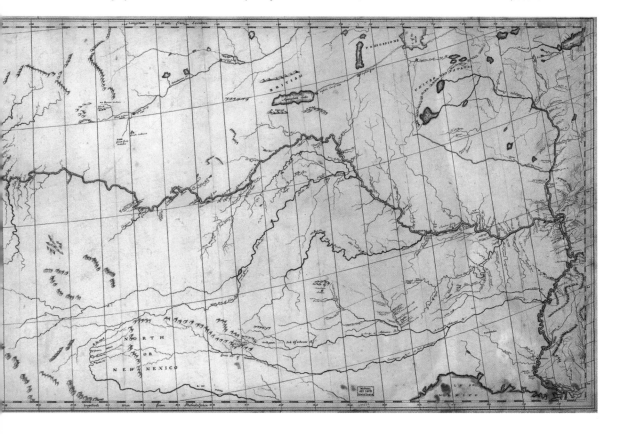

WILLIAM EDWARD PARRY PENETRATES THE ARCTIC ARCHIPELAGO 1819-20

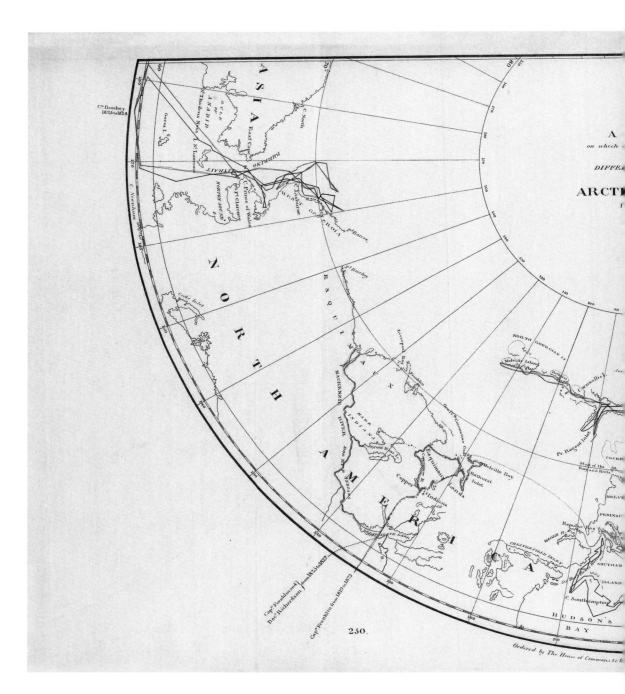

'It was evident that a very material change had taken place … we were now making a very near approach to the Magnetic Pole.'

William Edward Parry, Journal of a Voyage … (1821)

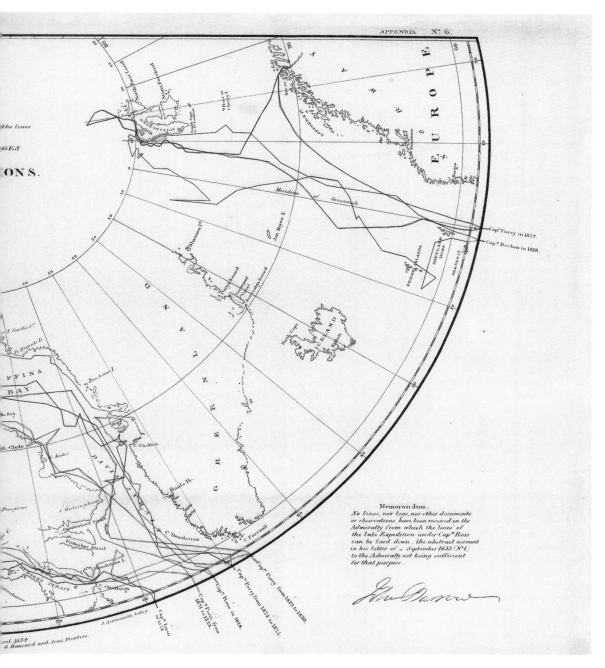

The first half of the nineteenth century saw a new flurry of Arctic expeditions resolved to find the Northwest Passage. One such search party was led by the British naval officer John Ross who made a strange decision, at 3 p.m. on 31 August 1818, to halt his expedition of two ships, the *Isabella* and the consort *Alexander*, not long after entering Lancaster Sound. There was something in the way ahead, said Ross. 'I distinctly saw the land', he recalled in *A Voyage of Discovery* … (1818), 'round the bottom of the bay, forming a connected chain of mountains with those which extended along the north and south sides.' This giant ridge of peaks, which he named 'Croker's Mountains' in honour of the first secretary of the Admiralty John Wilson Croker, blocked their path. Lancaster Sound, it seemed, was actually a bay. Ross gave the order for the ships to turn around and begin the journey home.

Receiving the return order on board the *Alexander*, Ross's young lieutenant William Edward Parry, could not believe his ears. He and his men had a clear view of the water ahead and all agreed without a doubt: there were no mountains. Had their commander lost his senses? Had he been fooled by a mirage visible only to himself? But Ross would not hear the protestations of his men. The *Isabella* and *Alexander* headed back to British docks, the crew's hopes of finding a Northwest Passage 'annihilated in a moment, without the shadow of a reason appearing', wrote the *Alexander*'s purser. Ross was forced to defend his decision from the moment he disembarked, and with the most vocal criticism coming from his furious men, including Parry, he was publicly pilloried for his incompetence.

Parry was adamant that Lancaster Sound (in the Qikiqtaaluk region, Nunavut, north of Canada and west of Greenland) was not only a strait, but that it could also well be the entrance to the fabled passage. Still a lieutenant, in 1819 Parry was dispatched by the Admiralty with his own strengthened ships, the bomb-vessel *Hecla* and the gun-brig *Griper*, to return to Lancaster Sound, break through Ross's imaginary mountains and, if possible, travel all the way to the Bering Strait. Sailing from Deptford in May, Parry reached Lancaster Sound by 1 August, almost a year after Ross had retreated home. They easily made their way through the Sound, with no mountains appearing and with remarkably little ice impeding their path. During this leg they moved

PREVIOUS PAGE: *A chart of the various British Arctic expeditions from 1818 to 1827 including those of John Ross and William Parry.*

Captain William Edward Parry.

through Barrow Strait and sighted a multitude of islands and inlets that would crop up in later exploratory missions, such as Admiralty Inlet, Wellington Channel, Prince Regent Inlet and other dutifully christened features.

At 9.15 p.m. on 4 September, Parry recorded the moment the ships made the landmark crossing of the meridian of 110° west from Greenwich, a record that entitled he and his men to a £5000 reward offered by Parliament. They continued on their westward way, but the pack ice was beginning to thicken. Before the sea had fully frozen up, Parry took refuge on the uninhabited Melville Island (which he named Winter Harbour). Here they were forced to overwinter, the first nineteenth-century expedition to do so in the Arctic, surviving off the ships' supplies.

Parry boosted morale with inventive means. 'The Royal Arctic Theatre' was founded by men from both ships, and fortnightly performances were complete with costumes and stage lighting. (Parry writes in his journal of putting on a

The Parry expedition ships Hecla *and* Griper *in Winter Harbour (Melville Island).*

Boats off Walden Island, in a snowstorm Aug 12 1827, *from Parry's* Narrative of an attempt to reach the North Pole... *(1828).*

7 p.m. show of *Miss in Her Teens* in which he played the female role of 'Fribble', while Frederick Beechey, who would later rise to rear admiral, reportedly shone as the lovely Miss Biddy.) They set up a school to teach literacy and an observatory to make magnetic measurements and astronomical observations. The men even produced their own newspaper, the *North Georgia Gazette and Winter Chronicle*.

After enduring ten months of scurvy, temperatures as low as -54°F (-48°C) and a three-month period of continuous darkness, by August the ice began to recede. Remarkably the men decided to push on, almost clearing the Canadian Arctic Archipelago with the Beaufort Sea (off the north coast of Alaska) so close it was almost in view, but their route remained locked with pack-ice resistant to summer warmth, and Parry was forced to concede it was time to return home. They arrived back in England in October 1820 having lost only one of ninety-four men, with a bundle of new discoveries and a sail-filling sense of progress in establishing the passage to the Pacific. Blessed with unusually ice-free waters, they had navigated three-quarters of the way through the Canadian Arctic Archipelago, rendering the expedition one of the most productive in the history of Arctic exploration.

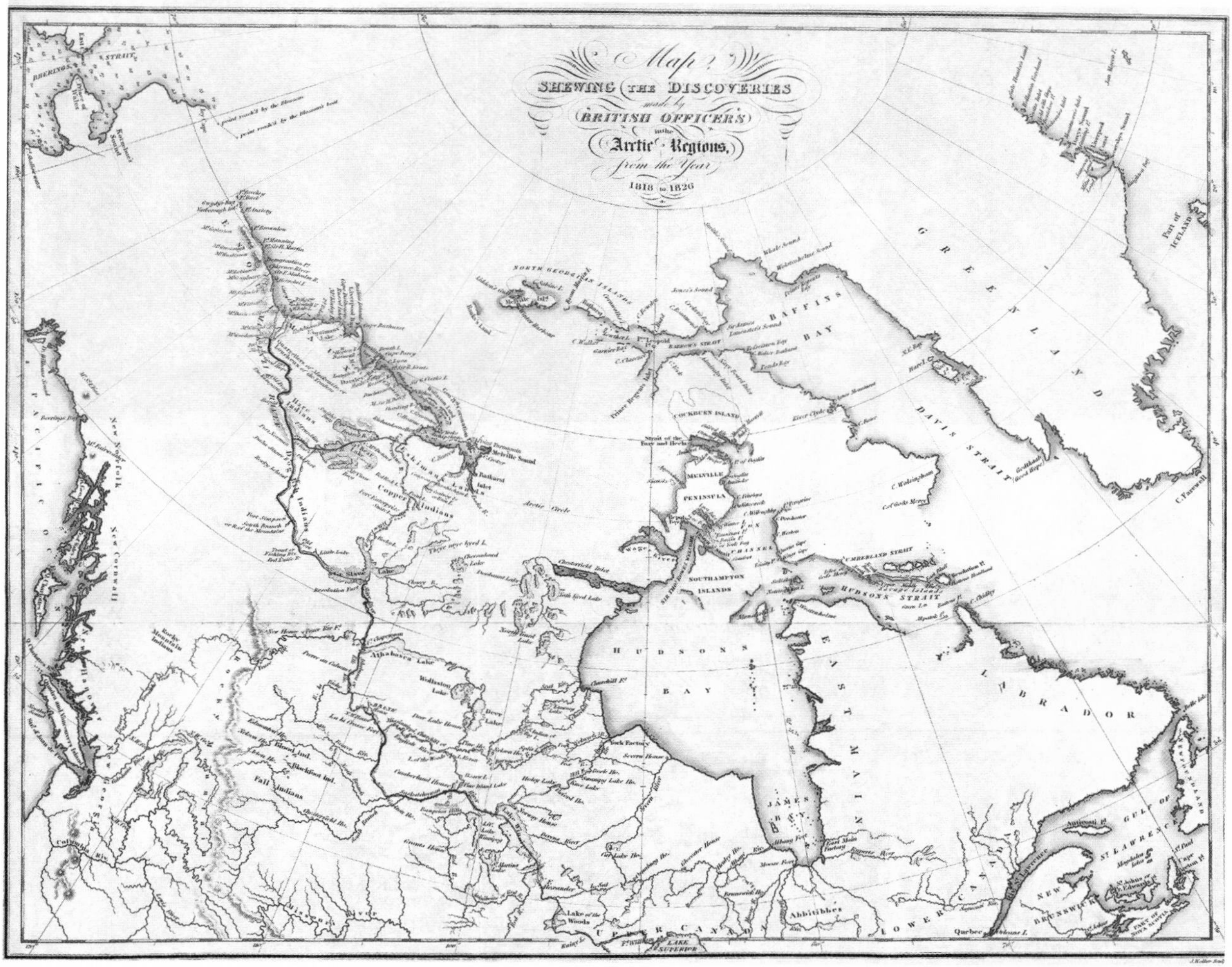

Map Shewing the Discoveries Made by British Officers in the Arctic Regions from the Year 1818 to 1826, *including those made by William Edward Parry.*

JAMES CLARK ROSS AND THE SEARCH FOR THE MAGNETIC POLES 1839-43

'The most persevering indefatigable man you can imagine.' CAPTAIN HUMPHREYS, ONE OF CLARK'S OFFICERS, IN A LETTER WRITTEN 28 JANUARY 1836

The magnetic compass was not initially used for navigation. On its invention in China during the Han Dynasty (between the second century BC and early third century AD), the 'south-governor' was a tool of geomancers – fortune-tellers who performed divinations by scattering sand or soil and interpreting the patterns. Practitioners of feng shui also

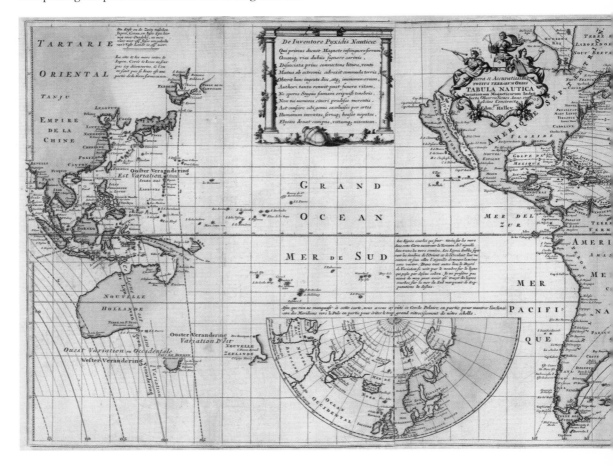

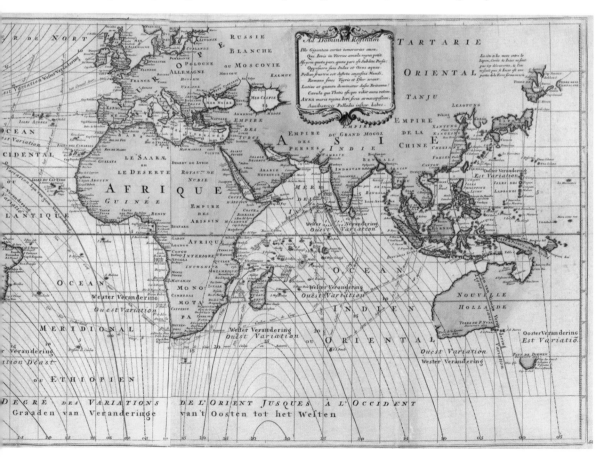

employed it for building structures in harmony with their environment. From what we can tell, it was between the ninth and eleventh centuries when Chinese navigators incorporated the compass as a navigational instrument; while in Europe we find the first reference to such a device in Alexander Neckam's *De naturis rerum* ('On the Nature of Things') produced in 1190.

By the sixteenth century, the compass needle's draw to the north was explained with the mythological belief in the Rupes Niger, a giant magnetic black mountain surrounded by a swirling vortex and lands of Arctic pygmies at the North Pole. The most famous early mapping of this is by Mercator, as a vignette on his 1569 world map (see page 114). The cartographer explained the idea to the astrologer and mathematician John Dee in 1577: 'right under the Pole there lies a bare Rock in the midst of the Sea. Its circumference is almost 33 miles [53km], and it is all of magnetic Stone'.

By 1600, oceanic sailors were familiar with the caveat of the compass for piloting, that rather than pointing consistently at

Edmond Halley's Nova et Accuratissima Totius Terrarum …, *the first world map to show his studies of magnetism variation in the year 1700, in the form of 'isogonal' lines, representing the Earth's magnetic fluctuations.*

true north (defined as north according to the Earth's axis) the needle pointed elsewhere, to a 'magnetic north' somewhere in the American Arctic, at an angle that varied depending on position. (Columbus had noticed the variations in September 1492, but decided not to mention it to his men so as not to cause panic.) In 1698 the future Astronomer Royal, Edmond Halley, set sail on England's first purely scientific voyage, the first of two navigations around the Atlantic in which he charted the compass variations throughout the ocean over a course of two years. The result was the groundbreaking map *A New and Correct Chart shewing the Variations of the Compass in the Western & Southern Oceans as observed in the year 1700* (see page 196-7), one of the earliest statistical graphics that outlines his data on Earth's magnetic field. But what of the magnetic poles themselves – where did they lie and what would be found there? And was there any substance to the Mercatorian myth of the black mountain?

It is here that John Ross, sighter of the illusory Croker's Mountains (see William Edward Parry Penetrates the Arctic Archipelago entry on pages 190-95), re-enters the picture. Disgraced from his failure to find the Northwest Passage, he proposed to the Admiralty that he return to Lancaster Sound with a steam-powered vessel to resume the search. The Admiralty passed on the plan, and so Ross approached a wealthy friend, the gin magnate Felix Booth, to fund the discovery. Booth hesitated over the reward offered by Parliament for finding the passage – how vulgar to be seen pursuing a cash prize of a meagre £20,000 – but when that was rescinded he agreed to provide the finances.

On 6 August 1829 John Ross entered Lancaster Sound aboard the steam-powered *Victory*, and by September was following the east coast of a great Arctic landmass he would name Boothia Felix (Boothia Peninsula). The ice swiftly set in and the crew of the *Victory* were trapped there for a year. When their ship was freed, they managed to move a few miles before being snared again by the ice, so two overland explorations were launched. It was while leading his group of six men and a sledge on 1 June 1831 across the Boothia Peninsula that James Clark Ross (nephew of John Ross) noticed his compass was set at within one minute of the vertical (i.e. if the needle was able to move in three dimensions, at this position it would point straight down). At this otherwise unremarkable stretch of frozen

Stephen Pearce's posthumous portrait of James Clark Ross, 1850.

landscape they were standing on the Magnetic North Pole. After raising the Union Jack, Ross returned to the *Victory*. Forced to overwinter twice more, the expedition would not return to England until late 1833.

The mystery of the Magnetic North Pole had been solved, but it wasn't until 1838, when southern voyages were becoming more frequent, that attention turned to its antipode. Plans for a mission to find the Magnetic South Pole were endorsed by the Royal Society and funded by Parliament, with James Clark Ross being the obvious choice to lead it. Ross was granted use of the 370-ton flagship *Erebus* and the 340-ton *Terror*, more famous for their later service in the mission of John Franklin to search for the Northwest Passage. The expedition left the Cornish coast on 5 October 1839, rounding the Cape of Good Hope in April 1840 on its way to the Desolation Islands (Kerguelen Islands) in the South Indian Ocean. All the while the men were making hourly magnetometric observations, while Ross himself performed astronomical and tidal experiments. He and his crew sailed south from New Zealand's Campbell Island and crossed the Antarctic Circle on New Year's Day 1841. The water became increasingly crowded with icebergs and floes, and the weather more hostile, but Ross pushed south regardless in the hope that the South Magnetic Pole was beneath what was named as the Ross Sea, to be found more easily than its counterpart ten years earlier. These hopes were dashed when land appeared – the coast of Victoria Land, and her giant line of mountains named Admiralty Range. Readings suggested the Pole was only 500 miles (800km) further, and so Ross and his men cruised south along its coast, reaching a record latitude and to their astonishment sighting a live volcano, until their progress was blocked by 'The Great Ice Barrier' (Ross Ice Shelf), Antarctica's largest ice shelf, which at 188,032 sq. miles (487,000 sq. km) is about the size of France. For future explorers this feature would mark the ingress to the South Pole, but to Ross it was a barrier of ice the size of the White Cliffs of Dover that signalled the end of the mission. He traced it for 200 miles (320km), then turned back for anchorage in Tasmania.

A second attempt was made a year later, but amid fierce gales once again the ice shelf rose up from the horizon to greet them and the mission was concluded. From this point in explorational history, Antarctica would be left in peace for decades, abandoned – no man would advance further south than the 78°10'S position of Ross for another sixty years.

Metrosideros robusta, which can grow to 82ft (25m) in height, as observed by Joseph Dalton Hooker during the Ross voyage to the Antarctic. From The Botany of the Antarctic Voyage of H.M. Discovery Ships Erebus and Terror, 1839-43.

THE MYSTERIOUS DISAPPEARANCE OF THE FRANKLIN EXPEDITION 1845-47

*'So little now remains to be done …
no reasonable doubt can be entertained …
and no objection with regard to any apprehension
of the loss of ships or men.'* Sir John Barrow, December 1844

The most famous disappearance in the history of exploration came in attempting to reveal its greatest mystery. In the four decades since the appointment of Sir John Barrow as Second Secretary of the Admiralty in 1804, British explorers had, at the cost of lost lives and vessels, cut swathes through the white secrecy of the Arctic in search of a passage west through to the Bering Sea, whittling down the uncharted territory to an angular zone of about 70,000 sq. miles (181,300 sq. km), with less than 310 miles (500km) of coastline left to chart. Barrow, now in his eighties, lobbied for one last assault, an expedition that would sail as far west as was possible to about 95°N, and then penetrate the frozen labyrinth southward and westward unrelentingly until reaching the Bering Strait. If this was found to be impossible then they should head north through the Wellington Channel and find an alternative route. Barrow approached William Edward Parry to lead the mission but he politely declined. James Clark Ross also turned down the offer, having promised his new wife he was done with the Arctic. Parry's third choice, James Fitzjames, was considered by the Admiralty too young for command while George Back was considered too argumentative, and Francis Crozier had no interest in leading. This left Barrow, somewhat reluctantly,

Sir John Franklin.

CAPTAIN AUSTIN'S
IN SEARCH OF
EXPEDITION
SIR JOHN FRANKLIN

INTREPID.   RESOLUTE.
ASSISTANCE.
PIONEER.

SIR JOHN FRANKLIN

with one remaining candidate, 59-year-old Sir John Franklin.

Though his age and lack of fitness were a concern, the immensely charming and popular Franklin was a veteran of three Arctic expeditions in which more than 3000 miles (4828km) of north Canadian coastline had been mapped, and he had recently returned from a lieutenant-governorship of Van Diemen's Land (Tasmania) assisting with passing Antarctic explorations, including that of James Ross. For the new expedition he was given a complement of 139 officers and crew to man the *Erebus* and *Terror*, which had been specially reinforced, generously stocked and fitted with steam engines from the London & Greenwich Railway. Francis Crozier commanded the *Terror*, while James Fitzjames was second-in-command to Franklin aboard the *Erebus*. They left the Thames on 19 May 1845, filled their stores at the Whalefish Islands on Greenland's west coast, enough for a three-year Arctic expedition. At the end of July the ships were spotted entering Lancaster Sound by the British whaling-vessels *Enterprise* and *Prince of Wales*. And then the best-equipped British navy expedition ever sent to the Arctic disappeared amid the ice.

By 1847, with not a word from the expedition, concern was growing in London. In January, John Ross offered to launch

As the search for Sir John Franklin continued, would-be rescuers resorted to increasingly inventive means. This broadside from 1852 (of which this is the only known copy) celebrates the use of hydrogen balloons by Horatio Austin's search party, to scatter message leaflets across the Arctic informing the survivors of the locations of relief vessels and food caches.

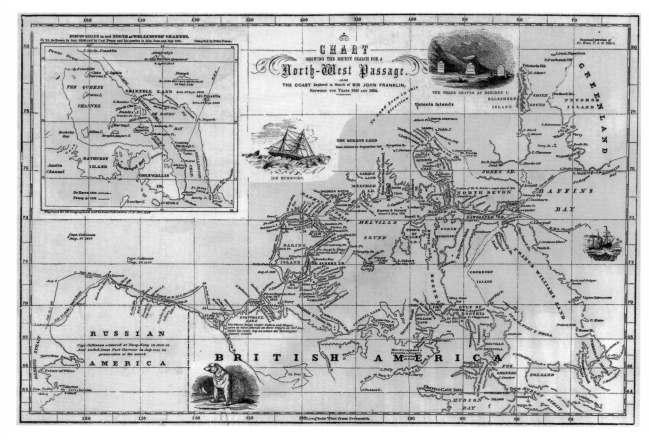

a search mission but the Admiralty affirmed their 'unlimited confidence in the skills and resources of Sir John Franklin', though this was undercut somewhat by their offer of a reward to whalers with information. Swiftly, the anxiety over the missing sailors would swell into a grand drama that filled newspapers and captivated the public imagination. In 1848 the Admiralty sent out a three-pronged search effort, led by John Richardson, Thomas Moore and James Clark Ross, but despite making various geographic discoveries in the region no trace of the missing men was found.

Over the next few decades thirty-six ships and overland expeditions set out to find the lost Franklin party, driven in large part by the urging of members of Parliament and Lady Franklin, who also wrote for aid from the US president and the czar of Russia. The Admiralty offered the reward of £20,000 (about £1,811,000 today) 'to any Party or Parties, of any country, who shall render assistance to the crews of the Discovery Ships under the command of Sir John Franklin'.

Chart showing the recent search for a North-west passage *by Charles Morse, 1856, New York.*

The first evidence was found in 1850, when four vessels convening at the southwestern tip of Devon Island found signs that Franklin had overwintered in that area. Then, in 1854, John Rae reported hearing from Inuit about a group of white men that had been seen dragging a boat along the west shore of King William Island.*

With no proof of their survival, by 1855 the British government declared Franklin and his men dead. The evidence was not conclusive for Lady Franklin, and she called for another search attempt. To the editor of *The Times* this would be 'wasting time on a search for dead men's bones', but Lady Franklin bought a schooner-rigged steam yacht, the *Fox*, and chose Leopold McClintock, who had joined Ross's previous search attempt, to captain.

McClintock and his second-in-command, William Hobson, made the most significant discovery at Point Victory near Cape Felix at the northern tip of King William Island: two stone cairns (piles of stones) under which the Franklin survivors had

* Rae also related the story he was told by the same Inuit, that the men had resorted to cannibalism. Lady Franklin condemned Rae for spreading lies, for it was unthinkable that a British navy man was capable of such a thing. However studies of the remains in the 1980s and 1990s found signs of knife marks on the bones, and a paper in the International Journal of Osteoarchaeology in 2016 presented evidence for the first time of desperate 'end-stage' cannibalism, in which the bones are broken and boiled, to be drained of the marrow.

The Arctic Council, including Sir John Barrow, James Clark Ross and William Edward Parry, planning a search for Sir John Franklin, by Stephen Pearce, 1851.

stashed their journey records. It turned out that the *Erebus* and *Terror* had indeed spent the winter of 1845-46 at Beechey Island. In 1846 Franklin had pushed south through the Peel and Franklin straits, but ice had prevented further progress. An update in the margin of the journal dated 1848 and signed by Fitzjames and Crozier stated that the ships had been trapped by the ice since 12 September 1846. Franklin had died on 11 June 1847, and in desperation on 22 April 1848 the men had deserted both ships. After Franklin's death, command fell to Crozier, who gave the order to the 105 remaining men to make their way over the ice towards the Great Fish River. All perished.

In the more than a century and a half since the crew made the decision to leave the supplies of their stranded ships and strike out across the ice, curiosity as to their fate never

20,000 POUNDS
STERLING
(100,000 Dollars)
REWARD!
TO BE GIVEN BY
HER BRITANNIC MAJESTY'S GOVERNMENT
to such private Ship, or distributed among such private Ships, or to any exploring party or parties, of any Country, as may, in the judgment of the **BOARD OF ADMIRALTY**, have rendered efficient assistance to

SIR JOHN FRANKLIN,
HIS SHIPS, OR THEIR CREWS,
and may have contributed directly to extricate them from the Ice.
H. G. WARD,
Secretary to the Admiralty.

LONDON, *March* 23, 1849.

The attention of **WHALERS**, or of any other Ships or parties disposed to aid in this service, is particularly directed to **SMITH'S SOUND** and **JONES'S SOUND**, in **BAFFIN'S BAY**, to **REGENT'S INLET** and the **GULF of BOOTHIA**, as well as to any of the Inlets or Channels leading out of **BARROW'S STRAIT**, particularly **WELLINGTON STRAIT**, or the Sea beyond, either Northward or Southward.

VESSELS entering through **BEHRING'S STRAITS** would necessarily direct their search North and South of **MELVILLE ISLAND**.

NOTE.—Persons desirous of obtaining information relative to the Missing Expedition, are referred to EDMUND A. GRATTAN, Esq., Her Britannic Majesty's Consul, BOSTON, MASSACHUSETTS; or ANTHONY BARCLAY, Esq., Her Britannic Majesty's Consul, NEW YORK.

An 1849 notice offering a reward for helping to extricate Sir John Franklin, his ships and crew from the ice.

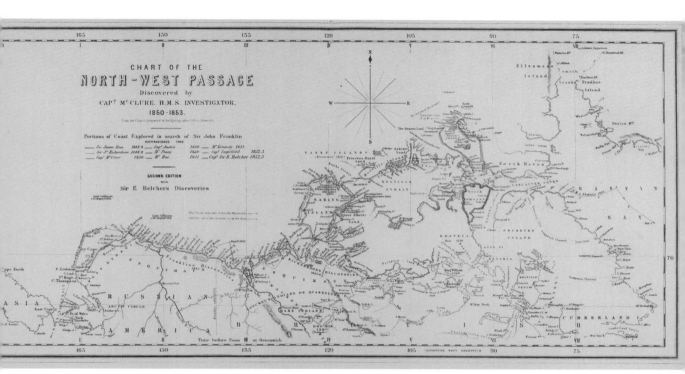

The various search missions for Sir John Franklin also improved mapping of the Canadian Arctic region, as shown by this chart of 1853.

diminished. The remains of a number of crew members have been discovered at sites across King William Island, and closely analysed for answers. The bodies of three of the crew who had died early in 1846 were disinterred in the 1980s, their autopsies showing signs of tuberculosis and death by pneumonia, as well as a high amount of lead in their blood. This prompted the theory that the men could have been poisoned by the solder of the hastily made food cans, or from the ships' customized water supply, which could explain the strange decisions made.

The most exciting developments in recent years, however, have been the discoveries of the wreck of the *Erebus*, in 2014, and two years later the *Terror*, found submerged in Terror Bay off the southwest coast of King William Island. At the time of writing the wrecks are yet to be fully explored, bar the salvage of a few items such as the bronze bell of the *Erebus*. The sites have been protectively designated National Historic Sites of Canada, and it remains to be seen what further insights they can provide. Although more than 170 years since the expedition was swallowed by the Arctic, the darkly compelling story of Franklin and his lost crew continues to unfold.

THE AGE OF THE FEMALE TRAVELLER BEGINS 1846

'To those bred under an elaborate social order, few such moments of exhilaration can come as that which stands at the threshold of wild travel. The gates of the enclosed garden are thrown open … behold! The immeasurable world.' GERTRUDE BELL, 1907

Though we are now firmly in the Victorian era, it will not have gone unnoticed that the chronology of exploration up to this point is a history almost entirely dominated by men. The dearth of female figures in the pantheon of those who discovered and mapped new lands hardly seems plausible, and yet when contextualized with the unwavering societal restrictions imposed on women it becomes less surprising. Women were simply not permitted the same education or freedom of movement as men. Banned from ships and prohibited from handling financial affairs, there was no question of the organization or command of what were essentially business ventures being handed to a member

A plate from The Honourable Impulsia Gushington's Egyptian travel account Lispings From Low Latitudes *(1863), actually written by the British aristocrat Lady Dufferin.*

A 1638 map of the Americas made by Maria Merian's father, the Swiss engraver Matthäus Merian.

of the fairer sex. Military, trade and scientific missions were sent by institutions that essentially rejected female participation, while missionary societies did not consider for a second sending women alone into the unknown. New worlds were dangerous tests of physical endurance, which the delicate female frame was considered incapable of withstanding. A woman leading an expedition was unthinkable. A woman exploring on her own was unimaginable.

Before European attitudes towards women travelling began to change – or, more specifically, began to be changed – in the mid-nineteenth century with the rise of the independent female traveller, the most notable journeywoman by far was Maria Sibylla Merian (1647-1717), a German-born naturalist and illustrator, daughter of the famed engraver Matthäus Merian. In 1665, at the age of eighteen, she married the painter

Johann Graff, and five years later dutifully relocated to Nuremberg with her husband and their two daughters.

As a devoted Protestant the study of nature was the study of God's splendour, and the depiction of its beauty and perfection an act of reverence. It was this adoration that led her to – scandalously – leave her husband in 1685, and with her daughters join a Protestant sect called the Labadists. Merian continued her work, and in 1691 set up her own shop in Amsterdam. With trade ships arriving there from across the world, she was perfectly placed to examine the exotic specimens that arrived daily. But it wasn't enough to study the corpses of these miraculous creatures – she wanted to see them in the wild. And so in 1699, at the age of fifty-two, she drew up her will and secured funds for a voyage independently, by selling 255 of her own paintings. With special permission granted by the City of Amsterdam, she bought passage to the Labadist colony of La Providence in Suriname, on the northeastern Atlantic coast of South America.

Such a self-funded enterprise was unprecedented, not just by a woman but by any European naturalist. Certainly Merian enjoyed the privilege of a respected family name and the comparatively greater leeway offered by Amsterdam society, but for a woman to make such a journey in the seventeenth

A Caiman alligator wrestling a snake, as observed by Maria Sibylla Merian during her South American travels.

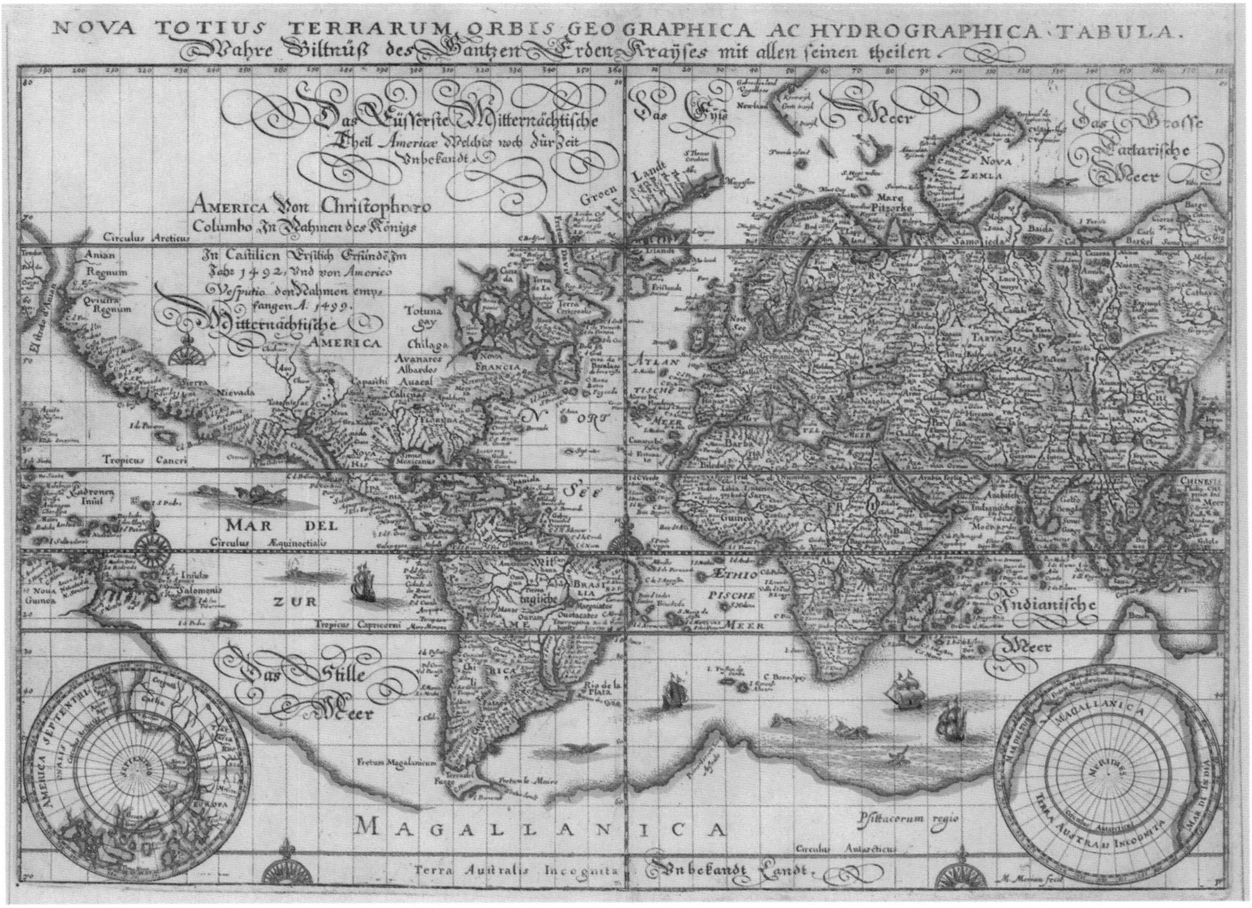

World map by Matthäus Merian.

century is extraordinary. With her younger daughter Dorothea, Merian spent two years in Suriname, collecting specimens and observing and painting more than ninety species of animals and over sixty species of plants. (It's believed that she remains the only person to have witnessed the metamorphoses of a number of these Surinamese species.)

On her return to Amsterdam she published the results of her adventure in 1705 with *Metamorphosis Insectorum Surinamensium* ('Transformation of the Surinamese insects'), one of the most beautiful works of natural history ever created. Merian's recordings would be instrumental in the revolutionary systematic botany of Carl Linnaeus, and her studies of the life cycles of insects formed one of the earliest demolishings of the popular belief in 'spontaneous generation', the prevailing notion that insects could burst into life out of non-living matter – insects were thought to be born from

Lady Mary Wortley Montagu,
by Godfrey Kneller,
c.1715-1720.

mud, maggots from dead flesh. Today Merian's work is
highly sought after, for both its scientific noteworthiness and
stunning artistry.

Following Merian's scientific mission, the genre of the
travel authoress was born with the indomitable Lady Mary
Wortley Montagu. Habitually defiant of convention, in 1710
at the age of twenty-one she spurned the advances of the
wonderfully named Clotworthy Skeffington to elope with Sir
Edward Wortley Montagu. When her husband was posted to
Constantinople in 1716 as British Ambassador to Turkey, she
shocked London society by insisting on accompanying him.
The letters she wrote reporting the cultures, geography and
hardships met on their travels became a sensation, and were
initially circulated in manuscript form before being published
after her death, in three volumes in 1763. The journey itself
was remarkable, it being a route that, as she wrote, 'has not

been undertaken by any Christian, since the time of the Greek Emperors'. After sailing to Rotterdam the Montagu party crossed overland through Holland into Germany, down the Danube to Vienna and, with the river freezing over, continued on land to Adrianople (Edirne) in northwest Turkey. One year after their departure from London, they reached Constantinople and their new palatial home in the hills of Pera (now Beyoğlu).

As well as being the first woman to make secular observations of the Muslim Orient, clearing up English misconceptions of the religion, Montagu is also remembered for introducing smallpox inoculation into Western medicine, after witnessing it practised during her Turkish travels. Seventy-nine years before Edward Jenner famously inoculated an 8-year-old boy with his vaccine drawn from cowpox in 1796, Montagu had in 1717 written excitedly about the Ottoman method of 'engrafting', in which fluid from smallpox sores was rubbed into the exposed skin of healthy subjects to give them immunity. Having lost her brother to the disease and surviving the pox herself, Montagu was so impressed by the treatment that she had her own 4-year-old son Edward inoculated with the technique, and promoted it widely on her return to England.

Following the adventures of Lady Montagu, eighteenth-century travel literature swelled with harrowing but popular journals made by women while accompanying their husbands on journeys through new continents. Isabel Godin des Odonais, for example, was a Peruvian who wrote of her grim but extraordinary 1769 journey from western Peru to the mouth of the Amazon river in search of her husband, who had been stranded in French Guiana for more than twenty years. In 1795, the English traveller Mary Ann Parker published *A Voyage Round the World, in the Gorgon Man of War*, the first female account of a circumnavigation and description of an Australian colony, having sailed around the globe aboard the frigate *Gorgon*, captained by her husband John Parker, between 1791 and 1792.

But it is the Austrian Ida Pfeiffer who is recognized as opening the age of the independent female traveller, with her trek through India, the Middle East and on around the world in 1846-48. On her return, Pfeiffer's story became so popular in Europe that shipping and rail companies offered her free

FOLLOWING PAGES: *Alexis-Hubert Jaillot's 1669 wall map of Africa, after Willem Blaeu's 1608 work.*

passage, and so between 1851 and 1854 she set off on a new sponsored global voyage, this time in the opposite direction. Pfeiffer couldn't understand the fuss around her best-selling books – she saw herself as an ordinary woman with 'an insatiable desire to travel'.

This was certainly a spirit shared by Isabella Bird, the archetypal Victorian lady traveller and first woman to be elected Fellow of the Royal Geographical Society. Bird spent the latter half of the nineteenth century in an almost permanent state of journeying, including east Asia, India, Persia and an 800 mile- (1287km-) trek through Colorado's Rocky Mountains. 'I have only one rival in Isabella's heart', lamented her suitor John Bishop, after years of proposing marriage in vain, 'and that is the high table-land of Central Asia.'

In many cases the literature produced by these late Victorian travellers is as enjoyable for the modern reader as it was for the contemporary audience, with the titles alone sometimes enough to give a sense of the bull-headed bravery and eccentricity of the women who left their husbands behind to see the world previously kept from them. Take, for example, Annie Hore's *To Lake Tanganyika in a Bath Chair* (1884), in which she recounts her 830 mile- (1336km-) trip across Tanzania from the Zanzibar coast inland to the lake on its western border, as an experiment organized by her husband, an engineer, to see if the crossing was possible. She rode the entire way in a wicker bath chair on wheels, with a pole for her porters to carry her over trickier ground. In the end she was borne the entire way, with her infant child bouncing in her lap, on a journey of ninety days.

A decade later, the American May French Sheldon strode unstoppably at the head of a train of 153 porters across east Africa, from Mombasa to the Maasai tribes beyond Mount Kilimanjaro and back again. Though lions claimed one of her party and she herself suffered a thorn to the eyeball, she maintained her travel uniform of gleaming white dresses, blonde wigs and a banner held aloft decorated with the warning in Latin: 'Noli me tangere' (Don't touch me).

Of similar attitude to proper field dress was Mary Kingsley ('You have no right to go about Africa in things you would be ashamed to be seen in at home'), the last great female explorer of the nineteenth century. Though the only European women to be found in west Africa at this time were the wives of

May French Sheldon.

missionaries, in 1893 Kingsley was travelling in Sierra Leone, from where she crossed to Angola and lived with the native people for months, learning local survival techniques. In 1894 she returned to Africa to live with and study the Fang people, who were reputed to be cannibals. (This was a common Victorian stereotyping based on reports of body parts on display in Fang villages. It was later discovered that the bones were, in fact, the remains of the tribe's loved ones, kept in open view for remembrance.)

Kingsley was happy to play to the comical image of a fish-out-of-water Englishwoman, and cheerfully recounts in her journal the time she survived falling into a hidden animal trap onto 12 in- (30cm-) ebony spikes ('It is at these moments you realize the blessings of a good thick skirt'). Elsewhere she writes of emerging from a mangrove swamp to discover a collar of leaches around her neck, and of her bemusement at upending a native purse into her hat to find 'a human hand, three big toes, four eyes, two ears, and other portions of the human frame'.

To paint her as a hapless comedienne, however, would be a great disservice. As a natural historian she made discoveries of new fish and lizard species in the Gulf of Guinea, and as an ethnologist became a highly respected authority and advocate of the African tribes she had encountered. She canoed Gabon's Ogooué river and the adjacent Rembwé river, and made the first ascent of Mount Cameroon. In mapmaking terms, there is little with which to illustrate her story. In fact her book, *Travels in West Africa* (1897), unusually has no map, for no cartography of any detail of the regions she explored had yet been drawn, and she certainly did not have the time to do it herself. And while this, and her detestation of European missionaries for importing 'second-hand rubbishy white culture', sets her quite apart from the most famous of African explorers and the subject of the next chapter, David Livingstone, where the two meet is with their love of the African continent. Having volunteered to return to Africa in 1900 to serve as a nurse in the Boer War, she died only three months later, and in accordance with her wishes Mary Kingsley was buried at sea, so that her soul might be carried along the coasts and among the rivers of the land that had never left her thoughts.

The dangers of leaving your palanquin transport unguarded. From May French Sheldon's journal Sultan to Sultan ... *(1892).*

Mary Kinglsey.

DAVID LIVINGSTONE, HENRY MORTON STANLEY AND THE 'DARK CONTINENT' 1853-73

'The mere animal pleasure of traveling in a wild unexplored country is very great … Africa is a wonderful country for appetite.' DAVID LIVINGSTONE

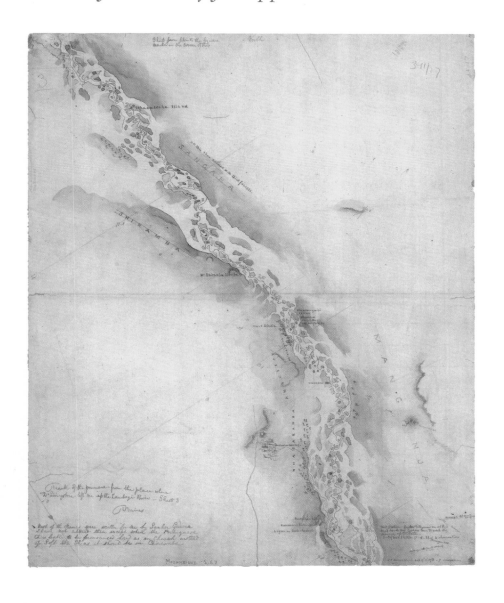

Missionaries were the great heroes of Victorian society. For a culture that saw itself as the leading moral light of the world, these explorer-proselytizers were revered for their devotion to bringing the radiance of Christianity and Western civilization to the benighted heathen masses of dark and distant continents. This was certainly the spirit that gripped David Livingstone, who had grown up outside Glasgow with a religious father and who from an early age had seized on the dream of medical missionary work, as it reconciled his dual passions to serve his faith and indulge his scientific interests. Freshly ordained and medically qualified, he joined the London Missionary Society hoping for a posting to China, but this was ruled out by the outbreak of the First Opium War of 1839. Instead he was dispatched to Kuruman in the Northern Cape province of South Africa on 8 December 1840. Disappointed by the missionary settlement he found there, he spent the next few years travelling throughout South Africa. In 1845 he married Mary Moffat, the daughter of a fellow missionary, insisting she join him on his travels despite her being pregnant. By now it was apparent that Livingstone had shifted interest from converting Africans to Christianity to more fully exploring the African continent. In 1852, he sent Mary and the children home to England, where they lived in penury while he continued his explorations in Africa.

In May 1853 Livingstone embarked on an immense journey. The goal of this expedition was to travel up the Zambezi river, which feeds into the Indian Ocean, in order to determine if it reached westward to the Atlantic. The source of the Zambezi, however, was in Zambia, so as they travelled west Livingstone's party was forced to abandon its canoes and trudge overland, reaching Luanda on the northeastern coast of Angola in May 1854, where a malaria-ridden Livingstone promptly collapsed.

Three months later Livingstone had recovered enough strength to lead his men back to the Zambezi, this time to explore its eastern path. Along this way he encountered the dazzling waterfall Mosi-oa-Tunya ('The Smoke that Thunders'), which he named Victoria Falls in 1855, writing: 'It had never been seen before by European eyes; but scenes so lovely must have been gazed on by angels in their flight.' Pushing on, Livingstone eventually reached Quelimane on Mozambique's east coast, and from there began the journey back to Britain, where he was greeted on the Southampton

David Livingstone.

Opposite: *Thomas Baine's original hand-painted map of his and Livingstone's route along the Zambezi in their steamer* Ma Robert.

dock by Mary on 12 December 1856.
Unbeknownst to Livingstone, the letters and
journals he had sent home had made him a
hero in his absence, winning him the Royal
Geographical Society's annual Founder's
Medal, and a public notoriety that ensured
his book, *Missionary Travels and Researches in
South Africa*, was a massive bestseller.

An observation made by a number of
Livingstone's biographers is the sense that,
with his dislike of Europeans, it was Africa
that felt more like home for him than Britain.
And indeed almost immediately did he begin
drawing up plans for a second expedition on the Zambezi,
this time sponsored by the British government interested in
establishing trade networks throughout Africa.

'The Zambezi Expedition' left England on 10 March 1858,
but it was beset with problems. Their steamship *Ma Robert* had
difficulty navigating rapids, the party was struck by dysentery,
and Livingstone frequently argued with his companions.
Frustrated by a lack of progress, and learning in March 1862
of the death of his wife from malaria in Mozambique, he
eventually returned to England in mid-1864, the expedition
having taken four years longer than its expected two.

In 1866 he was back in Africa to pursue an obsession with
discovering the source of the Nile, and this time embarked
with a party of only African and Arab helpers. To the outside
world Livingstone had disappeared, and just as with Sir John
Franklin his vanishing in the African interior filled headlines
around the world for years. This included those of the *New
York Herald*, whose owner and editor, James Gordon Bennett,
saw an opportunity for an exclusive adventure piece and
contacted one of his foreign correspondents, an immigrant
Welshman named John Rowlands, who had adopted the name
Henry Morton Stanley on first arriving in the United States.
On 12 October Stanley left Bombay for Zanzibar with the
order: 'Find Livingstone'.

In contrast to Livingstone's exploratory ambitions, Stanley
was solely focused on finding the man and getting the story.
Splitting his men into five caravans, Stanley set off within
a month of arriving in Zanzibar, following rumours of
an elderly white man living in Ujiji, on Lake Tanganyika

The Victoria Falls, of the
Leeambye or Zambesi
River called by the natives
Mosioatunya (smoke-
sounding), *from Livingstone's*
Missionary Travels *(1857).*

(divided between Tanzania, the Democratic Republic of the Congo, Burundi and Zambia). At that location on 10 November Stanley found Livingstone, and according to the subsequent *New York Herald* article, greeted him with the famous words: 'Dr Livingstone, I presume?' (Although it's possible the line may have been fabricated afterwards by Stanley, as he tore out the pages of his diary documenting the encounter.) The two men explored the north line of Lake Tanganyika, but failed to find an outlet to prove it was part of the White Nile watershed.

Stanley headed for England, while Livingstone, despite heavy illness, remained behind to continue the search for the Nile's source. Stanley's book *How I Found Livingstone* became a bestseller, but on hearing that Livingstone had finally succumbed to malaria and dysentery in 1873 he decided to complete Livingstone's great quest. By convincing both the London *Daily Telegraph* and the *New York Herald* to provide funds in return for the exclusive story, Stanley formed the Anglo-American Expedition, which he led over 999 days across central Africa between 1874 and 1877. Stanley had as much grit as Livingstone, having had a colourful martial career in the American Civil War (it's thought he is the only man to have served in the Confederate Army, the Union Army and the Union Navy). With unbreakable mettle he became the first European, if not the first person, to circumnavigate Lake Victoria and confirm John Hanning Speke's claim of it being the White Nile source. As well as mapping the lakes and river systems encountered along the way, Stanley also followed the massive north-flowing Lualaba river, which Livingstone had unsuccessfully pursued, and in another monumental achievement discovered it to be a source for the Congo river.

Stanley's expedition solved these great geographical enigmas, added a host of new place names to the African map, and placed him at the forefront in the pantheon of nineteenth-century explorers. He would return to England and use the notoriety gained from the publishing of his journal, *Through the Dark Continent*, in 1878, to urge Western governments to develop trade with Africa and by doing so reduce the slave trade still active in the interior, a freedom Livingstone had also hoped for the continent.

Stanley meeting Livingstone, from the Illustrated London News, *1872.*

BURKE AND WILLS'S DOOMED CROSSING OF AUSTRALIA 1860-61

'I am satisfied that the frame of man never was more severely taxed.' ROBERT O'HARA BURKE

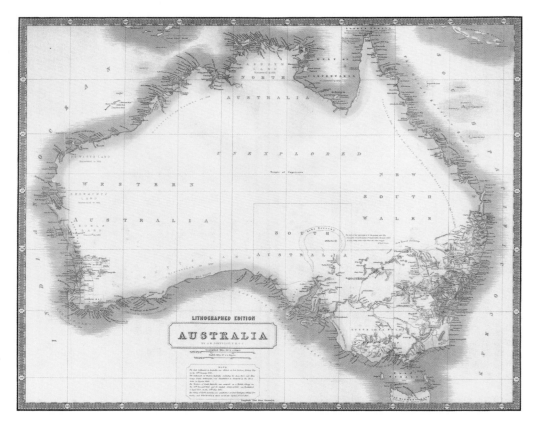

While Livingstone and then Stanley fought their way through the uncharted geography of the African continent, a comparable blankness of interior stared back at European cartographers of Australia. Though the heartland was yet unmapped, coastal colonization was booming. The 1850s were the gold-rush years of Australia: multiple discoveries of goldfields in Victoria drew huge numbers of migrants to the region, swiftly making Melbourne Australia's largest city, growing from 29,000 inhabitants in 1851 to 139,916 in 1861. Melbourne's new wealth stimulated not only great municipal

The 1850 edition of W. & A. K. Johnston's map of Australia, showing the vastness of the unexplored central and northern regions, before Robert O'Hara Burke and William John Wills set out.

growth but also ambition for international prestige. By 1855
the Australian Overland Telegraph Line was a national project
in development, intended to connect Australia to the new
telegraph cable in Java and on to Europe. The network would
most likely run through the centre of the Australian continent,
but this was an interior almost completely unexplored by
Europeans, though not for lack of effort. A four-man exploration
of the northern territory led by Prussian explorer and naturalist
Ludwig Leichhardt had disappeared along with their two
Aborigine guides in 1848 (a mystery that remains unsolved),
and in the same year Edmund Kennedy was speared to death by
Aborigines near the banks of the Escape River, 20 miles (32km)
from the Cape York Peninsula he had been sent to investigate.

To succeed where these had failed, in 1859 the Royal
Victorian Society drew up plans for the 'Victorian Exploring
Expedition', with £9,000 of the budget contributed by the
public. The selection of Irishman Robert O'Hara Burke to lead
the expedition was an unusual choice as he had no experience
in exploration or bushcraft, but he charmed the equally
inexperienced committee, and likely it was thought that the
appointment of the surveyor and navigator William John Wills
as third-in-command would compensate. The decision would
prove catastrophic.

Waved off by a 15,000-strong crowd, Burke embarked
with his expedition of fifteen men and twenty-five Karachi
camels from Melbourne on 20 August 1860, heading for the
Gulf of Carpentaria on the north coast. Arguments broke
out almost immediately. On top of the wretched weather,
difficult roads and failing wagons, there was William Landells,
Burke's second-in-command, to deal with, who refused to
stop giving rum to the cameleers (and the camels, in equal
measure). Landells soon quit, Wills was promoted, and the
party marched on to camp on the Darling river at Menindee
in October after 400 miles (644km). It had taken them two
months to make a journey regularly done by the mail coach in
little more than a week. Burke had heard about a rival effort to
make a south–north overland crossing, led by John McDouall
Stuart and so decided to split his party into an advance
group with the stronger horses and fittest men, and a slower
rearguard to follow them to Cooper's Creek, the appointed
halfway mark in central Australia. Aided by unseasonably
mild weather, Burke's advance party reached the camp on

The Explorer Robert
O'Hara Burke, *by William
Strutt (c.1860), an artist who
accompanied Robert O'Hara
Burke and William John Wills
on part of their exploration.*

11 November, swiftly relocating to nearby Bullah Bullah Waterhole after they were plagued by rats.

This was as far as Europeans had ever reached. Initially the plan was to wait out the scorching summer and leave in autumn (March) the next year, but Stuart's rivalry was ever on Burke's mind, and in a rash move he decided to strike out with his advance group for the north coast on 16 December, ordering the rest of the men to remain behind at Cooper's Creek to wait three months for their return. Burke, Wills, John King and Charles Gray went on ahead with six camels, one horse and supplies for three months, plunging into the northern summer temperatures that regularly hit 122°F (50°C) in the shade. They followed waterholes and reached the modern settlement of Boulia, continuing on to cross the Tropic of Capricorn. 'The frame of man', wrote Burke in his journal at this point, 'never was more severely taxed.' After fighting through 'soft and rotten' country, two months after their departure from Cooper's Creek they found their way blocked by marshes and mangrove swamps. They had no boat to navigate these, and with supplies running low, in frustration they decided to turn back.

Gradually the group began to disintegrate. Three of the camels were shot and eaten, and by 4 April Billy the horse was also killed for his meat. They shed their equipment piece by piece along the way, and resorted to eating portulaca (moss roses) for nourishment. When Gray was discovered stealing group rations, he was badly beaten by Burke. Gray died just under a month later from dysentery. Severely weakened, the remaining three managed to reach Cooper's Creek on the evening of 21 April 1861, only to discover the rear party, led by William Brahe, had abandoned the camp after waiting a month longer than ordered. Burke and his men found a blaze (marking) left on a tree for them, in which Brahe recorded the date of their departure: 21 April 1861. (They had missed them by only nine hours.)

Wills and King proposed heading south, retracing their path from Menindee in the hope of catching up with Brahe, but Burke overruled them and made the extraordinary decision to instead head southwest through 150 miles (240km) of desert to a remote police outstation near Mount Hopeless. Unbeknown to them Brahe had been struggling with guilt over abandoning his post, and hurried back to Cooper Creek to check for signs

William John Wills, c.1860.

of the Burke party – tragically Burke hadn't left his own blaze on the tree, and so Brahe left again.

Meanwhile, in the Strzelecki Desert, Burke, Wills and King had run out of supplies and had shot their last camel. Aboriginal tribesmen came to their aid, but Burke took a shot at one he thought was stealing, and the group fled. Soon, Wills could no longer walk. Burke and King left him with some food, and continued along the Cooper. After two days, Burke succumbed, and King returned to Wills but found he had also died. King survived with the help of Aborigines, and was eventually rescued by the anthropologist Alfred William Howitt, who also buried Burke and Wills before returning to Melbourne.

Though the shambolic mission had ended in tragedy, much detail of the Australian interior was added to the map as a result. The theory of an inland sea was proved false, and in fact the mangroves that had blocked their way to the north coast were found to be tidal, meaning they had technically succeeded in their mission. Howitt was sent back to recover the bodies, and on 21 January 1863 Burke and Wills were celebrated with a state funeral in Melbourne attended by 40,000 people.

A map of Australia showing explorers' routes, published with The Australian handbook for 1886.

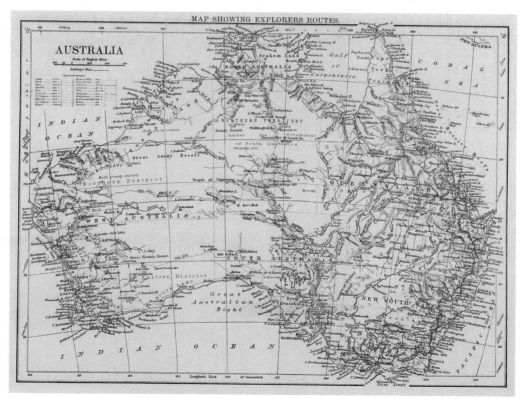

ADOLF NORDENSKIÖLD CIRCUMNAVIGATES THE ENTIRE EURASIAN LANDMASS 1878-80

'Thus finally was reached the goal towards which so many nations had struggled ...' ADOLF ERIK NORDENSKIÖLD, 1881

Just eighteen years after Robert O'Hara Burke and William John Wills had perished in the Australian desert, at a similar longitude another remarkable expedition arrived much farther north. At first glance there was nothing extraordinary about the European vessel *Vega* that drew into the Japanese harbour of Yokohama at 9.30 p.m. on 2 September 1879. Westerners had been a common sight for more than twenty years, ever since the diplomatic mission of the US navy commodore Matthew Perry had ended Japan's 220-year-old policy of isolation and initiated relations with Western powers. The former fishing village of Yokohama had opened to the commerce of the world, and transformed into a coastal city with a global citizenry of 70,000.

What set the ship apart was the way it had come. Its Finnish-Swedish commander, Adolf Nordenskiöld, disembarked and hurried through the streets to send home by telegram the historic news of their safe arrival. 'All are well. We left Winter quarters on the eighteenth, and doubled East Cape on the 20th of July. Proceeded thence to Lawrence Bay, Port Clarence and Behring's Island. Have had no sickness and no scurvy. The *Vega* is in excellent condition.' Nordenskiöld and his exhausted men had become the first to successfully navigate a Northeast Passage around Eurasia.

The name Adolf Nordenskiöld is today not one familiar to the general public, and yet in the last quarter of the nineteenth century the 'ever-memorable north-east passage' of the *Vega*, as the *New York Times* labelled the expedition, was headline news around the globe, its leader fêted by international scientific societies and appointed a commander of Sweden's Order of the Polar Star. *Vega*'s success capped centuries of piecemeal eastward progress along the Arctic

Some 300 years before the Vega *cruised through the Bering Strait, Stefano Bonsignori had in 1578 mapped the imagined polar lands north of Greenland, rumoured to be inhabited by pygmies.*

The Explorer, *a portrait of Adolf Erik Nordenskiöld by Georg Von Rosen, 1886.*

coast and explorations of the Siberian wilderness, of which the eighteenth century had seen a drastic increase after Vitus Bering had blazed the way. Particularly remarkable was the enterprise of the Russian polar explorer Semyon Chelyuskin, who had struck out with dogsleds across sea ice in 1742 to find Asia's northernmost point (now known as Cape Chelyuskin). By 1823, when Ferdinand von Wrangel recorded the Chukchi Sea (dividing Siberia and Alaska), clearing up any notion of a land bridge to North America, these numerous ventures had together resulted in coastal Arctic charts of near-modern accuracy. No one, though, had yet managed to sail the great distance directly along this coast from the Barents Sea to the Bering Strait.

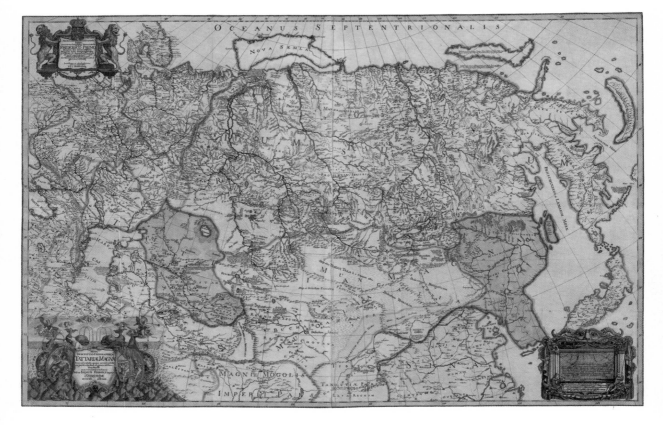

Philipp Strahlenberg's 1730 map of Russia.

In marked contrast to the kind of haphazard adventure of the inept Burke and Wills, when Nordenskiöld set out from the Swedish port of Karlskrona on 22 June 1878, it was in leadership of the best-equipped expedition of its kind. Careful planning was to be expected from a man with a scientific background in mineralogy, who in 1876 had been elected to the French Academy of Sciences to fill the chair left empty by the death of David Livingstone. He had also by that point participated in eight previous Arctic explorations, including an 1872 attempt to reach the North Pole using reindeer, which came to an abrupt end when the animals bolted at the first opportunity. The 299-ton, German, barque-rigged steamer *Vega* carried sufficient provisions for two years in case of unexpected overwintering, and a crew composed of experienced sailors, scientists, hydrographers and walrus hunters both old and young, so that the latter could learn from the former.

In three months the *Vega* had passed relatively easily from the Barents Sea into the Kara Sea. The smooth sailing continued, with their path almost completely ice-free. Encountering near-viscous fog they were forced to pause at Taymyr Island for three days, but once it cleared they were able to continue on to Cape Chelyuskin, which they rounded in celebration, for they were the first known expedition to do so. Their luck held as they made their way through the Laptev Sea, and it seemed as though their goal would be reached with almost anti-climactic ease. However, just 140 miles (225km) from their finishing line of the Bering Strait the waters grew thick with unbreakable ice sheets and the *Vega* was soon pinned in place by the frozen barrier.

The entrance of the Vega *into Stockholm on 24 April 1880.*

The end was agonizingly close yet out of reach, and there was no choice but to wait out the winter on board. Thanks to their commander's foresight and the assistance of the local indigenous Chukchi people this would be a fairly comfortable 264 days. The time was spent gathering meteorological and hydrographic data of the region, and geomagnetic recordings made from an observatory built on shore. With plenty of supplies and fuel remaining by the time the ice began to melt, the *Vega* happily emerged into the Bering Strait in July 1879 and headed for anchorage at Yokohama. After Nordenskiöld had sent his telegram, and after he and his crew enjoyed local festivities held in their honour while the *Vega* was overhauled, they continued their Eurasian circumnavigation, sailing west via the Suez Canal, Naples (where the *Vega* was 'literally exposed to storming by visitors'), Lisbon and Falmouth, before pulling into Stockholm on 24 April 1880, which to this day is celebrated as 'Vega Day' in Sweden. 'May the voyage', writes Nordenskiöld in his account of the journey, 'incite new exploratory expeditions to sea, which now, for the first time, has been ploughed by the keel of a sea-going vessel, and conduce to dissipate a prejudice which for centuries has kept the most extensive cultivable territory on the globe shut from the great Oceans of the World.'

THE RACE TO THE NORTH POLE
1893-1909

'There is something — I know not what to call it — in those frozen spaces, that brings a man face-to-face with himself and his companions.' Robert Peary

By the late nineteenth century, with the Northwest Passage finally discovered (though not yet completely navigated — see Roald Amundsen Conquers the Northwest Passage — and the Race to the South Pole entry on page 232-7), the geographic poles, as the last great parts unknown, beckoned. It remained

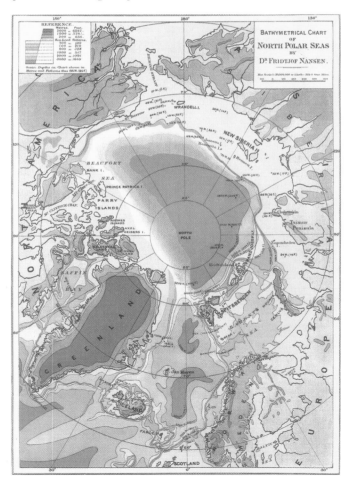

Bathymetrical chart of depth of North Polar Seas drawn by Fridtjof Nansen, 1893-96.

a complete mystery as to what would be found there. The possibility of an Arctic Ocean frozen solid, and therefore necessitating trek by foot, was unacceptable – surely there had to be a navigable route to the geographic North Pole. And so the early belief held by sixteenth-century explorers like Sir Martin Frobisher, in a liquid Arctic sea thawed by the sun's intensity, had not died but evolved through scientific conjecture. For Victorian Polar explorers this came in the theory of the respected German cartographer August Petermann, who proposed in the 1850s that warm southern currents created portals in the walls of the pack-ice barrier, leading to a negotiable channel. The suggestion of these Thermometric Gateways had fatal consequences – in 1879 the American explorer George Washington De Long pursued such an entrance aboard the *Jeanette* to this theoretical Open Polar Sea. The ship became trapped in ice beyond the Bering Strait, and the thirty-three-man expedition was forced to strike out with sleds and then small sailing boats for Siberia. De Long and nineteen of his crew died.

Three years after the *Jeanette* had been snared in the Arctic ice, remains of the ship were found to have been spat out and carried adrift all the way to the southwest coast of Greenland. This gave rise to one of the most ambitious ideas in the history of Polar exploration. In 1889, with the solidity of the Arctic ocean now reluctantly accepted, the Norwegian explorer and future Nobel Peace Prize laureate Fridtjof Nansen proposed that, instead of battling the ice and dodging the closing jaws of the floes in search of a way through, what if a ship were designed to be deliberately trapped in the ice, to ride the natural drift of the sheets as they – theoretically – carried the vessel effortlessly to the Pole. The *Fram* ('Forward') was constructed in Norway using the strongest oak available, with a rounded-hull design that would ensure the boat would be lifted upwards as the ice closed around it.

In June 1893 the most robust vessel ever built, and smaller than its predecessors, left Oslo with a crew of just twelve and followed the Siberian coast. Pack ice was sighted and Nansen led his ship into the stiffening field at a position of 78°49'N, 132°53'E, where he gave the order to stop the engine and raise the rudder. For sixteen months the Norwegians were borne by their ice-floe cradle towards the Pole, the men passing the time by reading from the 600-volume library and enjoying

Portrait of Fridtjof Nansen taken on his return in 1889 from an expedition to Greenland.

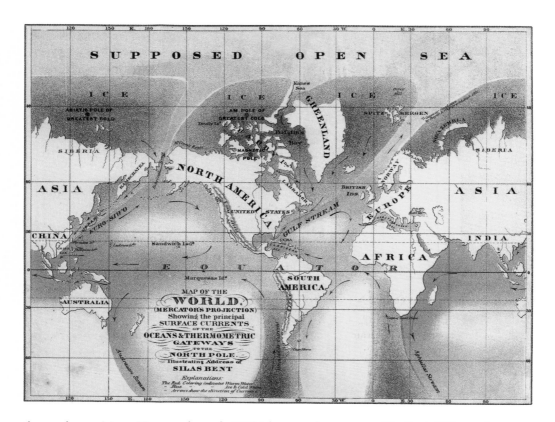

Silas Bent's 1872 map of Thermometric Gateways, showing in the far north the supposed 'Open Sea'.

the ample provisions. However by early 1895 it became clear that they would drift past the North Pole by some 300 miles (500km) and so with magnificent bravery Nansen left the ship and, with Hjalmar Johansen, set out to reach the North Pole by trekking across the ice. After hitting a record 86°N their chronometers stopped and they found themselves on a floe carrying them south faster than they could move north, and were forced to retreat, riding the floe south to Franz Josef Land. To the astonishment of both parties there they encountered a British expedition led by Frederick Jackson, and in September 1896 Nansen was reunited with the *Fram*.

Assaults on the Geographic North Pole continued into the twentieth century, and in September 1909 the front page of the *New York Herald* broke the news: 'The North Pole is Discovered by Dr Frederick A. Cook'. Cook, an American physician and explorer, had last been seen in February 1908, when he had set out from Greenland to cross Smith Sound to Ellesmere Island in the northern Canadian Arctic. With a party of ten Inuit assistants, eleven sledges and 105 dogs, he had crossed the frozen Bay fjord to reach Cape Thomas Howard, a headland that projected into the Arctic ocean. After three days of crossing the frozen Arctic Ocean only two Inuit companions, Ahwelaw and Etukishook, remained, and together the three men had disappeared into a Polar blizzard on a direct heading for the Pole. Now, back from the 'dead' after a year of mysterious wanderings through the Northland, Cook telegrammed home the news that he had reached the North Pole on 21 April 1908, after which he had been unable to return to Greenland because of open water, and so had waited out the season on Devon Island.

The news was celebrated around the world, and Cook received a celebrity reception on his arrival in Copenhagen en route home. The public was in for a shock, however, when just a week later the newspapers carried a second announcement: 'Peary Discovers the North Pole After Eight Trials in 23 Years.' Robert Peary, an American explorer and navy officer, had sent a telegram from Labrador declaring his own North Pole discovery made on 6 April 1909, and furiously contested Cook. Ahwelaw and Etukishook, he revealed, had testified to him that Cook had never left the mainland. Thus began the Cook–Peary controversy, which to this day has never been resolved – we still can't conclusively identify the first man to reach the Geographic North Pole. This is because the accounts of both explorers have been found to be seriously flawed, with neither providing sufficient supporting evidence. Cook's photographs of himself at the North Pole were found to be cropped pictures of Alaska taken years before (his photos supporting his earlier claim to have conquered Alaskan Mount McKinley have also been proven to be fake). He never produced detailed navigational records, and the diary he handed to Danish authorities was clearly written after the fact. He had also mapped a new landmass he called Bradley Land, 'with mountains and high valleys', which has been shown to be non-existent.

With so much cause to doubt Cook, then, what of Peary's claim? He too appears to have invented a landmass, named Crocker Land in honour of the banker George Crocker who had stumped up $50,000 for Peary's expedition. None of his Inuit helpers nor his servant Matthew Henson corroborated his calculations, and subsequent analysis of his logbook revealed troubling inconsistencies in his measurements. This includes the claim to have travelled 225 miles (362km) in the four days in which he went to and from the Pole, a daily speed of 56 miles (90km) that no one has ever come close to matching.

Robert Peary in Polar furs, 1909.

The deceptive Dr Frederick A. Cook, 1909.

ROALD AMUNDSEN CONQUERS THE NORTHWEST PASSAGE – AND THE RACE TO THE SOUTH POLE

1903-12

*'Victory awaits him who has everything in order –
luck, people call it. Defeat is certain for him who
has neglected to take the necessary precautions in
time; this is called bad luck.'* ROALD AMUNDSEN, 1912

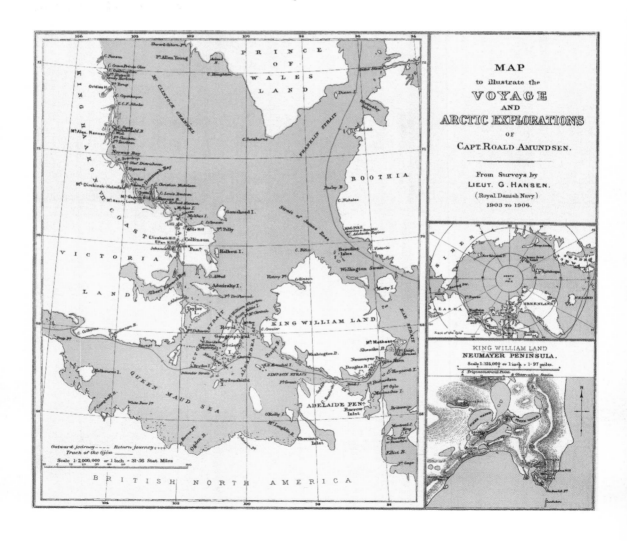

The knowledge necessary to complete a navigation of the Northwest Passage had by 1900 been collectively pieced together through centuries of Arctic ventures, but as yet no one had threaded the fragments with a successful continuous journey from east to west. This was finally achieved between 1903 and 1906 by the remarkable Norwegian Polar explorer Roald Amundsen, who rewrote the established rules of Arctic exploration to take the prize that had eluded the mighty British Admiralty for centuries. Amundsen's advanced approach to Polar survival was forged by his experiences serving in the gruelling Belgian Antarctic Expedition (BelgAE) of 1897-99, which was so poorly planned that there was insufficient food and warm clothing for everyone on board. From boyhood, Amundsen's dream had been that of his heroes: to navigate the Northwest Passage. 'A strange ambition burned within me …' he would later write of the idea. He began meticulous preparation for such a venture, seeking advice from Arctic veterans and studying magnetism.

Amundsen left Oslo in June 1903 in the small fishing sloop *Gjøø* (a day before debt collectors planned to seize it) with a crew of just six men, a miniaturization previously unthinkable. To the shock of his peers he also made the revolutionary decision to adopt the ways of the 'primitive' Inuit. He abandoned the porous cotton garb of previous European Polar explorations in favour of fur skins, and at Greenland he gathered dogs, sleds and kayaks. The *Gjøø* then followed Franklin's route through Lancaster Sound to the Boothia Peninsula, where John Ross had pinpointed the Magnetic North Pole in 1831 (see James Clark Ross and the Search for the Magnetic Poles entry on pages 196-9). Amundsen and his crew headed south down the east coast of King William Island, easily navigating shallow waters that would have blocked off larger vessels like those of the Franklin expedition, and finding there 'the finest little harbour in the world' made it their base of operations for the two winters they would be forced to wait out, just as Amundsen had anticipated. The seasons proved relatively comfortable and they continued heading west, following the northern Canadian coast on an unimpeded journey to emerge into the Beaufort Sea. The only significant problem occurred on arrival at Fort Yukon, Alaska, where Amundsen found there to be no working telegraph office to send out the news of his victory. Undaunted he sledged south over 200 miles

Roald Amundsen in fur skins, c.1912.

Opposite: *Map of Roald Amundsen's Arctic explorations, from the* Geographic Journal, *1907.*

(320km) to Eagle City, to make a $700 reverse-charge call to notify his countryman Fridtjof Nansen of the achievement that he dedicated to the newly independent Norway.

Amundsen barely paused before organizing an expedition to reach the North Pole and explore the Arctic Basin. Fridtjof Nansen graciously offered him the use of the *Fram* and, for the conquering hero of the Passage, funding was soon found. But then the news came of Cook and Peary's race to the north (see The Race to the North Pole entry on pages 228-31), and Amundsen made an extraordinary decision that he kept secret from everyone, including his backers and even his crew. Rather than abandon the idea and surrender the funds raised, he would depart for the Bering Strait as planned, but instead swing south and take the *Fram* to the Antarctic. 'If the expedition was to be saved … there was nothing left for me but to try and solve the last great problem – the South Pole,' he wrote. The much-publicized British *Terra Nova* expedition led by Captain Robert Falcon Scott had already departed in June 1910 with the goal 'to reach the South Pole, and to secure for the British Empire the honour of this achievement'. Though Scott was not yet aware of it, the journey had become a race. At Madeira, Amundsen informed his men of the plan, and sent a courtesy telegram to Scott, saying simply: 'Beg leave to inform you *Fram* proceeding Antarctic. Amundsen.'

Little was known about Antarctica at this time and the two competitors adopted very different approaches. Scott drew on his experience from his previous expedition of 1901-04 in charge of the *Discovery*, and the progress that Ernest

The Terra Nova *at the ice foot, Cape Evans.*

Robert Falcon Scott in the Cape Evans hut, October 1911.

Shackleton, his deputy on that expedition, had made on his own later venture in which ponies were used for hauling across the ice. Scott would also incorporate his own idea – motorized sledges. Amundsen, in contrast, relied on dogsleds and other adaptations picked up from the Inuit. He and his eighteen men arrived at the Bay of Whales on 2 January 1911, and established a camp they named Framheim.

After waiting in agonizing anticipation for the Antarctic winter to thaw, in September the Norwegians launched an impatient first assault on the South Pole but temperatures as low as -73°F (-58°C) claimed two of their dogs and a few frostbitten fingers and toes, and they were driven back to camp. Meanwhile, at Cape Evans, 370 miles (595km) to the west along the Ross Ice Shelf, the *Terra Nova*'s crew were preparing for their own march on the South Pole.

Amundsen and his men launched their second effort on 19 October, while Scott sent his motor party of mechanical sledges ahead on 24 October. The machines broke down in just a few weeks, and Scott's party of ponies caught up with them on 21 November. Amundsen had reached the Queen Maud mountains by this time, and after making the brutal ascent of the 10,600ft- (3230m-) high Axel Heiberg Glacier he set up camp and slaughtered twenty-four of their dogs for

Anton Omelchenko of the Terra Nova *Expedition stands at the end of the Barne Glacier on Ross Island, in the Ross Dependency of Antarctica, 2 December 1911.*

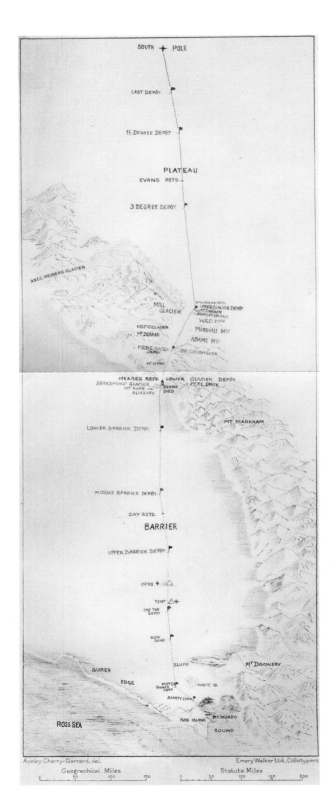

From Apsley Cherry-Garrard's
The Worst Journey in the World:
Antarctic 1910-13.

provisions at a spot they named the 'Butchers' Shop'. They struck out for the south, fighting through adverse conditions with poor visibility, until on 14 December 1911 they finally reached the South Pole. They planted the Norwegian flag and named the point King Haakon VII's Plateau. 'Never has a man achieved a goal so diametrically opposed to his wishes', reflected Amundsen. 'The area around the North Pole – devil take it – had fascinated me since childhood, and now here I was at the South Pole. Could anything be more crazy?'

The Norwegians spent three days at the Pole, taking care to leave a tent and markers for Scott to discover, so there could be no repeat of the Cook–Peary confusion. On 18 December they headed back to Framheim, taking care to move only 15 nautical miles (28km) per day to preserve their strength. They picked up the pace on 7 January, and on 25 January, at 4 a.m., they reached Framheim with all of the men and eleven of the fifty-two dogs surviving, after ninety-nine days and 1860 nautical miles (3445km) traversed. Amundsen telegrammed the news from Tasmania on 7 March, where he learnt there was still no news of the Scott expedition.

The fate of the British company would not be discovered until November 1912, when a search party from the Cape Evans base found the frozen bodies of the men just 11 miles (18km) from a supply depot.

The dejected Scott group at the South Pole, having learnt Amundsen had beaten them to it just thirty-four days earlier.

ERNEST SHACKLETON'S ANTARCTIC EXPEDITION IN THE *ENDURANCE* 1914-17

'Difficulties are just things to overcome, after all.'

ERNEST SHACKLETON

The discovery of the South Pole will not be the end of Antarctic exploration', wrote a defiant Ernest Shackleton in 1912. 'The next work of importance is the determination of the whole coastline of the Antarctic continent and then a trans-continental journey from sea to sea crossing the Pole.' Shackleton, the most beloved and charismatic of British explorers, had come to know Antarctica well, having served as Third Officer in Robert Falcon Scott's *Discovery* Expedition of 1901-04, the first British investigation of the region since that of James Clark Ross some sixty years before, and a trailbreaker for future efforts.

Charm personified, Shackleton inspired faithfulness in men to follow him anywhere. It was an appeal that also worked well in eliciting funds, and with £7000 (£680,000 today) provided by his employer, the wealthy industrialist William Beardmore, Shackleton announced his plan to the Royal Geographical Society and attracted further contributions. In January 1908 he was back in the Antarctic with the *Nimrod*, a vessel only half the size of Scott's *Discovery*, and a scientific team that included the Australian geologist Douglas Mawson. Two years were spent carrying out ostensible scientific and cartographic objectives, but these were punctuated with heroic escapades like the scaling of Mount Erebus, Antarctica's second highest volcano at 3794m (12,448ft). Shackleton's main target, though, was the South Pole. Though unsuccessful, the four-man Southern party that left camp on 29 October 1908 reached a farthest south latitude of 88°23'S, just 97½ nautical miles (180.6km) from the Pole. At this time, it was the closest anyone had got to either Pole.

Douglas Mawson had intended to spend only a year with Shackleton, but instead lasted the duration. In an age when society placed greater cachet on dramatic heroic struggles (with disaster only making the tales more seductive) over productive

Ernest Shackleton portrait by Jack Keith.

scientific collection, Mawson, in contrast to Shackleton, was
something of an anomaly. With his mentor, Edgeworth David,
Mawson was in the party that summited Mount Erebus
and made the trek to the Magnetic South Pole. The data he
collected was substantial, but so much about the continent
remained a mystery that its questions obsessed him: was
Antarctica a single vast landmass, or islands draped in a giant
ice sheet? And what secrets lay along its enormous uncharted
coastline from the Ross Sea (just south of New Zealand) to
the longitude of South Africa? Robert Falcon Scott invited
Mawson, a meticulous geographer, to join his disastrous *Terra
Nova* Expedition but the Australian declined – his sights were
set on leading his own mission to map the Antarctic shores.

The funds were raised from both the British and Australian
governments (a charted Antarctic would be invaluable to
mining and whaling industry), and the Australasian
Antarctic Expedition departed from Hobart, Tasmania on
2 December 1911 aboard the *Aurora*, intending to chart the
2000 mile- (3200km-) long coastline of Antarctica to the south
of Australia. They landed at Cape Denison, Commonwealth
Bay, where they set up the first of two camps to serve as home
for the next three years. Denison, referred to by Mawson as
'the windiest place on Earth', was the subject of fierce katabatic
winds ('descending' winds that fly down slopes, accelerated
by gravity) and the expedition often had to fight to remain on
their feet, as documented in the iconic photograph taken by
Frank Hurley (see page 240).

Mawson's men were divided into teams, five at Cape
Denison and three at the western base on the ice shelf at Queen
Mary Land, where the eight men overwintered together in a
20-sq. ft- (6-sq. m-) hut. Enduring constant blizzards, with
phenomenal local whirlwinds frequently hurling their gear
into the air, they explored with sledges and made excellent
progress delineating the miles of coastline. Despite his
assiduousness, drama in the Antarctic theatre was inevitable
and Mawson had a brush with death in the summer of
1912, when he, Xavier Mertz and Belgrave Ninnis surveyed
George V Land. Ninnis, who was jogging beside Mawson's
sled, plummeted down a crevasse to his death, taking with him
six of the dogs, their tent and their rations. Mawson and Mertz
were forced to survive by eating their dogs, but were poisoned
by the excessive amount of Vitamin A in the animals' liver.

Mertz went mad, biting off his own finger and flying into rages that Mawson had to suppress by sitting on his chest. Mertz died on 8 January 1913, and Mawson, with frostbitten fingers and crumbling shoes, cut his sledge in half with a pocket saw and dragged himself the last 100 miles (160km) solo. Mawson returned to Australia in 1914 a national hero, in what was considered the greatest Antarctic venture to date.

Shackleton, meanwhile, had been knighted by King Edward VII and awarded the Gold Medal by the Royal Geographical Society, but behind the scenes he was struggling to pay off the debts left him by the *Nimrod* Expedition. His thoughts returned to a transcontinental crossing.

Despite the outbreak of the First World War on 3 August 1914, Shackleton's Imperial Trans-Antarctic Expedition (1914-17) was directed to proceed by the First Lord of the Admiralty, Winston Churchill, and so left British waters on 8 August in two parties of men selected from a shortlist divided into 'Mad; Hopeless; Possible'. The *Endurance* would navigate the Weddell Sea to reach Vahsel Bay on Antarctica's Luitpold Coast, following Filchner's plan to use it as a base of operations

Frank Hurley's photograph, 'A Blizzard' – Mawson and his men routinely had to fight their way through winds of speeds reaching up to 320km/h (200mph).

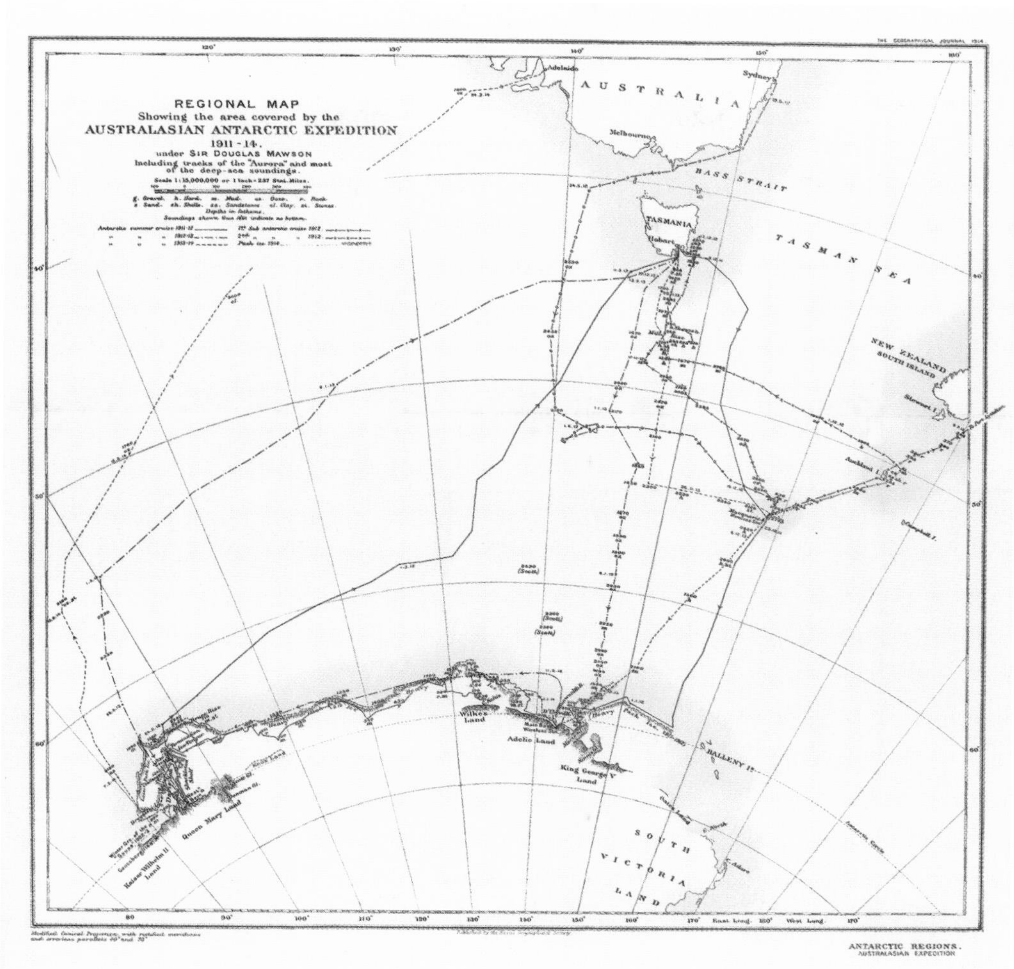

The area covered by Mawson's Australasian Antarctic Expedition, 1911-14.

for the continental crossing. Shackleton's second ship, the *Aurora*, would carry the Ross Sea party around to the other side of the continent, south of Australia, and lay supply depots to support the sledge team in the second half of their crossing. As *Endurance* entered the Weddell Sea in January 1915, however, a flash-freeze caught them in a trap of pack ice, and they were forced to drift helplessly for ten months until on 21 November the ice finally crushed the *Endurance*, and it disappeared below the floes. Before its loss, the twenty-eight-man crew had salvaged their equipment but were now stranded on the ice, with only the fabric of their tents for defence against the Antarctic winds.

After months in their makeshift camps with the ice audibly cracking beneath them, the men took the three rescued

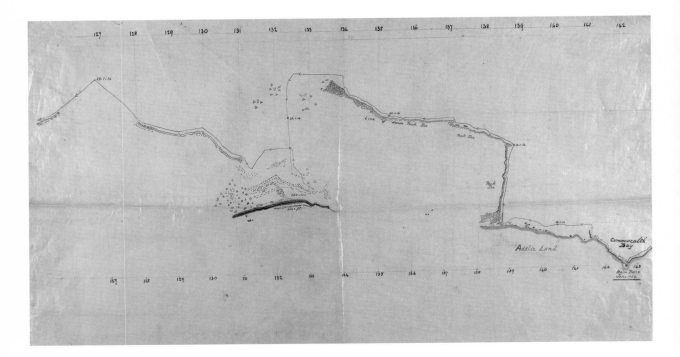

whaleboats and remaining provisions and set out for Elephant Island, just north of the Antarctic Peninsula. Ice-covered and mountainous, the barren island was no more hospitable but at least it was solid ground to rest on; but not a place that a rescue mission would investigate to seek them out. There was only one chance for survival: someone would have to take one of the 22ft- (7m-) long open boats out across the world's coldest and most violent waters to raise the alarm at the Norwegian whaling station on the island of South Georgia, about 870 miles (1400km) away.

Shackleton volunteered to lead the suicidal mission, taking with him five men chosen for their navigational skills (and, in Tom Crean's case, his near indestructability). On 24 April, in the face of approaching winter, they took the *James Caird* out into the Southern Ocean and into 'the highest, broadest and longest swells in the world', wrote one of the men, Frank Worsley. 'They race on their encircling course until they reach their birthplace again, and so, reinforcing themselves, sweep forward in fierce and haughty majesty.' Worsley had to be held in place by two of the men as he took measurements with his sextant, for even a slight error in calculation could send them wide of South Georgia. Shackleton and his men fought through heavy gales that tossed their boat with unrelenting

Original hand-drawn map showing the coast explored by the Australasian Antarctic Expedition during three seasons from 1911 to 1914.

savagery, threatening to sink it with the weight of forming ice that had to be routinely chipped away. The stars and horizon were obscured by the extreme weather, forcing them to rely on dead reckoning and sensing the wind on the back of the neck for course correction. After fourteen days, the peaks of South Georgia came into view and after enduring a final hurricane they landed on its southern shore. Rather than risk taking to the sea again to reach the whaling station on the north shore, Shackleton, Worsley and Crean left the others to recuperate and made a thirty-six-hour land crossing of the mountainous island territory, equipped with little more than a length of rope, before strolling into the station at Stromness Bay to the astonishment of the whalers. It took Shackleton four attempts to return through the ice to collect his men, but when he did, on 30 August 1916, it was ultimately without the loss of a single man.

Xavier Mertz at the snow-covered entrance of a hut.

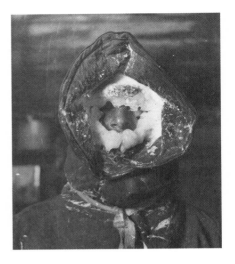

ABOVE: *Huskies pulling a sledge on the Adelie Land Plateau.*

BELOW: *Ernest Shackleton, Captain Frank Worsley and crew setting out in the* James Caird, *from Elephant Island, Easter Monday, 24 April 1916.*

The icy face of a member of the Australasian Antarctic Expedition team.

The Endurance *in the Antarctic*
winter darkness, trapped in
the Weddell Sea, Shackleton
expedition, 27 August 1915.

Map drawn from memory by
Frank Worsley on his return
from the Shackleton expedition.
It shows the route across South
Georgia trekked by himself,
Shackleton and Tom Crean in
May 1916.

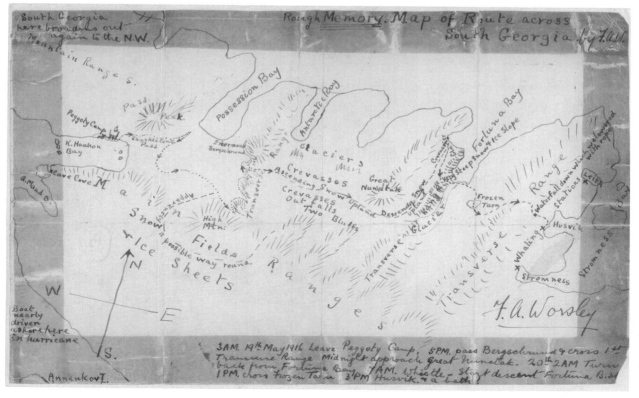

AFTERWORD

With the triumphant failure of the Shackleton expedition, the Heroic Age of exploration was brought to an exhausting close. Dividing lines must be drawn in histories, and the story of the *Endurance* traditionally forms an appropriate climax, before the next stage of modern discovery begins. Cartography too by this point had long shed its artistic plumage to take up residency in its modern division of scientific tool, and it feels right that a curation of its most splendid examples should end here also.

Of course, great geographical exploits follow on. With the incorporation of ground and air vehicles in the ensuing Mechanical Age, the few remaining blank spaces of found territory on maps were detailed at an unprecedented rate: the desert explorations of Gertrude Bell, T. E. Lawrence and Harry St John Philby, and later Wilfred Thesiger, brought into focus the last of the planet's great voids, and at the outbreak of the Second World War the cartography of these pioneers gained vital strategic value. In the Arctic, with the confusion of the Peary–Cook controversy left unresolved, it wasn't until April 1969 – the same year that Man first set foot on the Moon – that the North Pole was undisputedly reached by foot, by the British explorer Wally Herbert, in the longest Arctic journey in history.

It is fascinating to look back not just at the challenges faced, but also at the evolution of the explorer's motive as it shifts over centuries. Powered initially with desires of empire, trade, profit, proselytism and gold, with the scientific revolution came a new geographical curiosity that placed a duty of discovery of knowledge and precision of record above acquisition of personal wealth. As 'parts unknown' shrank to only the most extreme and inhospitable zones, the explorer refashioned as the solitary hero, championed so romantically by Victorian society. The Heroic Age, with its celebration of dramatic adventure regardless of success or failure, gave way to the Mechanical Age, when technology gifted the ability of prodigious data gathering and the means to comfortably endure the environments that so easily claimed those who first braved their hostility.

Andreas Cellarius's 1660 celestial map of the constellations.

The blanks spaces are gone, so where does that leave the modern explorer? Indeed, with our world now mapped one can today be prey to the almost dispiriting sense that its secrets are revealed. And yet the statistic remains that we have explored less than five per cent of our oceans, that we have discovered less than a quarter of the estimated total species with which we cohabit. And then there are the discoveries that await celestial adventurers, and star cartographers of future generations. Around and above us, mystery abounds. 'We shall not cease from exploration', assures T. S. Eliot, 'and the end of all our exploring will be to arrive where we started, and know the place for the first time.'

SELECT BIBLIOGRAPHY

Bannister, D. & Moreland, C. (1994) *Antique Maps*, London: Phaidon

Baynton-Williams, A. & Baynton-Williams, M. (2006) *New Worlds: Maps From the Age of Discovery*, London: Quercus

Baynton-Williams, A. & Armitage, G. (2012) *The World at Their Fingertips*, London: British Library Publishing

Bentley, J. H. (1993) *Old World Encounters*, Oxford: Oxford University Press

Brolsma, H., Clancy, R. & Manning, J. (2013) *Mapping Antarctica*, London: Springer

Cameron, I. (1980) *To the Farthest Ends of the Earth*, London: MacDonald

Crone (1953) *Maps and Their Makers*, London: Hutchinson's University Library

Dampier, W. (1697) *A New Voyage Round the World*, London: James Knapton

Dilke, O. A. W. (1985) *Greek and Roman Maps*, London: Thames & Hudson

Edson, E. (2007) *The World Map, 1300–1492*, Baltimore: John Hopkins University Press

Fisher, R. & Johnston, H. (1993) *From Maps to Metaphors*, Vancouver: University of British Columbia Press

Flinders, M. (1814) *A Voyage to Terra Australis*, London: G. and W. Nicol

Frankopan, P. (2016) *The Silk Roads: A New History of the World*, London: Bloomsbury

Garfield, S. (2012) *On the Map*, London: Profile

Hakluyt, R. (1582) *Divers Voyages*, London: Thomas Dawson

Hakluyt, R. (1589) *The Principall Navigations, Voiage and Discoveries of the English Nation, Made by Sea or over Land*, London: G. Bishop & R. Newberie

Hanbury-Tenison, R. (ed.) (2010) *The Great Explorers*, London: Thames & Hudson

Hanbury-Tenison, R. (ed.) (1993) *The Oxford Book of Exploration*, Oxford: Oxford University Press

Harris, N. (2002) *Mapping the World*, London: The Brown Reference Group

Hart, H. (1942) *Venetian Adventurer: Being an Account of the Life and Times and of the Book of Messer Marco Polo*, Stanford: Stanford University Press

Henderson, B. (2006) *True North, London: Norton*

Henry, D. (1773) *An Historical Account of All the Voyages Round the World*, London: printed for F. Newbery

Howgego, R. (2003-13) *Encyclopedia of Exploration*, Sydney: Hordern House

Howgego, R. (2009) *The Book of Exploration*, London: Weidenfeld & Nicolson

Hunter, D. (2012) *The Race to the New World*, London: Palgrave Macmillan

Huntford, R. (1985) *Shackleton*, London: Hodder & Stoughton

Jones, E. T. & Condon, M. M. (2016) *Cabot and Bristol's Age of Discovery*, Bristol: Cabot Project Publications

Koeman, C. K. (1970) *Joan Blaeu and His Grand Atlas*, London: George Philip

Larner, J. (1999) *Marco Polo and the Discovery of the World*, New Haven: Yale University Press

Levathes, L. (1994) *When China Ruled the Seas*, Oxford: Oxford University Press

Lister, R. (1965) *Old Maps and Globes*, London: Camelot Press

Moorehead, A. (1969) *Darwin and the Beagle*, New York: Harper & Row

Moreland, C. & Bannister, D. (1989) *Antique Maps*, London: Phaidon

Nebanzahl, K. (2011) *Mapping the Silk Road and Beyond*, London: Phaidon

Park, M. (1798) *Travels in the Interior Districts of Africa*, London: John Murray

Penrose, B. (1962) *Travel and Discovery in the Renaissance, 1420-1620*, London: Holiday House

Purchas, S. (1625-26) *Hakluytus Posthumus or Purchas His Pilgrimes ...* , London: H. Fetherston

Ridley, G. (2011) *The Discovery of Jeanne Baret*, London: Random House

Robinson, J. (1990) *Wayward Women*, Oxford: Oxford University Press

Shirley, R. W. (1983) *The Mapping of the World*, London: Holland Press

Skelton, R. A. (1964) *History of Cartography*, Cambridge: Harvard University Press

Thrower, N. (2007) *Maps and Civilization: Cartography in Culture and Society*, Chicago: University of Chicago Press

Wafer, L. (1699) *A New Voyage and Description of the Isthmus of America ...* , London: James Knapton

Watson, P. (2017) *Ice Ghosts: The Epic Hunt for the Lost Franklin Expedition*, London: Norton

Williams, G. (2002) *Voyages of Delusion*, London: HarperCollins

Wulf, A. (2015) *The Invention of Nature: The Adventures of Alexander von Humboldt, the Lost Hero of Science*, London: John Murray

INDEX

ACKNOWLEDGEMENTS

I would like to express my deep appreciation to all who provided such indispensable help in the creation of this book: to Charlie Campbell at Kingsford Campbell, to Ian Marshall at Simon & Schuster, and Laura Nickoll and Keith Williams for designing such a beautiful book. Thank you to Franklin Brooke-Hitching for enduring incessant questions and to my entire family for their support; to Alex and Alexi Anstey, Daisy Laramy-Binks, Matt and Gemma Troughton, Kate Awad, Katherine Anstey, Rosamund Urwin, Richard Jones, Katherine Parker, June Hogan, Georgie Hallett and Thea Lees. Thanks also to my friends at QI: John, Sarah and Coco Lloyd, Piers Fletcher, James Harkin, Alex Bell, Alice Campbell Davies, Anne Miller, Andrew Hunter Murray, Anna Ptaszynski, Dan Schreiber and Sandi Toksvig.

I am especially grateful to those who have been so generous in providing, and allowing the reproduction of, the magnificent maps and other items collected here: to Barry Ruderman of Barry Lawrence Ruderman Antique Maps for his boundless generosity in support of the book; to Massimo de Martini and Miles Baynton-Williams at Altea Antique Maps; Daniel Crouch and his staff at Daniel Crouch Rare Books and Maps; Richard Fattorini and Francesca Charlton-Jones at Sotheby's; Filip Devroe of Sanderus Antiquariaat; Charles Miller Ltd; and finally the wonderful (and wonderfully patient) staff of the Royal Geographical Society library and the British Library for their help and advice.

PICTURE AND MAP CREDITS

Altea Antique Maps Pg 9-10, 11, 15, 156-157; **Austrian National Library** Pg 24; **Barry Lawrence Ruderman Antique Maps** Pg 12, 18, 20, 23, 34 , 40, 53, 58-59, 61, 71, 77, 78, 85, 86, 87, 92, 94, 110, 112, 113, 116, 119, 122, 128, 137, 141, 146, 147, 150-1, 166, 170, 174, 184, 195, 196-7, 207, 209, 212-3, 220, 226, 247; **Bavarian State Library** Pg 51; **Beinecke Rare Book and Manuscript Library** Pg 69, 185; **Biblioteca Estense, Modena, Italy** Pg 64-5; **Biblioteca Nazionale Marciana, Venice** Pg 43, 46 (bottom); **Bibliothèque nationale de France** Pg 38, 50, 70; **Biodiversity Heritage Library** Pg 164; **Photo Bodleian Libraries** Pg 28, 29, 47; **Boston Public Library** Pg 63; **bpk / Stiftung Preussische Schlösser und Gärten Berlin-Brandenburg / Jörg P. Anders** Pg 182; **Bridgeman Images** Pg 96; **British Library, London, UK/Bridgeman Images** Pg 102-3; **Bruun Rasmussen** Pg 35; **Charles Miller Limited** Pg 17; **Christies Images Limited** Pg 1, 2; **Daniel Crouch Rare Books** Pg 89; **Daniel Villafruela** Pg 67; **The Florentine Civic Museums (CC BY 3.0)** Pg 48, 224; **Fridtjof Nansen Institute** Pg 228, 229 (top); **bpk / Gemäldegalerie, Staatliche Museen zu Berlin / Jörg P. Anders** Pg 80-81; **Geographicus Fine Antique Maps** Pg 168; **Hampell Auctions** Pg 208; **Harry Ransom Center, University of Texas at Austin** Pg 54-55; **Jan Dalsgaard Sørensen** Pg 229 (bottom); **Karen Green** Pg 19 (top); **Library of Congress** Pg 72, 101, 107, 187, 219 *Geography and Map Division* Pg 44, 56, 62, 74-5, 76, 82-3, 98, 164-5, 186, 188-9; **mapsorama.com** Pg 45; **Martayar Lan Fine Antique Maps and Rare Books** Pg 172-3; **Metropolitan Museum of Art** Pg 54, 178; **Missouri Historic Society, St Louis** Pg 188 (top); **Mitchell Library, State Library of New South Wales;** Pg 163; **The Museum Silhak** Pg 108-9; **bpk / Nationalgalerie, Staatliche Museen zu Berlin / Karin März** Pg 179; **National Libra of Australia** Pg 134, 136, 140, 148, 221, 222, 240, 243, 244 (top right), p244 (bottom), p245 (top) ; **National Lil of Norway** Pg 118, 231 (top); **National Museum of Fine Arts, Sweden** Pg 225; **Naval Museum of Madri** Pg 52, 60; **National Portrait Gallery, London** Pg 123, 203 ; **New York Public Library** Pg 135, 138, 158 (t **Peary-MacMillan Arctic Museum, Bowdoin College** Pg 230 (bottom), 231 (bottom); **Philadelphia Mus of Art** Pg 46 (top); **Royal Geographic Society** Pg 216; **Royal Museums Greenwich** Pg 198 (top); **Sande Antiquariaat, Ghent** Pg 26-7, 125; **licensed with permission of the University of Cambridge, Scott P Research Institute** Pg 245 (bottom); **Sir George Grey Special Collections, Auckland City Libraries** **Sotheby's** Pg 10, 30-1; **Stanford University** Pg 66; **State Library of New South Wales** Pg 132, 244 (t **State Library of Victoria** Pg 238, 242; **Stephen Chambers** Pg 198 (bottom); **Uppsala University Libra** Pg 90-91; **Walters Art Museum** Pg 33; **Yale Center for British Art** Pg 210; **Yale University** Pg 37; Στσ

All other images courtesy of the author.

First published in Great Britain by Simon & Schuster UK Ltd, 2018
A CBS company

Copyright © 2018 by Edward Brooke-Hitching

This book is copyright under the Berne Convention.
No reproduction without permission.
All rights reserved.

The right of Edward Brooke-Hitching to be identified as the author of this work has been asserted by him in accordance with sections 77 and 78 of the Copyright, Designs and Patents Act, 1988.

Editorial Director: Ian Marshall
Design: Keith Williams, sprout.uk.com
Project Editor: Laura Nickoll

1 3 5 7 9 10 8 6 4 2

Simon & Schuster UK Ltd
1st Floor
222 Gray's Inn Road
London WC1X 8HB

www.simonandschuster.co.uk

Simon & Schuster Australia,
Sydney

Simon & Schuster India,
New Delhi

The author and publishers have made all reasonable efforts to contact copyright-holders for permission, and
ologise for any omissions or errors in the form of credits given. Corrections may be made to future printings.

P catalogue record for this book is available from the British Library

k ISBN: 978-1-4711-6682-2
BN: 978-1-4711-6683-9

hina

MIX
aper from
sible sources
104723

ry
);
m
s
ar
204;
left);
Sweden
poc Pg 20

ments and Credits   PAGE 255

ACKNOWLEDGEMENTS

I would like to express my deep appreciation to all who provided such indispensable help in the creation of this book: to Charlie Campbell at Kingsford Campbell, to Ian Marshall at Simon & Schuster, and Laura Nickoll and Keith Williams for designing such a beautiful book. Thank you to Franklin Brooke-Hitching for enduring incessant questions and to my entire family for their support; to Alex and Alexi Anstey, Daisy Laramy-Binks, Matt and Gemma Troughton, Kate Awad, Katherine Anstey, Rosamund Urwin, Richard Jones, Katherine Parker, June Hogan, Georgie Hallett and Thea Lees. Thanks also to my friends at QI: John, Sarah and Coco Lloyd, Piers Fletcher, James Harkin, Alex Bell, Alice Campbell Davies, Anne Miller, Andrew Hunter Murray, Anna Ptaszynski, Dan Schreiber and Sandi Toksvig.

I am especially grateful to those who have been so generous in providing, and allowing the reproduction of, the magnificent maps and other items collected here: to Barry Ruderman of Barry Lawrence Ruderman Antique Maps for his boundless generosity in support of the book; to Massimo de Martini and Miles Baynton-Williams at Altea Antique Maps; Daniel Crouch and his staff at Daniel Crouch Rare Books and Maps; Richard Fattorini and Francesca Charlton-Jones at Sotheby's; Filip Devroe of Sanderus Antiquariaat; Charles Miller Ltd; and finally the wonderful (and wonderfully patient) staff of the Royal Geographical Society library and the British Library for their help and advice.

PICTURE AND MAP CREDITS

Altea Antique Maps Pg 9-10, 11, 15, 156-157; **Austrian National Library** Pg 24; **Barry Lawrence Ruderman Antique Maps** Pg 12, 18, 20, 23, 34 , 40, 53, 58-59, 61, 71, 77, 78, 85, 86, 87, 92, 94, 110, 112, 113, 116, 119, 122, 128, 137, 141, 146, 147, 150-1, 166, 170, 174, 184, 195, 196-7, 207, 209, 212-3, 220, 226, 247; **Bavarian State Library** Pg 51; **Beinecke Rare Book and Manuscript Library** Pg 69, 185; **Biblioteca Estense, Modena, Italy** Pg 64-5; **Biblioteca Nazionale Marciana, Venice** Pg 43, 46 (bottom); **Bibliothèque nationale de France** Pg 38, 50, 70; **Biodiversity Heritage Library** Pg 164; **Photo Bodleian Libraries** Pg 28, 29, 47; **Boston Public Library** Pg 63; **bpk / Stiftung Preussische Schlösser und Gärten Berlin-Brandenburg / Jörg P. Anders** Pg 182; **Bridgeman Images** Pg 96; **British Library, London, UK/Bridgeman Images** Pg 102-3; **Bruun Rasmussen** Pg 35; **Charles Miller Limited** Pg 17; **Christies Images Limited** Pg 1, 2; **Daniel Crouch Rare Books** Pg 89; **Daniel Villafruela** Pg 67; **The Florentine Civic Museums (CC BY 3.0)** Pg 48, 224; **Fridtjof Nansen Institute** Pg 228, 229 (top); **bpk / Gemäldegalerie, Staatliche Museen zu Berlin / Jörg P. Anders** Pg 80-81; **Geographicus Fine Antique Maps** Pg 168; **Hampell Auctions** Pg 208; **Harry Ransom Center, University of Texas at Austin** Pg 54-55; **Jan Dalsgaard Sørensen** Pg 229 (bottom); **Karen Green** Pg 19 (top); **Library of Congress** Pg 72, 101, 107, 187, 219 *Geography and Map Division* Pg 44, 56, 62, 74-5, 76, 82-3, 98, 164-5, 186, 188-9; **mapsorama.com** Pg 45; **Martayan Lan Fine Antique Maps and Rare Books** Pg 172-3; **Metropolitan Museum of Art** Pg 54, 178; **Missouri Historical Society, St Louis** Pg 188 (top); **Mitchell Library, State Library of New South Wales**; Pg 163; **The Museum of Silhak** Pg 108-9; **bpk / Nationalgalerie, Staatliche Museen zu Berlin / Karin März** Pg 179; **National Library of Australia** Pg 134, 136, 140, 148, 221, 222, 240, 243, 244 (top right), p244 (bottom), p245 (top) ; **National Library of Norway** Pg 118, 231 (top); **National Museum of Fine Arts, Sweden** Pg 225; **Naval Museum of Madrid** Pg 52, 60; **National Portrait Gallery, London** Pg 123, 203 ; **New York Public Library** Pg 135, 138, 158 (top); **Peary-MacMillan Arctic Museum, Bowdoin College** Pg 230 (bottom), 231 (bottom); **Philadelphia Museum of Art** Pg 46 (top); **Royal Geographic Society** Pg 216; **Royal Museums Greenwich** Pg 198 (top); **Sanderus Antiquariaat, Ghent** Pg 26-7, 125; **licensed with permission of the University of Cambridge, Scott Polar Research Institute** Pg 245 (bottom); **Sir George Grey Special Collections, Auckland City Libraries** Pg 204; **Sotheby's** Pg 10, 30-1; **Stanford University** Pg 66; **State Library of New South Wales** Pg 132, 244 (top left); **State Library of Victoria** Pg 238, 242; **Stephen Chambers** Pg 198 (bottom); **Uppsala University Library, Sweden** Pg 90-91; **Walters Art Museum** Pg 33; **Yale Center for British Art** Pg 210; **Yale University** Pg 37; **Σταυρός** Pg 20

All other images courtesy of the author.

First published in Great Britain by Simon & Schuster UK Ltd, 2018
A CBS company

Copyright © 2018 by Edward Brooke-Hitching

This book is copyright under the Berne Convention.
No reproduction without permission.
All rights reserved.

The right of Edward Brooke-Hitching to be identified as the author of this work has been asserted by him in accordance with sections 77 and 78 of the Copyright, Designs and Patents Act, 1988.

Editorial Director: Ian Marshall
Design: Keith Williams, sprout.uk.com
Project Editor: Laura Nickoll

1 3 5 7 9 10 8 6 4 2

Simon & Schuster UK Ltd
1st Floor
222 Gray's Inn Road
London WC1X 8HB

www.simonandschuster.co.uk

Simon & Schuster Australia,
Sydney

Simon & Schuster India,
New Delhi

The author and publishers have made all reasonable efforts to contact copyright-holders for permission, and apologise for any omissions or errors in the form of credits given. Corrections may be made to future printings.

A CIP catalogue record for this book is available from the British Library

Hardback ISBN: 978-1-4711-6682-2
Ebook ISBN: 978-1-4711-6683-9

Printed in China

MIX
Paper from
responsible sources
FSC® C104723